Absolutely Positively

A Collection of Specific Commands for the Christian Life,
Taken from the Writings of Ellen G. White
and the Holy Scriptures

*Compiled By
Timothy & Eriann Hullquist,
and their daughter, Sarah Prowant*

TEACH Services, Inc.
P U B L I S H I N G
www.TEACHServices.com • (800) 367-1844

World rights reserved. This book or any portion thereof may not be copied or reproduced in any form or manner whatever, except as provided by law, without the written permission of the publisher, except by a reviewer who may quote brief passages in a review.

This book was written to provide truthful information in regard to the subject matter covered. The author assumes full responsibility for the accuracy of all facts and quotations as cited in this book. The opinions expressed in this book are the author's personal views and interpretation of the Bible, Spirit of Prophecy, and/or contemporary authors and do not necessarily reflect those of TEACH Services, Inc.

This book is sold with the understanding that the publisher is not engaged in giving spiritual, legal, medical, or other professional advice. If authoritative advice is needed, the reader should seek the counsel of a competent professional.

Copyright © 2013 TEACH Services, Inc.
ISBN-13: 978-1-4796-0202-5 (Paperback)
ISBN-13:978-1-4796-0203-2 (ePub)
ISBN-13: 978-1-4796-0204-9 (Kindle/Mobi)
Library of Congress Control Number: 2013940731

Published by

TEACH Services, Inc.
P U B L I S H I N G
www.TEACHServices.com • (800) 367-1844

Table of Contents

Chapter 1	Character	5
Chapter 2	Diet & Exercise	19
Chapter 3	The Sabbath	33
Chapter 4	Education	39
Chapter 5	Faith & Prayer	52
Chapter 6	Relationships	60
Chapter 7	The Bible	65
Chapter 8	Communication	73
Chapter 9	Family	86
Chapter 10	God	100
Chapter 11	Stewardship	106
Chapter 12	Health & Healing	113
Chapter 13	Dress	120
Chapter 14	Romance & Marriage	126
Chapter 15	Entertainment	136
Chapter 16	The Church	143
Chapter 17	Evangelism	158
Chapter 18	Heaven	166
Chapter 19	Encouragement	171

Chapter 1

Character

With energy and fidelity our youth should meet the demands upon them, and this will be a guarantee of success. Young men who have never made a success in the temporal duties of life will be equally unprepared to engage in the higher duties. A religious experience is gained only through conflict, through disappointment, through severe discipline of self, through earnest prayer. The steps to heaven must be taken one at a time, and every advance step gives strength for the next (*Counsels to Parents, Teachers, and Students*, p. 100).

Physical labor will not prevent the cultivation of the intellect. Far from this. The advantages gained by physical labor will so balance the mind that it shall not be overworked. The toil will then come upon the muscles, and relieve the wearied brain. There are many listless, useless girls who consider it unladylike-like to engage in active labor. But their characters are too transparent to deceive sensible persons in regard to their real worthlessness. They will simper and giggle, and are all affectation. They appear as though they could not speak fairly and squarely, but torture all they say with lisping and simpering. Are these ladies? They are not born fools, but were educated such. It does not require a frail, helpless, over-dressed, simpering thing to make a lady. A sound body is required for a sound intellect. Physical soundness, and a practical knowledge in all the necessary household duties, is never a hindrance to a well-developed intellect, but is highly important for a lady (*Christian Education*, p. 17).

Judicious labor is a healthful tonic for the human race. It makes the feeble strong, the poor rich, the wretched happy. Satan lies in ambush, ready to destroy those whose leisure gives him opportunity to approach them under some attractive disguise. He is never more successful than when he comes to men in their idle hours (*Counsels to Parents, Teachers, and Students*, p. 278).

Children, never prove unfaithful stewards in the home. Never shirk your duty. Good hard work makes firm sinews and muscles. In promoting the prosperity of the home, you will bring the richest blessing to yourselves (*Child Guidance*, p. 124).

Young men who desire to exercise their gifts in the work of the ministry, will find a helpful lesson in the example of Paul at Thessalonica, Corinth, Ephesus, and other places. Although an eloquent speaker, and chosen by God to do a special work, he was never above labor, nor did he ever weary of sacrificing for the cause he loved (*Acts of the Apostles*, p. 354).

All self-uplifting works out the natural result—making character of which God cannot approve. Work and teach; work in Christ's lines, and then you will never work in your own weak ability, but will have the cooperation of the divine (*Counsels to Parents, Teachers, and Students*, p. 283).

But we all, with open face beholding as in a glass the glory of the Lord, are changed into the same image from glory to glory, even as by the Spirit of the Lord (2 Corinthians 3:18).

The policy principle is one that will assuredly lead into difficulties. He who regards the favor of men as more desirable than the favor of God will fall under the temptation to sacrifice principle for worldly gain or recognition. Thus fidelity to God is constantly being sacrificed. Truth, God's truth, must be cherished in the soul and held in the strength of heaven, or the power of Satan will wrest it from you (*Counsels to Parents, Teachers, and Students*, p. 485).

Exercise in household labor is of the greatest advantage to young girls. Physical labor will not prevent the cultivation of the intellect: far from it. The advantages gained by physical labor will balance a person and prevent the mind from being overworked. The toil will come upon the muscles and relieve the wearied brain... A sound body is required for a sound intellect. Physical soundness and a practical knowledge of all the necessary household duties will never be a hindrance to a well-developed intellect; both are highly important (*Counsels to Parents, Teachers, and Students*, p. 287).

Those who prove untrue are to be dealt with in accordance with the wisdom that God will impart. Never are God's servants to look upon disaffection, scheming, and deception as virtues; those in responsibility are to manifest their decided disapproval of all unfaithfulness in business and spiritual matters. And they are to choose as counselors in every line of work, only those men in whom they can repose the utmost confidence (*Christian Leadership*, p. 10).

It is essential that honesty be practiced in all the details of the mother's life, and it is important in the training of children to teach the youthful girls as well as boys never to prevaricate or to deceive in the least (*Child Guidance*, p. 152).

Those who are hiding their talents in the earth are throwing away their opportunities to obtain a star-gemmed crown. Until the great disclosures of the final judgment shall be made, it will never be known how many men and women have done this, nor how many lives have gone out in darkness because God-given talents have been buried in business instead of being used in the service of the Giver (*Counsels on Stewardship*, p. 125).

A good man out of the good treasure of his heart bringeth forth that which is good; and an evil man out of the evil treasure of his heart bringeth forth that which is evil: for of the abundance of the heart his mouth speaketh (Luke 6:45).

Honor, integrity, and truth must be preserved at any cost to self. Our every thought, word, and action should be subject to the will of Christ (*Christian Leadership*, p. 16).

The religion of Christ never degrades the receiver. It never makes him coarse or rough, discourteous or self-important, passionate or hardhearted. On the contrary, it refines the taste, sanctifies the judgment, and purifies and ennobles the thoughts, bringing them into captivity to Jesus Christ (*Counsels to Parents, Teachers, and Students*, p. 365).

Many Christians do not have works corresponding to the name they bear. They act as if they had never heard of the plan of redemption wrought out at infinite cost. The majority aim to make a name for themselves in the world; they adopt its forms and ceremonies, and live for the indulgence of self. They follow out their own purposes as eagerly as do the world, and thus they cut off their power to help in establishing the kingdom of God (*Counsels on Stewardship*, p. 54).

God will accept only those who are determined to aim high. He places every human agent under obligation to do his best. Moral perfection is required of all. Never should we lower the standard of righteousness in order to accommodate inherited or cultivated tendencies to wrong-doing. We need to understand that imperfection of character is sin. All righteous attributes of character dwell in God as a perfect, harmonious whole, and every one who receives Christ as a personal Saviour is privileged to possess these attributes (*Christ Object Lessons*, p. 330).

The love of God will never lead to the belittling of sin; it will never cover or excuse an unconfessed wrong. It has to do with all our acts and thoughts and feelings. It follows us, and reaches every secret spring of action. By indulgence in sin, men are led to lightly regard the law of God. Many conceal their transgressions from their fellow men, and flatter themselves that God will not be strict to mark iniquity. But His law is the great standard of right, and with it every act of life must be compared in that day when God shall bring every work into judgment, with every secret thing, whether it be good or evil. Purity of heart will lead to purity of life. All excuses for sin are vain. Who can plead for the sinner when God testifies against him? (*Conflict and Courage*, p. 120).

Never before was there so much at stake; never were there results so mighty depending upon a generation as upon these now coming upon the stage of action. Not for one moment should the youth think that they can acceptably fill any position of trust without possessing a good character. Just as well might they expect to gather grapes of thorns, or figs of thistles (*Counsels to Parents, Teachers, and Students*, p. 536).

Patience as well as courage has its victories. By meekness under trial, no less than by boldness in enterprise, souls may be won to Christ. The Christian who manifests patience and cheerfulness under bereavement and suffering, who meets even death itself with the peace and calmness of an unwavering faith, may accomplish for the gospel more than he could have effected by a long life of faithful labor. Often when the servant of God is withdrawn from active duty, the mysterious providence which our shortsighted vision would lament is designed by God to accomplish a work that otherwise would never have been done (*Acts of the Apostles*, p. 465).

Never utter sentiments of doubt. Christ's teaching was always positive in its nature. With a tone of assurance bear an affirmative message. Lift up the Man of Calvary higher and still higher; there is power in the exaltation of the cross of Christ (*Counsels to Parents, Teachers, and Students*, p. 434).

Therefore being justified by faith, we have peace with God through our Lord Jesus Christ: By whom also we have access by faith into this grace wherein we stand, and rejoice in hope of the glory of God. And not only so, but we glory in tribulations also: knowing that tribulation worketh patience; And patience, experience; and experience, hope: And hope maketh not ashamed; because the love of God is shed abroad in our hearts by the Holy Ghost which is given unto us. For when we were yet without strength, in due time Christ died for the ungodly (Romans 5:1–6).

Often the Christian life is beset by dangers, and duty seems hard to perform. The imagination pictures impending ruin before and bondage or death behind. Yet the voice of God speaks clearly, "Go forward." We should obey this command, even though our eyes cannot penetrate the darkness, and we feel the cold waves about our feet. The obstacles that hinder our progress will never disappear before a halting, doubting spirit. Those who defer obedience till every shadow of uncertainty disappears and there remains no risk of failure or defeat, will never obey at all. Unbelief whispers, "Let us wait till the obstructions are removed, and we can see our way clearly:" but faith courageously urges an advance, hoping all things, believing all things (*Conflict and Courage*, p. 92).

Without Christ we can do nothing. The pure principles of uprightness, virtue, and goodness are all from God. A conscientious discharge of duty, Christ-like sympathy, love for souls and love for your own soul, because you belong to God, and have been bought with the precious blood of Christ, will make you a laborer together with God, and endow you with persuasive, drawing power. You must respect your own faith in order successfully to introduce it to others (*Christian Education*, p. 92).

Beyond the discipline of the home and the school, all have to meet the stern discipline of life. How to meet this wisely is a lesson that should be made plain to every child and to every youth. It is true that God loves us, that He is working for our happiness, and that, if His law had always been obeyed, we should never have known suffering; and it is no less true that, in this world, as the result of sin, suffering, trouble, burdens, come to every life. We may do the children and the youth a lifelong good by teaching them to meet bravely these troubles and burdens. While we should give them sympathy, let it never be such as to foster self-pity. What they need is that which stimulates and strengthens rather than weakens (*Child Guidance*, p. 157).

Character building is the most important work ever entrusted to human beings, and never before was its diligent study so important as now. never was any previous generation called to meet issues so momentous; never before were young men and young women confronted by perils so great as confront them today (*Child Guidance*, p. 169).

Never underrate the importance of little things. Little things supply the actual discipline of life. It is by them that the soul is trained that it may grow into the likeness of Christ, or bear the likeness of evil. God help us to cultivate habits of thought, word, look, and action that will testify to all about us that we have been with Jesus and learned of Him! (*Child Guidance*, p. 129).

If men would give less attention to the artificial and would cultivate greater simplicity, they would come far nearer to answering the purpose of God in their creation. Pride and ambition are never satisfied, but those who are truly wise will find substantial and elevating pleasure in the sources of enjoyment that God has placed within the reach of all (*Adventist Home*, p. 132).

Character

There is great need of the cultivation of true refinement in the home. This is a powerful witness in favor of the truth. In whomsoever they may appear, vulgarity of language and of demeanor indicate a vitiated heart. Truth of heavenly origin never degrades the receiver, never makes him coarse or rough. Truth is softening and refining in its influence. When received into the heart, it makes the youth respectful and polite. Christian politeness is received only under the working of the Holy Spirit. It does not consist in affection or artificial polish, in bowing and simpering. This is the class of politeness possessed by those of the world, but they are destitute of true Christian politeness. True polish, true politeness, is obtained only from a practical knowledge of the gospel of Christ. True politeness, true courtesy, is a kindness shown to all, high or low, rich or poor (*Adventist Home*, p. 422).

The most careful cultivation of the outward proprieties of life is not sufficient to shut out all fretfulness, harsh judgment, and unbecoming speech. True refinement will never be revealed so long as self is considered as the supreme object (*Adventist Home*, p. 425).

Never lose sight of the fact that you belong to God, that He has bought you with a price, and you must render an account to Him for all His entrusted talents (*Adventist Home*, p. 463).

We are living in a most solemn period of this earth's history. There is never time to sin; it is always perilous to continue in transgression, but in a special sense is this true at the present time. We are now upon the very borders of the eternal world and stand in a more solemn relation to time and to eternity than ever before. Now let every person search his own heart and plead for the bright beams of the Sun of Righteousness to expel all spiritual darkness and cleanse from defilement (*Adventist Home, p. 549*).

Other dishonest, intriguing actions were done in a secret, artful manner, People were turned away from their rights. Some of these things have never been adjusted. Men were inspired by the suggestions of the great adversary of souls to turn aside the counsels of God for human inventions. God declares, "Neither will I be with you any more until you put away all these unholy things from you." (*Spaulding and Magan Collection*, p. 152).

Many changes are made that might better never be made. Often, when workers become discontented, instead of being encouraged to stay where they are, and make a success of their work, they are sent to another place. But they take with them the same traits of character that have marred their work in the past. They will manifest the same unchristlike spirit; for they have not learned the lesson of patient, humble service. Thus our working force has often been weakened (*Spaulding and Magan Collection*, p. 234).

This is the position taken by many today who claim to be the children of God. They do not understand what it means to receive Christ as a personal Saviour. They have never crucified self (*Spaulding and Magan Collection*, p. 273).

Take unto you the whole armor of God, and never forget the gospel shoes of peace. Go not to any man with a heavy tread or with anger in your voice. Let all God's servants, from those occupying the highest positions to those in the lowest service, walk humbly before Him (*Spaulding and Magan Collection*, p. 281).

Those who know the truth, but who walk contrary to the truth, may never place their foot in the path that Christ followed (*Spaulding and Magan Collection*, p. 307).

All human ambition, all boasting, is to be laid in the dust. Self, sinful self, is to be abased, not exalted. By holiness to God in the daily life here below, we are to manifest the Christ-life. The corrupt nature is to become pure and undefiled; subdued, not exalted. We are to be humble, faithful men and women. Never are we to sit upon the judgment-seat. God demands that his representatives shall be pure vessels, revealing the beauty of sanctified character. The channel is always to remain unobstructed, that the Holy Spirit may have free course; otherwise, spiritual leaders will gloss over the work that must be done in the natural heart in order to perfect Christian character; and they will present their own imperfections in such a way that they make of none effect God's truth, which is as steadfast as the eternal throne. And while God calls upon all his watchmen to lift the danger-signal, at the same time he presents before them the life character of the Saviour as an example of what they must be and do in order to be saved (*Spaulding and Magan Collection*, p. 313).

Never feel that it is your prerogative to humiliate a fellow-worker. If mistakes have been made, learn about them, not from a desire to crush the one who has made them, but from a desire to help, that no one be separated from God's work. Help those who have erred, by telling them of your experiences, showing how, when you have made grave mistakes, patience and fellowship, kindness and helpfulness, on the part of your fellow-workers, gave you courage and hope. Harsh judgment is not becoming. Be afraid to condemn where God has not condemned. Remember that your brethren love God, and that they are striving to keep his commandments as verily as you are. You have been in the Battle, and you carry the scars of conflict. Will you not deal merciful with those who are fiercely assailed? (*Spaulding and Magan Collection*, p. 347).

The children of God should never be rough and discourteous in their bearing toward one another. They should never blame and condemn. To those who want to give vent to a spirit of fault-finding, I would say, Go out among the rocks and stumps, and there relieve your mind of its evil thoughts; for these inanimate objects will not be harmed by your words. Only your own soul will suffer. After you have talked it all out, consider that it is written in the books of heaven what manner of spirit you are of. Then come to God with a broken heart and a contrite spirit, confess your need, and plead for his grace to make you one of his humble children. Let the ambition you have be exercised in a way that will bless needy souls (*Spaulding and Magan Collection*, p. 407).

It is a dangerous work to invest men with authority to judge and rule their fellowmen. Not to you nor to any other man has been given power to control the actions of God's people, and the effort to do this must be no longer continued. God has been dishonored by the education that has been given to the churches in Southern California in looking to one man as conscience and judgment for them. God has never authorized any man to exercise a ruling power over his fellow workers; and those who have allowed a dictatorial spirit to come into their official work need to experience the converting power of God upon their hearts. They have placed man where God should be (*Spaulding and Magan Collection*, p. 413).

All the learning they may acquire will never undo the evil resulting from lax discipline in childhood. One neglect, often repeated, forms habit. One wrong act prepares the way for another. Bad habits are more easily formed than good ones and are given up with more difficulty (*Child Guidance*, p. 202).

I beseech you to bring yourselves under God's control. When tempted to speak provokingly, refrain from saying anything. You will be tempted on this point because you have never overcome this objectionable trait of character. But every wrong habit must be overcome. Make a complete surrender to God. Fall on the Rock, Christ Jesus, and be broken. As husband and wife, discipline yourselves. Go to Christ for help. He will willingly supply you with His divine sympathy, His free grace (*Adventist Home*, p. 342).

In our character building we must build on Christ. He is the sure foundation—a foundation which can never be moved. The tempest of temptation and trial cannot move the building which is riveted to the Eternal Rock (*Child Guidance*, p. 166).

O generation of vipers, how can ye, being evil, speak good things? for out of the abundance of the heart the mouth speaketh. A good man out of the good treasure of the heart bringeth forth good things: and an evil man out of the evil treasure bringeth forth evil things (Matthew 12:34, 35).

Purity of life and a character molded after the divine Pattern are not obtained without earnest effort and fixed principles. A vacillating person will not succeed in attaining Christian perfection. Such will be weighed in the balances and found wanting. Like a roaring lion, Satan is seeking for his prey. He tries his wiles upon every unsuspecting youth ... Satan tells the young that there is time enough yet, that they may indulge in sin and vice this once and never again; but that one indulgence will poison their whole life. Do not once venture on forbidden ground. In this perilous day of evil, when allurements to vice and corruption are on every hand, let the earnest, heartfelt cry of the young be raised to heaven: "Wherewithal shall a young man cleanse his way?" And may his ears be open and his heart inclined to obey the instruction given in the answer, "By taking heed thereto, according to thy word." (*Child Guidance*, p. 466).

You cannot do an evil work and others not be affected by it. While your course of action reveals what kind of material is used in your own character building, it also has a powerful influence over others (*Adventist Home*, p. 463).

We never needed close connection with God more than we need it today. One of the greatest dangers that besets God's people has ever been from conformity to worldly maxims and customs. The youth especially are in constant peril. Fathers and mothers should be on their guard against the wiles of Satan. While he is seeking to accomplish the ruin of their children, let not parents flatter themselves that there is no particular danger. Let them not give thought and care to the things of this world, while the higher, eternal interests of their children are neglected (*Child Guidance*, p.471).

Let this mind be in you, which was also in Christ Jesus: (Philippians 2:5).

That which will make the character lovely in the home is that which will make it lovely in the heavenly mansions. The measure of your Christianity is gauged by the character of your home life. The grace of Christ enables its possessors to make the home a happy place, full of peace and rest. Unless you have the Spirit of Christ, you are none of His and will never see the redeemed saints in His kingdom, who are to be one with Him in the heaven of bliss. God desires you to consecrate yourself wholly to Him and represent His character in the home circle (*Child Guidance*, p. 481).

The nearer we come to Jesus and the more clearly we discern the purity of His character, the more clearly we shall discern the exceeding sinfulness of sin and the less we shall feel like exalting ourselves. Those whom heaven recognizes as holy ones are the last to parade their own goodness. The apostle Peter became a faithful minister of Christ, and he was greatly honored with divine light and power; he had an active part in the upbuilding of Christ's church; but Peter never forgot the fearful experience of his humiliation; his sin was forgiven; yet well he knew that for the weakness of character which had caused his fall only the grace of Christ could avail. He found in himself nothing in which to glory (*Christ Object Lessons*, p. 160).

All who have wrought with unselfish spirit will behold the fruit of their labors. The outworking of every right principle and noble deed will be seen. Something of this we see here. But how little of the result of the world's noblest work is in this life manifest to the doer! How many toil unselfishly and unweariedly for those who pass beyond their reach and knowledge! Parents and teachers lie down in their last sleep, their lifework seeming to have been wrought in vain; they know not that their faithfulness has unsealed springs of blessing that can never cease to flow; only by faith they see the children they have trained become a benediction and an inspiration to their fellow men, and the influence repeat itself a thousandfold... Men sow the seed from which, above their graves, others reap blessed harvests. They plant trees that others may eat the fruit. They are content here to know that they have set in motion agencies for good. In the hereafter the action and reaction of all these will be seen (*Child Guidance*, p. 564).

Remember that you will never reach a higher standard than you yourself set. Then set your mark high, and step by step, even though it be by painful effort, by self-denial and sacrifice, ascend the whole length of the ladder of progress. Let nothing hinder you. Fate has not woven its meshes about any human being so firmly that he need remain helpless and in uncertainty. Opposing circumstances should create a firm determination to overcome them. The breaking down of one barrier will give greater ability and courage to go forward. Press with determination in the right direction, and circumstances (*Christ Object Lessons*, p. 344).

Now is the time to prepare. The seal of God will never be placed upon the forehead of an impure man or woman. It will never be placed upon the forehead of the ambitious, world-loving man or woman. It will never be placed upon the forehead of men or women of false tongues or deceitful hearts. All who receive the seal must be without spot before God; candidates for heaven. Search the Scriptures for yourselves, that you may understand the fearful solemnity of the present hour (*Christian Experience and Teachings,* p. 191).

Oh, how different are the standards by which God and men measure character. God sees many temptations resisted of which the world and even near friends never know—temptations in the home, in the heart. He sees the soul's humility in view of its own weakness; the sincere repentance over even a thought that is evil. He sees the wholehearted devotion to His service. He has noted the hours of hard battle with self-battle that won the victory. All this God and angels know. A book of remembrance is written before Him for them that fear the Lord and that think upon His name (*Christ Object Lessons,* p. 403).

We can never be saved in indolence and inactivity. There is no such thing as a truly converted person living a helpless, useless life. It is not possible for us to drift into heaven. No sluggard can enter there.... Those who refuse to co-operate with God on earth, would not co-operate with Him in heaven. It would not be safe to take them to heaven (*Christian Service,* p. 89).

Success in this life, success in gaining the future life, depends upon a faithful, conscientious attention to the little things. Perfection is seen in the least, no less than in the greatest, of the works of God. The hand that hung the worlds in space is the hand that wrought with delicate skill the lilies of the field. And as God is perfect in his sphere, so we are to be perfect in ours. The symmetrical structure of a strong, beautiful character is built up by individual acts of duty. And faithfulness should characterize our life in the least as well as in the greatest of its details. Integrity in little things, the performance of little acts of fidelity and little deeds of kindness, will gladden the path of life; and when our work on earth is ended, it will be found that every one of the little duties faithfully performed, has exerted an influence for good,—an influence that can never perish (*Christian Education,* p. 217).

Man will rise no higher than his conceptions of truth, purity, and holiness. If the mind is never exalted above the level of humanity, if it is not uplifted by faith to contemplate infinite wisdom and love, the man will be constantly sinking lower and lower. The worshipers of false gods clothed their deities with human attributes and passions, and thus their standard of character was degraded to the likeness of sinful humanity (*Conflict and Courage,* p. 32).

Until the judgment you will never know the influence of a kind, considerate course toward the inconsistent, the unreasonable, the unworthy. When we meet with ingratitude and betrayal of sacred trusts, we are roused to show our contempt or indignation. This the guilty expect, they are prepared for it. But kind forbearance takes them by surprise, and often awakens their better impulses, and arouses a longing for a nobler life (*Counsels on Stewardship,* p. 101).

To talk of religion in a casual way, to pray without soul hunger and living faith, avails nothing. A nominal faith in Christ, which accepts Him merely as the Saviour of the world, can never bring healing to the soul... It is not enough to believe about Christ; we must believe in Him. The only faith that will benefit us is that which embraces Him as a personal Saviour; which appropriates His merits to ourselves (*Conflict and Courage*, p. 298).

Evil habits and practices are bringing upon men disease of every kind. Let the understanding be convinced by education as to the sinfulness of abusing and degrading the powers that God has given (*Counsels on Health*, p. 504).

We should never forget that we are placed on trial in this world, to determine our fitness for the future life. None can enter heaven whose characters are defiled by the foul blot of selfishness. Therefore, God tests us here, by committing to us temporal possessions, that our use of these may show whether we can be entrusted with eternal riches (*Counsels on Stewardship*, p. 22).

Character building is the most important work ever entrusted to human beings; and never before was its diligent study so important as now. Never was any previous generation called to meet issues so momentous; never before were young men and young women confronted by perils so great as confront them today (*Education*, p. 225).

The Lord gave you your work, not to be done in a rush, but in a calm, considerate manner. The Lord never compels hurried, complicated movements (*Evangelism*, p. 146).

This world is not the Christian's heaven, but merely the workshop of God, where we are to be fitted up to unite with the sinless angels in a holy heaven. We should be constantly training the mind to noble, unselfish thoughts. This education is necessary to so bring into exercise the powers which God has given us that His name shall best be glorified upon the earth. We are accountable for all the noble qualities which God has given us, and to put these faculties to a use He never designed we should is showing base ingratitude to Him. The service of God demands all the powers of our being, and we fail of meeting the design of God unless we bring these powers to a high state of cultivation, and educate the mind to love to contemplate heavenly things, and strengthen and ennoble the energies of the soul by right actions, operating to the glory of God (*God's Amazing Grace*, p. 297).

And be not conformed to this world: but be ye transformed by the renewing of your mind, that ye may prove what is that good, and acceptable, and perfect, will of God (Romans 12:2).

There must be men who will begin a work in the right way, and hold to it and push it forward firmly. Everything must be done according to a well-matured plan, and with system. God has entrusted His sacred work to men, and He asks that they shall do it carefully. Regularity in all things is essential. Never be late to an appointment. In no department or office should time be lost in unnecessary conversations. The work of God requires things which it does not receive, because men do not learn from the God of wisdom. They press too many things into their life, postpone until tomorrow that which demands their attention today, and much time is lost in painfully picking up the lost stitches (*Evangelism*, p. 649).

Love, courtesy, self-sacrifice—these are never lost. When God's chosen ones are changed from mortality to immortality, their words and deeds of goodness will be made manifest, and will be preserved through the eternal ages... Through the merits of Christ's imputed righteousness, the fragrance of such words and deeds is forever preserved (*Faith I Live By*, p. 239).

To make God's grace our own, we must act our part. The Lord does not propose to perform for us either the willing or the doing. His grace is given to work in us to will and to do, but never as a substitute for our effort (*God's Amazing Grace*, p. 142).

You need to become acquainted with the weak as well as the strong points in your characters, that you may be constantly guarded lest you engage in enterprises and assume responsibilities for which God has never designed you. You should not compare your actions and measure your lives by any human standard, but with the rule of duty revealed in the Bible (*Gospel Workers*, 1915, p. 319).

Let no one seek to exalt himself by talking of his deeds, extolling his abilities, displaying his knowledge, and cultivating self-conceit ... Christ was never self-confident or conceited (*In Heavenly Places*, p. 221).

The Saviour of the world would have His co-laborers represent Him; and the more closely a man walks with God, the more faultless will be his manner of address, his deportment, his attitude, and his gestures. Coarse and uncouth manners were never seen in our pattern, Christ Jesus. He was a representative of heaven, and His followers must be like Him (*Gospel Workers*, 1915, p. 91).

There are men and women who invite temptation; they place themselves in positions where they will be tempted, where they cannot but be tempted, when they place themselves in society that is objectionable. The best way to keep safe from sin is to move with due consideration at all times and under all circumstances, never to move or act from impulse. Move with the fear of God ever before you and you will be sure to act right; then leave your reputation with God. Slander cannot then sully your character one particle. No one can degrade our character but ourselves, by our own course of action (*In Heavenly Places*, p. 197).

Of all people in the world, reformers should be the most unselfish, the most kind, the most courteous. In their lives should be seen the true goodness of unselfish deeds. The worker who manifests a lack of courtesy, who shows impatience at the ignorance or waywardness of others, who speaks hastily or acts thoughtlessly, may close the door to hearts so that he can never reach them (*Gospel Workers*, 1915, p. 507).

The ability to give a reason for our faith is a good accomplishment, but if the truth does not go deeper than this, the soul will never be saved. The heart must be purified from all moral defilement (*Last Day Events*, p. 70).

Angels of God are watching the development of character. They are weighing moral worth. If you bestow your attentions upon those who have no need, you are doing the recipients harm, and you will yourself receive condemnation, rather than reward. Remember that when by your conversation you descend to the level of frivolous characters, you are encouraging them in the path that leads to perdition. Your unwise attentions may prove the ruin of their souls. You degrade their conceptions of what constitutes Christian life and character. You confuse their ideas, and make impressions that may never be effaced. The harm thus done to souls that needed to be strengthened, refined, and ennobled, is often a sin unto death. They cannot associate these men with the sacred positions which they occupy. The ministers, the officers of the church, all are regarded as no better than themselves. Then where is their example? (*Medical Missionary*, p. 146).

You can never secure a good character by merely wishing for it. It can be gained only by labor. Your desires in this direction must be expressed in earnest, honest endeavor and patient toil. By taking advance steps each day up the ladder of progress, you will find at last at the top,—a conqueror, yes, more than a conqueror, through Him who has loved you (*Messages to Young People*, p. 348).

It makes every difference what material is used in the character building. The long-expected day of God will soon test every man's work. "The fire shall try every man's work of what sort it is" (1 Corinthians 3:13). As fire reveals the difference between gold, silver, and precious stones and wood, hay, and stubble, so the day of judgment will test characters, showing the difference between characters formed after Christ's likeness and characters formed after the likeness of the selfish heart. All selfishness, all false religion, will then appear as it is. The worthless material will be consumed; but the gold of true, simple, humble faith will never lose its value. It can never be consumed, for it is imperishable. One hour of transgression will be seen to be a great loss, while the fear of the Lord will be seen to be the beginning of wisdom. The pleasure of self-indulgence will perish as stubble, while the gold of steadfast principle, maintained at any cost, will endure forever (*Mind, Character and Personality*, Volume 2, p. 548).

Love must dwell in the heart. A thoroughgoing Christian draws his motives of action from his deep heart love for his Master. Up through the roots of his affection for Christ springs an unselfish interest in his brethren. Love imparts to its possessor grace, propriety, and comeliness of deportment. It illuminates the countenance and subdues the voice; it refines and elevates the whole being (*Ministry of Healing*, p. 490).

Wherever there is an impulse of love and sympathy, wherever the heart reaches out to bless and uplift others, there is revealed the working of God's Holy Spirit. In the depths of heathenism men who have had no knowledge of the written law of God, who have never even heard the name of Christ, have been kind to His servants, protecting them at the risk of their own lives. Their acts show the working of a divine power. The Holy Spirit has implanted the grace of Christ in the heart of the savage, quickening his sympathies contrary to his nature, contrary to his education (*My Life Today*, p. 237).

Those who live for a purpose, seeking to benefit and bless their fellowmen and to honor and glorify their Redeemer, are the truly happy ones on the earth, while the man who is restless, discontented, and seeking this and testing that, hoping to find happiness, is always complaining of disappointment. He is always in want, never satisfied, because he lives for himself alone. Let it be your aim to do good, to act your part in life faithfully (*Mind, Character and Personality*, Volume 2, p. 806).

You need not wait for your way to be made smooth before you; go to work to improve your entrusted talents. You have nothing to do with what the world will think of you. Let your words, your spirit, your actions, be a living testimony to Jesus, and the Lord will take care that the testimony for His glory, furnished in a well-ordered life and a godly conversation, shall deepen and intensify in power. Its results may never be seen on earth, but they will be made manifest before God and angels (*A New Life*, p. 35)

We are never to rest in a satisfied condition, and cease to make advancement, saying, "I am saved." When this idea is entertained, the motives for watchfulness, for prayer, for earnest endeavor to press onward to higher attainments, cease to exist. No sanctified tongue will be found uttering these words till Christ shall come, and we enter in through the gates into the city of God. Then, with the utmost propriety, we may give glory to God and to the Lamb for eternal deliverance. As long as man is full of weakness—for of himself he cannot save his soul—he should never dare to say, "I am saved." (*A New Life*, p. 43

The religion of Jesus Christ is a system of the true heavenly politeness and leads to a practical exhibition of habitual tenderness of feeling, kindness of deportment. He who possesses godliness will also add this grace, taking a step higher on the ladder. The higher he mounts the ladder, the more of the grace of God is revealed in his life, his sentiments, his principles. He is learning, ever learning the terms of his acceptance with God, and the only way to obtain an inheritance in the heavens is to become like Christ in character. The whole scheme of mercy is to soften down what is harsh in temper, and refine whatever is rugged in the deportment. The internal change reveals itself in the external actions. The graces of the Spirit of God work with hidden power in the transformation of character. The religion of Christ never will reveal a sour, coarse, and uncourteous action. Courtesy is a Bible virtue. The virtue of this grace of brotherly kindness characterized the life of Christ. Never was such courtesy exhibited upon the earth as Christ revealed, and we cannot overestimate its value (*Our High Calling*, p. 72).

The human mind becomes dwarfed and enfeebled when dealing with commonplace matters only, never rising above the level of time and sense to grasp the mysteries of the unseen. The understanding is gradually brought to the level of the things with which it is constantly familiar ease to grow intellectually and spiritually during his lifetime (*Our High Calling* p. 106)

Absolutely Positively

Chapter 2

Diet & Exercise

Never cheat the stomach out of that which health demands, and never abuse it by placing upon it a load which it should not bear. Cultivate self-control. Restrain appetite; keep it under the control of reason. Do not feel it necessary to load down your table with unhealthful food when you have visitors. The health of your family and the influence upon your children should be considered, as well as the habits and tastes of your guests (*Counsels on Diets and Foods*, p. 176).

For the kingdom of God is not meat and drink; but righteousness, and peace, and joy in the Holy Ghost (Romans 14:17).

Where wrong habits of diet have been indulged there should be no delay in reform. When dyspepsia has resulted from the abuse of the stomach, efforts should be made carefully to preserve the remaining strength of the vital forces, by removing every overtaxing burden. The stomach may never entirely recover health after long abuse; but a proper course of diet will save further debility, and many will recover more or less fully. It is not easy to prescribe rules that will meet every case; but with attention to right principles in eating, great reforms may be made, and the cook need not be continually toiling to tempt the appetite (*Counsels on Diets and Foods*, p. 126).

The character of the food and the manner in which it is eaten exert a powerful influence on the health. Many students have never made a determined effort to control the appetite or to observe proper rules in regard to eating. Some eat too much at their meals, and some eat between meals whenever the temptation is presented (*Counsels to Parents, Teachers, and Students*, p. 297).

Many make a mistake in drinking cold water with their meals. Taken with meals, water diminishes the flow of the salivary glands; and the colder the water, the greater the injury to the stomach. Ice water or ice lemonade, drunk with meals, will arrest digestion until the system has imparted sufficient warmth to the stomach to enable it to take up its work again. Hot drinks are debilitating; and besides, those who indulge in their use become slaves to the habit. Food should not be washed down; no drink is needed with meals. Eat slowly, and allow the saliva to mingle with the food. The more liquid there is taken into the stomach with the meals, the more difficult it is for the food to digest; for the liquid must first be absorbed. Do not eat largely of salt; give up bottled pickles; keep fiery spiced food out of your stomach; eat fruit with your meals, and the irritation which calls for so much drink will cease to exist. But if anything is needed to quench thirst, pure water, drunk some little time before or after the meal, is all that nature requires (*Counsels on Diets and Foods*, p. 420).

We are to teach the people how to prepare dishes that are not expensive, but wholesome and palatable. And never is a recipe to appear in our health journals that will injure our reputation as health reformers (*Counsels to Writers and Editors*, p. 129).

Wine is a mocker, strong drink is raging: and whosoever is deceived thereby is not wise (Proverbs 20:1).

In his association with those whom he meets, the canvasser can do much to show the value of healthful living. Instead of staying at a hotel, he should, if possible, obtain lodging with a private family. As he sits at the table with the family, let him practice the instruction given in the health works he is selling, holding up the banner of strict temperance. As opportunity is offered, let him speak of the value of a healthful diet. He should never be ashamed to say, "No, thank you; I do not eat meat." If tea is offered, let him refuse it, explaining that it is harmful, that though for a time stimulating, the stimulating effect passes off, and a corresponding depression is left. Let him explain the injurious effect of intoxicating drinks, and of tobacco, tea, and coffee, on the digestive organs and the brain (*Counsels on Health*, p. 463).

Those who would work in God's service must not be seeking worldly gratification and selfish indulgence (*Counsels on Diets and Foods*, p. 35).

And God said, Behold, I have given you every herb bearing seed, which is upon the face of all the earth, and every tree, in the which is the fruit of a tree yielding seed; to you it shall be for meat (Genesis 1:29).

Fashionable visiting is made an occasion of gluttony. Hurtful food and drinks are partaken of in such a measure as to greatly tax the organs of digestion. The vital forces are called into unnecessary action in the disposal of it, which produces exhaustion, and greatly disturbs the circulation of the blood, and, as a result, want of vital energy is felt throughout the system. The blessings which might result from social visiting, are often lost for the reason that your entertainer, instead of being profited by your conversation, is toiling over the cookstove, preparing a variety of dishes for you to feast upon. Christian men and women should never permit their influence to countenance such a course by eating of the dainties thus prepared. Let them understand that your object in visiting them is not to indulge the appetite, but that your associating together, and interchange of thoughts and feelings, might be a mutual blessing. The conversation should be of that elevated, ennobling character which could afterward be called to remembrance with feelings of the highest pleasure (*Counsels on Diets and Foods*, p. 88).

Intemperance has cursed the world almost from its infancy. Noah's son was so debased by the excessive use of wine that he lost all sense of propriety, and the curse which followed his sin has never been lifted from his descendants (*Christian Temperance and Bible Hygiene*, p. 28).

The stomach must have careful attention. It must not be kept in continual operation. Give this misused and much-abused organ some peace and quiet and rest (*Child Guidance*, p. 389).

Great care should be taken when the change is made from a flesh meat to a vegetarian diet to supply the table with wisely prepared, well-cooked articles of food. So much porridge eating is a mistake. The dry food that requires mastication is far preferable. The health food preparations are a blessing in this respect. Good brown bread and rolls, prepared in a simple manner yet with painstaking effort, will be healthful (*Counsels on Diets and Foods*, p. 108).

Many turn from light and knowledge, and sacrifice principle to taste. They eat when the system needs no food, and at irregular intervals, because they have no moral stamina to resist inclination. As the result, the abused stomach rebels, and suffering follows. Regularity in eating is very important for health of body and serenity of mind. Never should a morsel of food pass the lips between meals (*Christian Temperance and Bible Hygiene*, p. 50).

By taking too much food, we not only improvidently waste the blessings of God, provided for the necessities of nature, but do great injury to the whole system. We defile the temple of God; it is weakened and crippled; and nature cannot do its work wisely and well, as God has made provision that it should. Because of the selfish indulgence of his appetite, man has oppressed nature's power by compelling it to do work it should never be required to do (*Counsels on Diets and Foods*, p. 131).

Your child has a nervous temperament, and her diet should be carefully guarded. She should not be allowed to choose that food which will gratify the taste without affording proper nourishment.... Never let her go from home to school without her breakfast. Do not venture to give full scope to your inclinations in this matter. Place yourself entirely under the control of God, and He will help you to bring all your desires into harmony with His requirements (*Child Guidance*, p. 390).

Cheese should never be introduced into the stomach (*Counsels on Diets and Foods*, p. 368).

Flesh was never the best food; but its use is now doubly objectionable, since disease in animals is so rapidly increasing (*Counsels on Diets and Foods*, p. 384).

The tissues of the swine swarm with parasites. Of the swine, God said, "It is unclean unto you; ye shall not eat of their flesh, nor touch their dead carcass." This command was given because swine's flesh is unfit for food. Swine are scavengers, and this is the only use they were intended to serve. Never, under any circumstances, was their flesh to be eaten by human beings (*Counsels on Diets and Foods*, p. 392).

And now, as in the days of Israel, every youth should be instructed in the duties of practical life. Each should acquire a knowledge of some branch of manual labor, by which, if need be, he may obtain a livelihood. This is essential, not only as a safeguard against the vicissitudes of life, but from its bearing upon physical, mental, and moral development. Even if it were certain that one would never need to resort to manual labor for his support, still he should be taught to work. Without physical exercise, no one can have a sound constitution and vigorous health; and the discipline of well-regulated labor is no less essential to the securing of a strong and active mind and a noble character (*Christian Education* p. 69).

Absolutely Positively

Education in health principles was never more needed than now. Notwithstanding the wonderful progress in so many lines relating to the comforts and conveniences of life, even to sanitary matters and to the treatment of disease, the decline in physical vigor and power of endurance is alarming. It demands the attention of all who have at heart the well-being of their fellow men (*Counsels on Diets and Foods*, p. 441).

Many students are deplorably ignorant of the fact that diet exerts a powerful influence upon the health. Some have never made a determined effort to control the appetite, or to observe proper rules in regard to diet. They eat too much, even at their meals, and some eat between meals whenever the temptation is presented. If those who profess to be Christians desire to solve the questions so perplexing to them, why their minds are so dull, why their religious aspirations are so feeble, they need not, in many instances, go farther than the table; here is cause enough, if there were no other (*Christian Education*, p. 184).

Many turn from light and knowledge, and sacrifice principle to taste. They eat when the system needs no food and at irregular intervals, because they have no moral stamina to resist inclination. As the result, the abused stomach rebels and suffering follows. Regularity in eating is very important for health of body and serenity of mind. Never should a morsel of food pass the lips between meals (*Counsels on Health*, p. 118).

Cooking schools are to be held. The people are to be taught how to prepare wholesome food. They are to be shown the need of discarding unhealthful foods. But we should never advocate a starvation diet. It is possible to have a wholesome, nutritious diet without the use of tea, coffee, and flesh food. The work of teaching the people how to prepare a dietary that is at once wholesome and appetizing, is of the utmost importance (*Counsels on Diets and Foods*, p. 469).

It is a religious duty for every Christian girl and woman to learn to make good, sweet, light bread from unbolted wheat flour. Mothers should take their daughters into the kitchen with them when very young, and teach them the art of cooking. The mother cannot expect her daughters to understand the mysteries of housekeeping without education. She should instruct them patiently, lovingly, and make the work as agreeable as she can by her cheerful countenance and words of approval. If they fail once, twice, or thrice, censure not. Already discouragement is doing its work, and tempting them to say, "It is no use; I can't do it." This is not the time for censure. The will is becoming weakened. It needs the spur of encouraging, cheerful, hopeful words: "Never mind the mistakes you have made. You are but a learner, and must expect to make blunders. Try again. Put your mind on what you are doing. Be very careful, and you will certainly succeed" (*Christian Temperance and Bible Hygiene*, p. 157).

Pork, although one of the most common articles of diet, is one of the most injurious. God did not prohibit the Hebrew from eating swine's flesh merely to show His authority, but because it is not a proper article of food for man. God never created the swine to be eaten under any circumstances. It is impossible for the flesh of any living creature to be healthful when filth is its natural element, and when it feeds upon every detestable thing (*Counsels on Health*, p. 116).

Carefully consider your diet. Study from cause to effect. Cultivate self-control. Keep appetite under the control of reason. never abuse the stomach by overeating, but do not deprive yourself of the wholesome, palatable food that health demands (*Counsels on Diets and Foods*, p. 168).

Pork, although one of the most common articles of diet, is one of the most injurious. God did not prohibit the Hebrews from eating swine's flesh merely to show his authority, but because it is not a proper article of food for man. God never created the swine to be eaten under any circumstances. It is impossible for the flesh of any living creature to be healthful when filth is its natural element, and when it feeds upon every detestable thing (*Christian Temperance and Bible Hygiene*, p. 48).

Plain, simple pie may serve as dessert, but when one eats two or three pieces merely to gratify an inordinate appetite, he unfits himself for the service of God. Some, after partaking largely of other food, will take dessert, not because they need it, but because it tastes good. If they are asked to take a second piece, the temptation is too great to be resisted, and two or three pieces of pie are added to the load placed upon the already overworked stomach. He who will do this has never educated himself to practice self-denial. The victim of appetite is so wedded to his own way that he cannot see the injury he is doing to himself (*Counsels on Diets and Foods*, p. 333).

Our economy must never be of that kind which would lead to providing meager meals. Students should have an abundance of wholesome food. But let those in charge of the cooking gather up the fragments that nothing be lost (*Adventist Home*, p. 377).

The digestive organs should never be burdened with a quantity or quality of food which it will tax the system to appropriate. All that is taken into the stomach, above what the system can use to convert into good blood, clogs the machinery; for it cannot be made into either flesh or blood, and its presence burdens the liver, and produces a morbid condition of the system. The stomach is overworked in its efforts to dispose of it, and then there is a sense of languor, which is interpreted to mean hunger, and without allowing the digestive organs time to rest from their severe labor, to recruit their energies, another immoderate amount is taken into the stomach, to set the weary machinery again in motion. The system receives less nourishment from too great a quantity of food, even of the right quality, than from a moderate quantity taken at regular periods (*Counsels on Diets and Foods*, p. 103).

Many indulge in the pernicious habit of eating just before retiring. They may have taken their regular meals, yet because they feel a sense of faintness, they think they must have a lunch. By indulging this wrong practice it becomes a habit, and they feel as though they could not sleep without food. In many cases this faintness comes because the digestive organs have been too severely taxed through the day in disposing of the great quantities of food forced upon them. These organs need a period of entire rest from labor, to recover their exhausted energies. A second meal should never be eaten until the stomach has had time to recover from the labor of digesting the preceding meal. When we lie down at night, the stomach should have its work all done, that it, as well as other portions of the body, may enjoy rest. But if more food is forced upon it, the digestive organs are put in motion again, to perform the same round of labor through the sleeping hours. The sleep of such is often disturbed with unpleasant dreams, and in the morning they awake unrefreshed. When this practice is followed, the digestive organs lose their natural vigor, and the person finds himself a miserable dyspeptic. And not only does the transgression of nature's laws affect the individual unfavorably, but others suffer more or less with him. Let any one take a course that irritates him in any way, and see how quickly he manifests impatience! He cannot, without special grace, speak or act calmly. He casts a shadow wherever he goes. How can any one say, then, "It is nobody's business what I eat or drink?" (*Christian Temperance and Bible Hygiene*, p. 50).

The habit of enjoying useful labor, once formed, will never be lost. You are then prepared to be placed in any circumstances in life, and you will be fitted for the position. You will learn to love activity. If you enjoy useful labor, your mind will be occupied with your employment, and you will not find time to indulge in dreamy fancies (*Adventist Home*, p. 90).

A second meal should never be eaten until the stomach has had time to rest from the labor of digesting the preceding meal. If a third meal be eaten at all, it should be light, and several hours before going to bed (*Counsels on Diets and Foods*, p. 158).

God calls upon parents to guard their children against the indulgence of appetite, and especially against the use of stimulants and narcotics. The tables of Christian parents should never be loaded with food containing condiments and spices. They are to study to preserve the stomach from any abuse (*Child Guidance*, p. 405).

Never take tea, coffee, beer, wine, or any spirituous liquors. Water is the best liquid possible to cleanse the tissues (*Counsels on Diets and Foods*, p. 421).

You are to make no prescription that no flesh meats shall never be used, but you are to educate the mind, and let the light shine in. Let the individual conscience be awakened in regard to self-preservation and self-purity from every perverted appetite. The variety of food at one meal causes unpleasantness, and destroys the good which each article, if taken alone, would do the system. This practice causes constant suffering, and often death (*Spaulding and Magan Collection*, p. 31).

There is a natural and a depraved appetite. Parents who have taught their children to eat unhealthful, stimulating food all their lives—until the taste is perverted, and they crave clay, slate pencils, burned coffee, tea grounds, cinnamon, cloves, and spices—cannot claim that the appetite demands what the system requires. The appetite has been falsely educated, until it is depraved. The fine organs of the stomach have been stimulated and burned, until they have lost their delicate sensitiveness. Simple, healthful food seems to them insipid. The abused stomach will not perform the work given it, unless urged to it by the most stimulating substances. If these children had been trained from their infancy to take only healthful food, prepared in the most simple manner, preserving its natural properties as much as possible, and avoiding flesh meats, grease, and all spices, the taste and appetite would be unimpaired. In its natural state, it might indicate, in a great degree, the food best adapted to the wants of the system" (*Child Guidance*, p. 381).

Intemperance in eating and drinking, intemperance in labor, intemperance in almost everything, exists on every hand. Those who make great exertions to accomplish just so much work in a given time, and continue to labor when their judgment tells them they should rest, are never gainers. They are living on borrowed capital. They are expending the vital force which they will need at a future time. And when the energy they have so recklessly used is demanded, they fail for want of it. The physical strength is gone, the mental powers fail. They realize that they have met with a loss, but do not know what it is. Their time of need has come, but their physical resources are exhausted. Every one who violates the laws of health must some time be a sufferer to a greater or less degree. God has provided us with constitutional force, which will be needed at different periods of our lives. If we recklessly exhaust this force by continual overtaxation, we shall sometime be losers. Our usefulness will be lessened, if not our life itself destroyed (*Christian Education*, p. 166).

The custom of placing different courses of food upon the table would better never have been invented. Let that which is provided for the meal be placed upon the table at the beginning, and then let each one eat that which will be the most healthful for him. Let each have an opportunity to choose what shall compose his meal. If the extras which are provided for dessert were dispensed with altogether it would be a blessing (*Spaulding and Magan Collection*, p. 42).

We are already suffering because of the wrong habits of our fathers, and yet how many take a course in every way worse than theirs! Opium, tea, coffee, tobacco, and liquor are rapidly extinguishing the spark of vitality still left in the race. Every year millions of gallons of intoxicating liquors are drank, and millions of dollars are spent for tobacco. And the slaves of appetite, while constantly spending their earnings in sensual indulgence, rob their children of food and clothing and the advantages of education. There can never be a right state of society while these evils exist (*Christian Temperance and Bible Hygiene*, p. 36).

The same rule of eating can not be made for all. I make it a rule never to eat custards; for when I eat them, they always make a disturbance in my stomach. But there are those in my family who suffer no inconvenience from eating custards, and because I can not eat them, I do not say that they ought not to eat them. We must each experiment and know for ourselves what is best for us to eat. We may have to abstain from many things that others can eat without inconvenience (*Spaulding and Magan Collection*, p. 260).

Bread should be light and sweet. Not the least taint of sourness should be tolerated. The loaves should be small, and so thoroughly baked that, as far as possible, the yeast germs shall be destroyed. When hot, or new, raised bread of any kind is difficult of digestion. It should never appear on the table. This rule does not, however, apply to unleavened bread. Fresh rolls made of wheaten meal, without yeast or leaven, and baked in a well-heated oven, are both wholesome and palatable (*Counsels on Diets and Foods*, p. 316).

And put a knife to thy throat, if thou be a man given to appetite. Be not desirous of his dainties: for they are deceitful meat (Proverbs 23:2, 3).

The more liquid there is taken into the stomach with the meals, the more difficult it is for the food to digest; for the liquid must first be absorbed. Do not eat largely of salt; give up spiced pickles; keep fiery food out of the stomach; eat fruit with the meals, and the irritation that calls for so much drink will cease to exist. But if anything is needed to quench thirst, pure water is all that nature requires. Never take tea, coffee, beer, wine, or any spirituous liquor (*Christian Temperance and Bible Hygiene*, p. 51).

Some cannot be impressed with the necessity of eating and drinking to the glory of God. The indulgence of appetite affects them in all the relations of life. It is seen in their family, in their church, in the prayer meeting, and in the conduct of their children. It has been the curse of their lives. You cannot make them understand the truths for these last days. God has bountifully provided for the sustenance and happiness of all His creatures; and if His laws were never violated, and all acted in harmony with the divine will, health, peace, and happiness, instead of misery and continual evil, would be experienced (*Counsels on Diets and Foods*, p. 54).

For the drunkard and the glutton shall come to poverty: and drowsiness shall clothe a man with rags (Proverbs 23:21).

Because we, from principle, discard the use of those things which irritate the stomach and destroy health, the idea should never be given that it is of little consequence what we eat. I do not recommend an impoverished diet. Many who need the benefits of healthful living, and from conscientious motives adopt what they believe to be such, are deceived by supposing that a meager bill of fare, prepared without painstaking, and consisting mostly of mushes and so-called gems, heavy and sodden, is what is meant by a reformed diet. Some use milk and a large amount of sugar on mush, thinking that they are carrying out health reform. But the sugar and milk combined are liable to cause fermentation in the stomach, and are thus harmful. The free use of sugar in any form tends to clog the system, and is not infrequently a cause of disease. Some think that they must eat only just such an amount, and just such a quality, and confine themselves to two or three kinds of food. But in eating too small an amount, and that not of the best quality, they do not receive sufficient nourishment (*Christian Temperance and Bible Hygiene*, p. 56).

Even if you are strict in the quality of your food, do you glorify God in your bodies and spirits which are His, by partaking of such a quantity of food? Those who place so much food upon the stomach, and thus load down nature, could not appreciate the truth should they hear it dwelt upon. They could not arouse the benumbed sensibilities of the brain to realize the value of the atonement, and the great sacrifice that has been made for fallen man. It is impossible for such to appreciate the great, the precious, and the exceedingly rich reward that is in reserve for the faithful overcomers. The animal part of our nature should never be left to govern the moral and intellectual (*Counsels on Diets and Foods*, p. 47).

I have never felt that it was my duty to say that no one should ever taste of meat under any circumstances. To say this when people have been educated to live on flesh to so great an extent, would be to carry matters to extremes. I have never felt that it was my duty to make sweeping assertions. What I have said, I have said under a sense of duty, but I have been guarded in my statements, because I did not want to give occasion for any one to be a conscience for another (*Spaulding and Magan Collection*, p. 80).

Some of our people conscientiously abstain from eating improper food, and at the same time neglect to eat the food that would supply the elements necessary for the proper sustenance of the body. Let us never bear testimony against health reform by failing to use wholesome, palatable food in place of the harmful articles of diet that we have discarded. Much tact and discretion should be employed in preparing nourishing food to take the place of that which has constituted the diet of many families. This effort requires faith in God, earnestness of purpose, and a willingness to help one another. A diet lacking in the proper elements of nutrition brings reproach upon the cause of health reform. We are mortal, and must supply ourselves with food that will give proper sustenance to the body (*Counsels on Diets and Foods*, p. 92).

God has written His law upon every nerve and muscle, every fiber and function of the human body. The indulgence of unnatural appetite, whether for tea, coffee, tobacco, or liquor, is intemperance, and is at war with the laws of life and health. By using these forbidden articles a condition of things is created in the system which the Creator never designed. This indulgence in any of the members of the human family is sin... The eating of food that does not make good blood is working against the laws of our physical organism, and is a violation of the law of God. The cause produces the effect. Suffering, disease, and death are the sure penalty of indulgence (*Evangelism*, p. 265).

Because it is the fashion, in harmony with morbid appetite, rich cake, pies, and puddings, and every hurtful thing, are crowded into the stomach. The table must be loaded down with a variety, or the depraved appetite cannot be satisfied. In the morning, these slaves to appetite often have impure breath, and a furred tongue. They do not enjoy health, and wonder why they suffer with pains, headaches, and various ills. Many eat three times a day, and again just before going to bed. In a short time the digestive organs are worn out, for they have had no time to rest. These become miserable dyspeptics, and wonder what has made them so. The cause has brought the sure result (*Counsels on Diets and Foods*, p. 158).

It is impossible to prescribe by weight the quantity of food which should be eaten. It is not advisable to follow this process, for by so doing the mind becomes self-centered. Eating and drinking become altogether too much a matter of thought. Those who do not make a god of the stomach will carefully guard the appetite. They will eat plain, nourishing food... They will eat slowly and will masticate their food thoroughly. After eating they will take proper exercise in the open air. Such need never trouble themselves to measure out precise quantities (*Mind, Character and Personality*, Volume 2, p. 392).

Those who have overtaxed their physical powers should not be encouraged to forgo manual labor entirely. But labor, to be of the greatest advantage, should be systematic and agreeable. Outdoor exercise is the best; it should be so planned as to strengthen by use the organs that have become weakened; and the heart should be in it; the labor of the hands should never degenerate into mere drudgery (*Ministry of Healing*, p. 238).

The stomach is not fevered with meat, and overtaxed, but is in a healthy condition, and can readily perform its task. There should be no delay in reform. Efforts should be made to preserve carefully the remaining strength of the vital forces, by lifting off every overtaxing burden. The stomach may never fully recover health, but a proper course of diet will save further debility, and many will recover more or less, unless they have gone very far in gluttonous self-murder (*Counsels on Diets and Foods*, p. 159).

Where wrong habits of diet have been indulged, there should be no delay in reform. When dyspepsia has resulted from abuse of the stomach, efforts should be made carefully to preserve the remaining strength of the vital forces by removing every overtaxing burden. The stomach may never entirely recover health after long abuse; but a proper course of diet will save further debility, and many will recover more or less fully. It is not easy to prescribe rules that will meet every case; but, with attention to right principles in eating, great reforms may be made, and the cook need not be continually toiling to tempt the appetite (*Ministry of Healing*, p. 308).

Eating much flesh will diminish intellectual activity. Students would accomplish much more in their studies if they never tasted meat. When the animal part of the human nature is strengthened by meat eating, the intellectual powers diminish proportionately (*Healthful Living*, p. 101).

But even health reformers can err in the quantity of food. They can eat immoderately of a healthful quality of food. Some in this house err in the quality. They have never taken their position upon health reform. They have chosen to eat and drink what they pleased and when they pleased. They are injuring their systems in this way. Not only this, but they are injuring their families by placing upon their tables a feverish diet, which will increase the animal passions of their children, and lead them to care but little for heavenly things. The parents are thus strengthening the animal, and lessening the spiritual powers of their children. What a heavy penalty will they have to pay in the end! And then they wonder that their children are so weak morally! (*Counsels on Diets and Foods*, p. 244).

Bread should never have the slightest taint of sourness. It should be cooked until it is most thoroughly done. Thus all softness and stickiness will be avoided... Milk should not be used in place of water in bread making. All this is extra expense, and is not wholesome. If the bread thus made is allowed to stand over in warm weather, and is then broken open, there will frequently be seen long strings like cobwebs. Such bread soon causes fermentation to take place in the stomach... Every housekeeper should feel it her duty to educate herself to make good sweet bread in the most inexpensive manner, and the family should refuse to have upon the table bread that is heavy and sour, for it is injurious (*Healthful Living*, p. 80).

If we would work for the restoration of health, it is necessary to restrain the appetite, to eat slowly, and only a limited variety at one time. This instruction needs to be repeated frequently. It is not in harmony with the principles of health reform to have so many different dishes at one meal. We must never forget that it is the religious part of the work, the work of providing food for the soul, that is more essential than anything else (*Counsels on Diets and Foods*, p. 275).

Where plenty of good milk and fruit can be obtained there is rarely any excuse for eating animal food; it is not necessary to take the life of any of God's creatures to supply our ordinary needs. In certain cases of illness or exhaustion it may be thought best to use some meat, but great care should be taken to secure the flesh of healthy animals. It has come to be a very serious question whether it is safe to use flesh food at all in this age of the world. It would be better never to eat meat than to use the flesh of animals that are not healthy. When I could not obtain the food I needed, I have sometimes eaten a little meat; but I am becoming more and more afraid of it (*Counsels on Diets and Foods*, p. 394).

Great care should be taken when the change is made from a flesh meat to a vegetarian diet, to supply the table with wisely prepared, well-cooked articles of food. So much porridge eating is a mistake. The dry food that requires mastication is far preferable. The health food preparations are a blessing in this respect. Good brown bread and rolls, prepared in a simple manner, yet with painstaking effort, will be healthful. Bread should never have the slightest taint of sourness. It should be cooked until it is thoroughly done. Thus all softness and stickiness will be avoided (*Counsels on Diets and Foods*, p. 318).

Young girls who have health never know how to appreciate its value. If their employment is sedentary, they have a distaste for other branches of labor. They complain of great weariness if they take exercise. This should be to them a convincing fact that they need to train their muscles (*Sons and Daughters of God*, p. 173).

Hot biscuit raised with soda or baking powder should never appear upon our tables. Such compounds are unfit to enter the stomach. Hot raised bread of any kind is difficult of digestion. Graham gems, which are both wholesome and palatable, may be made from the unbolted flour, mixed with pure cold water and milk. But it is difficult to teach our people simplicity. When we recommend graham gems, our friends say, "Oh, yes, we know how to make them." We are much disappointed when they appear raised with baking powder or with sour milk and soda. These give no evidence of reform. The unbolted flour, mixed with pure soft water and milk, makes the best gems we have ever tasted. If the water is hard, use more sweet milk, or add an egg to the batter. Gems should be thoroughly baked in a well-heated oven, with a steady fire (*Counsels on Diets and Foods*, p. 319).

Make fruit the article of diet to be placed on your table, which shall constitute the bill of fare. The juices of it mingled with bread will be highly enjoyed. Good, ripe, undecayed fruit is a thing we should thank the Lord for, because it is beneficial to health. Try it. To educate your children to subsist on a meat diet is harmful to them. It is much easier not to create an unnatural appetite than to correct it and reform the taste after it has become second nature. Our Sanitariums should never be conducted after the manner of a hotel. I am sorry it is such a difficult matter for you to deny your appetites and reform your habits of eating and drinking (*Spaulding and Magan Collection*, p. 81).

The cook fills an important place in the household. She is preparing food to be taken into the stomach, to form brain, bone, and muscle. The health of all members of the family depends largely upon her skill and intelligence. Household duties will never receive the attention they demand until those who faithfully perform them are held in proper respect (*Counsels on Diets and Foods*, p. 252).

It is important that the food should be prepared with care, that the appetite, when not perverted, can relish it. Because we from principle discard the use of meat, butter, mince pies, spices, lard, and that which irritates the stomach and destroys health, the idea should never be given that it is of but little consequence what we eat (*Counsels on Diets and Foods*, p. 259).

I am instructed to say that the health food work is not at present being conducted as to greatly advance the work of God. The Lord has presented before me many dangers that threaten the management of this business. The Lord never designed that the manufacture and sale of health foods should become such a commercial [business] as it now is. This is not to become a speculative business, in which a few shall receive large personal profits. To many minds God has given wisdom to devise healthful food preparations (*The Health Food Ministry*, p. 73).

Thousands have indulged their perverted appetites, have eaten a good meal, as they called it, and as the result, have brought on a fever, or some other acute disease, and certain death. That was enjoyment purchased at immense cost. Yet many have done this, and these self-murderers have been eulogized by their friends and the minister, and carried directly to heaven at their death. What a thought! Gluttons in heaven! No, no; such will never enter the pearly gates of the golden city of God. Such will never be exalted to the right hand of Jesus, the precious Saviour, the suffering Man of Calvary, whose life was one of constant self-denial and sacrifice. There is a place appointed for all such among the unworthy, who can have no part in the better life, the immortal inheritance (*Counsels on Diets and Foods*, p. 125).

The Bible nowhere teaches the use of intoxicating wine, either as a beverage or as a symbol of the blood of Christ. We appeal to the natural reason whether the blood of Christ is better represented by the pure juice of the grape in its natural state, or after it has been converted into a fermented and intoxicating wine... We urge that the latter should never be placed upon the Lord's table... We protest that Christ never made intoxicating wine; such an act would have been contrary to all the teachings and examples of his life... The wine which Christ manufactured from water by a miracle of his power was the pure juice of the grape (*Healthful Living*, p. 113).

The mince pies and the pickles, which should never find a place in any human stomach, will give a miserable quality of blood (*Counsels on Diets and Foods*, p. 345).

Drug takers are never well. They are always taking cold, which causes extreme suffering, because of the poison all through their system (*Healthful Living*, p. 209).

We have always used a little milk and some sugar. This we have never denounced, either in our writings or in our preaching. We believe cattle will become so much diseased that these things will yet be discarded, but the time has not yet come for sugar and milk to be wholly abolished from our tables (*Counsels on Diets and Foods*, p. 330).

Thousands are sick and dying around us who might get well and live if they would; but their imagination holds them. They fear that they will be made worse if they labor or exercise, when this is just the change they need to make them well. Without this they never can improve. They should exercise the power of the will, rise above their aches and debility, engage in useful employment, and forget that they have aching backs, sides, lungs, and heads. Neglecting to exercise the entire body, or a portion of it, will bring on morbid conditions. Inaction of any of the organs of the body will be followed by a decrease in size and strength of the muscles and will cause the blood to flow sluggishly through the blood vessels (*Medical Missionary*, p. 105).

Some of our people conscientiously abstain from eating improper food, and at the same time neglect to eat food that would supply the elements necessary for the proper sustenance of the body. Let us never bear a testimony against health reform by failing to use wholesome, palatable food in place of the harmful articles of diet that we have discarded. Much tact and discretion should be employed in preparing nourishing food to take the place of that which has constituted the diet of many families. This effort requires faith in God, earnestness of purpose, and a willingness to help one another. A diet lacking in the proper elements of nutrition brings reproach upon the cause of health reform. We are mortal, and must supply ourselves with food that will give proper sustenance to the body (*Medical Missionary*, p. 273).

The Lord will teach many in all parts of the world to combine fruits, grains, and vegetables into foods that will sustain life and will not bring disease. Those who have never seen the recipes for making the health foods now on the market will work intelligently, experimenting with the food productions of the earth, and will be given light regarding the use of these productions. The Lord will show them what to do (*Counsels on Health*, p. 471).

Keep the work of health reform to the front, is the message I am given to bear. Show so plainly the value of health reform that a widespread need for it will be felt. But never advocate a starvation diet. It is possible to have a wholesome, nutritious diet without using flesh-meat (*Medical Missionary*, p. 275).

The less that condiments and desserts are placed upon our tables, the better it will be for all who partake of the food. All mixed and complicated foods are injurious to the health of human beings. Dumb animals would never eat such a mixture as is often placed in the human stomach (*Counsels on Diets and Foods*, p. 113).

You should never let a morsel pass your lips between your regular meals. Eat what you ought, but eat it at one meal, and then wait until the next (*Counsels on Diets and Foods*, p. 180).

Some who are never considered really drunk are always under the influence of mild intoxicants. They are feverish, unstable in mind, unbalanced. Imagining themselves secure, they go on and on, until every barrier is broken down, every principle sacrificed. The strongest resolutions are undermined, the highest considerations are not sufficient to keep the debased appetite under the control of reason (*Ministry of Healing*, p. 332).

Absolutely Positively

It is quite a common custom with people of the world to eat three times a day, beside eating at irregular intervals between meals; and the last meal is generally the most hearty, and is often taken just before retiring. This is reversing the natural order; a hearty meal should never be taken so late in the day. Should these persons change their practice, and eat but two meals a day, and nothing between meals, not even an apple, a nut, or any kind of fruit, the result would be seen in a good appetite and greatly improved health (*Counsels on Diets and Foods*, p. 181).

Poor, half-decayed fruit and vegetables should never be placed upon the table because it is a savings of a few pennies. This kind of management is a loss, and the body that should be nourished as a temple of the Holy Ghost and be fitted to do the very best kind of work is neglected. Many speeches were made in regard to self-denial and self-sacrifice that were wholly inappropriate and uncalled for (*The Retirement Years*, p. 127).

You are to make no prescriptions that flesh meats shall never be used, but you are to educate the mind, and let the light shine in. Let the individual conscience be awakened in regard to self-preservation and self-purity from every perverted appetite (*Counsels on Diets and Foods*, p. 291).

For a healthy young man, stern, severe exercise is strengthening to brain, bone, and muscle. And it is an essential preparation for the difficult work of a physician. Without such exercise the mind cannot be in working order. It cannot put forth the sharp, quick action that will give scope to its powers. It becomes inactive. Such a youth will never, never become what God designed he should be. He has established so many resting places that he becomes like a stagnant pool. The atmosphere surrounding him is charged with moral miasma (*Letter 103*, p. 1900).

Water can be used in many ways to relieve suffering. Drafts of clear, hot water taken before eating (half a quart, more or less), will never do any harm, but will rather be productive of good (*Counsels on Diets and Foods* 303).

Chapter 3

The Sabbath

If thou turn away thy foot from the sabbath, from doing thy pleasure on my holy day; and call the sabbath a delight, the holy of the LORD, honourable; and shalt honour him, not doing thine own ways, nor finding thine own pleasure, nor speaking thine own words: Then shalt thou delight thyself in the LORD; and I will cause thee to ride upon the high places of the earth, and feed thee with the heritage of Jacob thy father: for the mouth of the LORD hath spoken it (Isaiah 58:13, 14).

When the Sabbath is thus remembered, the temporal will not be allowed to encroach upon the spiritual. No duty pertaining to the six working days will be left for the Sabbath. During the week our energies will not be so exhausted in temporal labor that on the day when the Lord rested and was refreshed, we shall be too weary to engage in His service (*Child Guidance*, p. 528).

Often when our workers present the testing Sabbath truth to the people, some stand hesitating for fear of bringing poverty and hardship upon themselves and their families. They say, Yes, I see what you are trying to show me in regard to the observance of the seventh-day Sabbath; but I am afraid if I keep the Sabbath I shall lose my position, and shall not be able to provide for my family. And so, many keep their worldly position and disobey the command of God. But these scriptures teach us that the Lord knows all about our experiences; He understands about our inconveniences; and He has a care for all who follow on to know the Lord. He will never allow His children to be tempted above that they are able to bear (*Evangelism*, p. 237).

Moreover also I gave them my sabbaths, to be a sign between me and them, that they might know that I am the LORD that sanctify them (Ezekiel 20:12).

In order to keep the Sabbath holy, it is not necessary that we enclose ourselves in walls, shut away from the beautiful scenes of nature and from the free, invigorating air of heaven. We should in no case allow burdens and business transactions to divert our minds upon the Sabbath of the Lord, which He has sanctified. We should not allow our minds to dwell upon things of a worldly character even. But the mind cannot be refreshed, enlivened, and elevated by being confined nearly all the Sabbath hours within walls, listening to long sermons and tedious, formal prayers. The Sabbath of the Lord is put to a wrong use if thus celebrated. The object for which it was instituted is not attained. The Sabbath was made for man, to be a blessing to him by calling his mind from secular labor to contemplate the goodness and glory of God. It is necessary that the people of God assemble to talk of Him, to interchange thoughts and ideas in regard to the truths contained in His word, and to devote a portion of time to appropriate prayer. But these seasons, even upon the Sabbath, should not be made tedious by their length and lack of interest (*Testimonies to the Church*, Volume 2, p. 583).

Absolutely Positively

Fathers and mothers should make it a rule that their children attend public worship on the Sabbath, and should enforce the rule by their own example. It is our duty to command our children and our household after us, as did Abraham. By example as well as precept we should impress upon them the importance of religious teaching. All who have taken the baptismal vow have solemnly consecrated themselves to the service of God; they are under covenant obligation to place themselves and their children where they may obtain all possible incentives and encouragement in the Christian life (*Child Guidance*, p. 530).

Never need anyone fear that observance of the true Sabbath will result in starvation. These promises are a sufficient answer to all the excuses that man may invent for refusing to keep the Sabbath. Even if, after beginning to keep God's law, it seems impossible to support one's family, let every doubting soul realize that God has promised to care for those who obey His commandments (*Evangelism*, p. 240).

The question has been asked, "Should our restaurants be opened on the Sabbath?" My answer is, No, no! The observance of the Sabbath is our witness to God—the mark, or sign, between Him and us that we are His people. Never is this mark to be obliterated (*Counsels on Health*, p. 489).

And God blessed the seventh day, and sanctified it: because that in it he had rested from all his work which God created and made (Genesis 2:3).

The Sabbath should be made so interesting to our families that its weekly return will be hailed with joy. In no better way can parents exalt and honor the Sabbath than by devising means to impart proper instruction to their families and interesting them in spiritual things, giving them correct views of the character of God and what He requires of us in order to perfect Christian characters and attain to eternal life. Parents, make the Sabbath a delight, that your children may look forward to it and have a welcome in their hearts for it (*Testimonies to the Church*, Volume 2, p. 585).

The Sabbath is God's memorial of His creative work, and it is a sign that is to be kept before the world (*Selected Messages*, Volume 2, p. 384).

In the Holiest I saw an ark; on the top and sides of it was purest gold. On each end of the ark was a lovely cherub, with their wings spread out over it. Their faces were turned towards each other, and they looked downwards. Between the angels was a golden censer. Above the ark, where the angels stood, was an exceeding bright glory, that appeared like a throne where God dwelt. Jesus stood by the ark. And as the saints' prayers came up to Jesus, the incense in the censer would smoke, and he offered up the prayers of the saints with the smoke of the incense to his Father. In the ark, was the golden pot of manna, Aaron's rod that budded, and the tables of stone which folded together like a book. Jesus opened them, and I saw the ten commandments written on them with the finger of God. On one table was four, and on the other six. The four on the first table shone brighter than the other six. But the fourth (the Sabbath commandment,) shone above them all; for the Sabbath was set apart to be kept in honor of God's holy name. The Holy Sabbath looked glorious—a halo of glory was all around it. I saw that the Sabbath was not nailed to the cross. If it was, the other nine commandments were; and we are at liberty to go forth and break them all, as well as to break the fourth. I saw that God had not changed the Sabbath, for he never changes. But the Pope had changed it from the seventh to the first day of the week; for he was to change times and laws (*A Sketch of the Christian Experience and Views of Ellen G. White*, p. 16).

None should permit themselves, through the week, to become so absorbed in their temporal interests, and so exhausted by their efforts for worldly gain, that on the Sabbath they have no strength or energy to give to the service of God. We are robbing the Lord when we unfit ourselves to worship Him upon His holy day. And we are robbing ourselves as well; for we need the warmth and glow of association, as well as the strength to be gained from the wisdom and experience of other Christians (*Child Guidance*, p. 530).

As a means of intellectual training, the opportunities of the Sabbath are invaluable. Let the Sabbath school lesson be learned, not by a hasty glance at the lesson scripture on Sabbath morning, but by careful study for the next week on Sabbath afternoon, with daily review or illustration during the week. Thus the lesson will become fixed in the memory, a treasure never to be wholly lost (*Counsels on Stewardship*, p. 43).

Had the Sabbath always been sacredly observed, there could never have been an atheist or an idolater (*Faith I Live By*, p. 32).

Jesus sought to impress upon the narrow minds of the Jews a sense of the folly of their view of the Sabbath. He showed them that God's work never ceases. It is even greater upon the Sabbath than upon ordinary occasions, for at that time his people leave their usual employments and spend the time in prayerful meditation and worship. They ask more favors of him upon the Sabbath than upon other days, they demand his special attention, they crave his choicest blessings, they offer importunate prayers for special favors. God does not wait for the Sabbath to pass before he grants those requests, but he deals to the petitioners, with judicious wisdom, whatever is best for them to have (*Spirit of Prophecy*, Volume 2, p. 164).

On Friday let the preparation for the Sabbath be completed. See that all the clothing is in readiness, and that all the cooking is done. Let the boots be blacked, and the baths be taken. It is possible to do this. If you make it a rule, you can do it. The Sabbath is not to be given to the repairing of garments, to the cooking of food, to pleasure seeking, or to any other worldly employment. Before the setting of the sun, let all secular work be laid aside, and all secular papers be put out of sight. Parents, explain your work and its purpose to your children, and let them share in your preparation to keep the Sabbath according to the commandment (*Child Guidance*, p. 528).

And it came to pass, that he went through the corn fields on the sabbath day; and his disciples began, as they went, to pluck the ears of corn. And the Pharisees said unto him, Behold, why do they on the sabbath day that which is not lawful? And he said unto them, Have ye never read what David did, when he had need, and was an hungred, he, and they that were with him? How he went into the house of God in the days of Abiathar the high priest, and did eat the shewbread, which is not lawful to eat but for the priests, and gave also to them which were with him? And he said unto them, The sabbath was made for man, and not man for the sabbath: Therefore the Son of man is Lord also of the sabbath (Mark 2:24–28).

The fourth commandment, which Rome has endeavored to set aside, is the only precept of the Decalogue that points to God as the Creator of the heavens and the earth, and thus distinguishes the true God from all false gods. The Sabbath was instituted to commemorate the work of creation, and thus to direct the minds of men to the true and living God. The fact of his creative power is cited throughout the Scriptures as proof that the God of Israel is superior to heathen deities. Had the Sabbath always been kept, man's thoughts and affections would have been led to his Maker as the object of reverence and worship, and there would never have been an idolater, an atheist, or an infidel (*Spirit of Prophecy, Volume 4*, p. 281).

The Sabbath was instituted in Eden before the Fall, and was observed by Adam and Eve, and all the heavenly host. God rested on the seventh day, and blessed and hallowed it. I saw that the Sabbath never will be done away; but that the redeemed saints, and all the angelic host, will observe it in honor of the great Creator to all eternity (*Faith I Live By*, p. 303).

Since the Sabbath is the memorial of creative power, it is the day above all others when we should acquaint ourselves with God through His works. In the minds of the children the very thought of the Sabbath should be bound up with the beauty of natural things. Happy is the family who can go to the place of worship on the Sabbath as Jesus and His disciples went to the synagogue—across the fields, along the shores of the lake, or through the groves. Happy the father and mother who can teach their children God's written word with illustrations from the open pages of the book of nature; who can gather under the green trees, in the fresh, pure air, to study the word and to sing the praise of the Father above (*Education*, p. 251).

There are those who hold that the Sabbath was given only for the Jews; but God has never said this. He committed the Sabbath to His people Israel as a sacred trust; but the very fact that the desert of Sinai, and not Palestine, was the place selected by Him in which to proclaim His law, reveals that He intended it for all mankind. The law of ten commandments is as old as creation. Therefore the Sabbath institution has no special relation to the Jews, any more than to all other created beings. God has made the observance of the Sabbath obligatory upon all men. "The sabbath," it is plainly stated, "was made for man." Let every one, therefore, who is in danger of being deceived on this point give heed to the Word of God rather than the assertions of men (*Lift Him Up*, p. 53).

Speak thou also unto the children of Israel, saying, Verily my sabbaths ye shall keep: for it is a sign between me and you throughout your generations; that ye may know that I am the LORD that doth sanctify you (Exodus 31:13).

I was shown that the law of God would stand fast forever, and exist in the new earth to all eternity. At the creation, when the foundations of the earth were laid, the sons of God looked with admiration upon the work of the Creator, and all the heavenly host shouted for joy. It was then that the foundation of the Sabbath was laid. At the close of the six days of creation, God rested on the seventh day from all his work which he had made; and he blessed the seventh day and sanctified it, because that in it he had rested from all his work. The Sabbath was instituted in Eden before the fall, and was observed by Adam and Eve, and all the heavenly host. God rested on the seventh day, and blessed and hallowed it; and I saw that the Sabbath would never be done away; but the redeemed saints, and all the angelic host, will observe it in honor of the great Creator to all eternity (*Spiritual Gifts*, Volume 1, p. 113)

Ye shall kindle no fire throughout your habitations upon the sabbath day (Exodus 35:3)

The day before the Sabbath should be made a day of preparation, that everything may be in readiness for its sacred hours. In no case should our own business be allowed to encroach upon holy time. God has directed that the sick and suffering be cared for; the labor required to make them comfortable is a work of mercy, and no violation of the Sabbath; but all unnecessary work should be avoided. Many carelessly put off till the beginning of the Sabbath little things that might have been done on the day of preparation. This should not be. Work that is neglected until the beginning of the Sabbath should remain undone until it is past. This course might help the memory of these thoughtless ones, and make them careful to do their own work on the six working days (*Patriarchs and Prophets*, p. 296).

Heaven's work never ceases, and we should never rest from doing good. Our own work the law forbids us to do on the rest day of the Lord. The toil for a livelihood must cease; no labor for worldly pleasure or profit is lawful upon that day. But the Sabbath is not to be spent in useless inactivity. As God ceased from His labor of creating, and rested upon the Sabbath, so we are to rest. He bids us lay aside our daily occupations, and devote those sacred hours to healthful rest, to worship, and to holy deeds (*Story of Jesus*, p. 74).

Neither carry forth a burden out of your houses on the sabbath day, neither do ye any work, but hallow ye the sabbath day, as I commanded your fathers (Jeremiah 17:22)

Cooking on the Sabbath should be avoided; but it is not therefore necessary to eat cold food. In cold weather the food prepared the day before should be heated. And let the meals, however simple, be palatable and attractive. Especially in families where there are children, it is well, on the Sabbath, to provide something that will be regarded as a treat, something the family do not have every day (*Ministry of Healing*, p. 307).

Thus saith the LORD; Take heed to yourselves, and bear no burden on the sabbath day, nor bring it in by the gates of Jerusalem; Neither carry forth a burden out of your houses on the sabbath day, neither do ye any work, but hallow ye the sabbath day, as I commanded your fathers (Jeremiah 17:21–22)

Everyone should feel that he has a part to act in making the Sabbath meetings interesting. You are not to come together simply as a matter of form, but for the interchange of thought, for

Absolutely Positively

the relation of your daily experiences, for the expression of thanksgiving, for the utterance of your sincere desire for divine enlightenment, that you may know God, and Jesus Christ, whom He has sent. Communing together in regard to Christ will strengthen the soul for life's trials and conflicts. Never think that you can be Christians and yet withdraw yourselves within yourselves. Each one is a part of the great web of humanity, and the experience of each will be largely determined by the experience of his associates (*Lift Him Up*, p. 303).

And it shall come to pass, that from one new moon to another, and from one sabbath to another, shall all flesh come to worship before me, saith the LORD (Isaiah 66:23)

Remember the sabbath day, to keep it holy. Six days shalt thou labor, and do all thy work: But the seventh day is the sabbath of the LORD thy God: in it thou shalt not do any work, thou, nor thy son, nor thy daughter, thy manservant, nor thy maidservant, nor thy cattle, nor thy stranger that is within thy gates: For in six days the LORD made heaven and earth, the sea, and all that in them is, and rested the seventh day: wherefore the LORD blessed the sabbath day, and hallowed it (Exodus 20:8–11)

Chapter 4

Education

The school work in a place where a church school has been established should never be given up unless God plainly directs that this should be done. Adverse influences may seem to conspire against the school, but with God's help the teacher can do a grand, saving work in changing the order of things. If he labors patiently, earnestly, perseveringly, in Christ's lines, the reformatory work done in the school may extend to the homes of the children, bringing into them a purer, more heavenly atmosphere. This is indeed missionary work of the highest order (*Counsels to Parents, Teachers, and Students*, p. 157).

Superintendents, never scold nor complain before your teachers or scholars. If you wish to influence the school for good, put away the whip, and exert a heaven-inspiring influence, which will carry the minds of all with you. In making plans and regulations for the school, let them represent, as nearly as possible, the voice of the school. In some schools there is a sharp, critical spirit. Much is made of forms and rules, while the weightier matters, mercy and the love of God, are neglected. Let all be cheerful. If any have clouds encompassing their souls, let them work out into the sunlight before they enter the Sabbath school. A mother who is constantly relating her discouragements, and complaining to her children of their lack of appreciation, cannot have proper control of them. So will it be with you, teachers and superintendents. If you see a lack in this respect, do not lessen your influence by speaking of it; but in a quiet way set influences to work that will correct the evil. Plan, study how to secure a well-organized, well-disciplined school (*Counsels on Stewardship*, p. 168).

In choosing retired localities for our schools, we do not for a moment suppose that we are placing the youth beyond the reach of temptation. Satan is a very diligent worker, and is untiring in devising ways to corrupt every mind that is open to his suggestions. He meets families and individuals on their own ground, adapting his temptations to their inclinations and weaknesses. But in the large cities his power over minds is greater, and his nets for the entanglement of unwary feet are more numerous. In connection with our schools, ample grounds should be provided. There are some students who have never learned to economize, and have always spent every shilling they could get. These should not be cut off from the means of gaining an education. Employment should be furnished them, and with their study of books should be mingled a training in industrious, frugal habits. Let them learn to appreciate the necessity of helping themselves (*Fundamentals of Christian Education*, p. 422).

Train up a child in the way he should go: and when he is old, he will not depart from it (Proverbs 22:6)

Absolutely Positively

In educating children and youth, teachers should never allow one passionate word or gesture to mar their works for in so doing they imbue the students with the same spirit that they themselves possess. The Lord would have our primary as well as our more advanced schools, of that character that angels of God can walk through the room, and behold in the order and principles of government, the order and government of heaven. This is thought by many to be impossible; but every school should begin with this, and should work most earnestly to preserve the spirit of Christ in temper, in communications, in instruction, the teachers placing themselves in the channel of light where the Lord can use them as his agents, to reflect his own likeness of character upon the students. They may know that as God-fearing instructors they have helpers every hour to impress upon the hearts of the children the valuable lessons given (*Spaulding and Magan Collection*, p. 101).

Do not think that the Bible will become a tiresome book to the children. Under a wise instructor the word will become more and more desirable. It will be to them as the bread of life, it will never grow old. There is in it a freshness and beauty that attract and charm the children and youth. It is like the sun shining upon the earth, giving its brightness and warmth, yet never exhausted. By lessons from Bible history and doctrine, the children and youth can learn that all other books are inferior to this. They can find here a fountain of mercy and love (*Counsels to Parents, Teachers, and Students*, p. 171).

God help the managers of our schools never to allow the outgoes to exceed the incomes, if the school has to be closed. There has not been the talent that is needed in the management of our schools financially. These things God will require of the managers. Every needless, expensive habit is to be laid aside, every unnecessary indulgence cut away. When the principles so manifestly indicated by the Word of God to all schools are taken hold of as earnestly as they should be, the debts will not accumulate (*Spaulding and Magan Collection*, p. 117).

Nothing is of greater importance than the education of our children and young people. The church should arouse and manifest a deep interest in this work; for now as never before, Satan and his host are determined to enlist the youth under the black banner that leads to ruin and death (*Counsels to Parents, Teachers, and Students*, p. 165).

Never will education accomplish all that it might and should accomplish until the importance of the parents' work is fully recognized, and they receive a training for its sacred responsibilities (*Child Guidance*, p. 64).

The work of teachers is an important one. They should make the word of God their meditation. God will communicate by His own Spirit with the soul. Pray as you study, "Open Thou mine eyes, that I may behold wondrous things out of Thy law," Psalm 119:18. When the teacher will rely upon God in prayer, the Spirit of Christ will come upon him, and God will work through him by the Holy Spirit upon the mind of the student. The Holy Spirit fills mind and heart with hope and courage and Bible imagery, which will be communicated to the student. The words of truth will grow in importance, and will assume a breadth and fullness of meaning of which he has never dreamed. The beauty and virtue of the word of God have a transforming influence upon mind and character; the sparks of heavenly love will fall upon the hearts of the children as an inspiration. We may bring hundreds and thousands of children to Christ if we will work for them (*Counsels to Parents, Teachers, and Students*, p. 172).

A teacher may have sufficient education and knowledge in the sciences to instruct, but has it been ascertained that he has tact and wisdom to deal with human minds? If instructors have not the love of Christ abiding in their hearts, they are not fit to bear the grave responsibilities placed upon those who educate the youth. Lacking the higher education themselves, they know not how to deal with human minds. Their own insubordinate hearts are striving for control; and to subject the plastic minds and characters of the children to such discipline is to leave upon the mind scars and bruises that will never be removed (*Counsels to Parents, Teachers, and Students*, p. 193).

We have many lessons to learn, and many, many to unlearn. God and heaven alone are infallible. Those who think that they will never have to give up a cherished view, never have occasion to change an opinion, will be disappointed. As long as we hold to our own ideas and opinions with determined persistency, we cannot have the unity for which Christ prayed (*Counsels to Writers and Editors*, p. 37).

Let the teacher bring peace and love and cheerfulness into his work. Let him not allow himself to become angry or provoked. The Lord is looking upon him with intense interest, to see if he is being molded by the divine Teacher. The child who loses his self-control is far more excusable than the teacher who allows himself to become angry and impatient. When a stern reproof is to be given, it may still be given in kindness. Let the teacher beware of making the child stubborn by speaking to him harshly. Let him follow every correction with drops of the oil of kindness. He should never forget that he is dealing with Christ in the person of one of Christ's little ones (*Counsels to Parents, Teachers, and Students*, p. 212).

Heart education is of more importance than the education gained from books. It is well, even essential, to obtain a knowledge of the world in which we live; but if we leave eternity out of our reckoning, we shall make a failure from which we can never recover (*Child Guidance*, p. 497).

Give instruction to a wise man, and he will be yet wiser: teach a just man, and he will increase in learning (Proverbs 9:9).

The youth in all our institutions are to be molded and fashioned and disciplined for God; and in this work the Lord's mercy and love and tenderness are ever to be revealed. This is not to degenerate into weakness and sentimentality. We are to be kind, yet firm. And let teachers remember that while decision is needful, they are never to be harsh or condemnatory, never to manifest an overbearing spirit. Let them keep calm, revealing the better way by refusing to be provoked to anger (*Counsels to Parents, Teachers, and Students*, p. 214).

Every teacher has his own particular traits of character to watch, lest Satan should use him as his agent to destroy souls, by his own unconsecrated traits of character. The only safety for teachers is to learn daily in the school of Christ, his meekness, his lowliness of heart; then self will be hid in Christ, and he will meekly wear the yoke of Christ, and consider that he is dealing with his heritage (*Spaulding and Magan Collection*, p. 144).

No man or woman is fitted for the work of teaching who is fretful, impatient, arbitrary, or dictatorial. These traits of character work great harm in the schoolroom. Let not the teacher excuse his wrong course by the plea that he has naturally a hasty temper or that he has erred ignorantly. In his position he stands where ignorance or lack of self-control is sin. He is writing upon souls lessons that will be carried all through life, and he should train himself never to speak a hasty word, never to lose his self-control (*Counsels to Parents, Teachers, and Students*, p. 233).

Teacher, weed from your talks all that is not of the highest and best quality. Keep before the students those sentiments only that are essential. Never should the physician, minister, or teacher prolong his talks until the alpha is forgotten in long-drawn-out assertions that are not of the least benefit. When this is done, the mind is swamped with a multitude of words that it cannot retain. Let the talks given be short and right to the point. Let the mind be kept sweet and pure, and open to heaven's first law, "Thou shalt love the Lord thy God with all thy heart, and with all thy soul, and with all thy strength, and with all thy mind; and thy neighbor as thyself." Luke 10:27. If those who act a part in the training of the youth will leave many things unsaid, and present before the students the importance of the principles they must obey in order to have eternal life, there will be seen a work of true reform (*Counsels to Parents, Teachers, and Students*, p. 403).

In all your teaching never forget that the greatest lesson to be taught and to be learned is the lesson of copartnership with Christ in the work of salvation. The education to be secured by searching the Scriptures is an experimental knowledge of the plan of salvation. Such an education will restore the image of God in the soul. It will strengthen and fortify the mind against temptation and fit the learner to become a worker with Christ in His mission of mercy to the world. It will make him a member of the heavenly family, prepare him to share the inheritance of the saints in light (*Counsels to Parents, Teachers, and Students*, p. 434).

Teachers and students are to come close together in Christian fellowship. The youth will make many mistakes, and the teacher is never to forget to be compassionate and courteous. Never is he to seek to show his superiority. The greatest of teachers are those who are most patient, most kind. By their simplicity and their willingness to learn they encourage their students to climb higher and still higher (*Counsels to Parents, Teachers, and Students*, p. 269).

What we need is knowledge that will strengthen mind and soul, that will make us better men and women. Heart education is of far more importance than mere book learning. It is well, even essential, to have a knowledge of the world in which we live; but if we leave eternity out of our reckoning we shall make a failure from which we can never recover (*Counsels to Parents, Teachers, and Students*, p. 388).

Man is finite; there is no light in his wisdom. His unaided reason can explain nothing in the deep things of God, nor can he understand the spiritual lessons that God has placed in the material world. But reason is a gift of God, and His Spirit will aid those who are willing to be taught. Man's words, if of any value, echo the words of God. In the education of youth they should never take the place of the divine word (*Counsels to Parents, Teachers, and Students*, p. 423).

Exercise the mental powers, and in no case neglect the physical. Let not intellectual slothfulness close up your path to greater knowledge. Learn to reflect as well as to study, that your minds may expand, strengthen, and develop. Never think that you have learned enough and that you may now relax your efforts. The cultivated mind is the measure of the man. Your education should continue during your lifetime; every day you should be learning and putting to practical use the knowledge gained (*Counsels to Parents, Teachers, and Students*, p. 475).

Students should be willing to work under those of experience, to heed their suggestions, to follow their advice, and to go as far as possible in thought, training, and intelligent enterprise; but they should never infringe upon a rule, never disregard one principle, that has been interwoven with the upbuilding of the institution. The dropping down is easy enough; the disregard of regulations is natural to the heart inclined to selfish ease and gratification. It is much easier to tear down than to build up. One student with careless ideas may do more to let down the standard than ten men with all their effort can do to counteract the demoralizing influence (*Counsels to Parents, Teachers, and Students*, p. 481).

As an educating power, the Bible is without a rival. Nothing will so impart vigor to all the faculties as requiring students to grasp the stupendous truths of revelation. The mind gradually adapts itself to the subjects upon which it is allowed to dwell. If occupied with commonplace matters only, to the exclusion of grand and lofty themes, it will become dwarfed and enfeebled. If never required to grapple with difficult problems, or put to the stretch to comprehend important truths, it will, after a time, almost lose the power of growth (*Christian Education*, p. 37).

If your life is hid with Christ in God, a divine Helper will stand beside you, and you will be one with the Saviour and one with those you are teaching. Never exalt self; exalt Christ, glorify Him, honor Him before the world. Say, I stand under the bloodstained banner of Prince Immanuel. I am wholly on the Lord's side. Show sympathy and tenderness in dealing with your pupils. Reveal the love of God. Let the words you speak be kind and encouraging. Then as you work for your students, what a transformation will be wrought in the characters of those who have not been properly trained in the home! The Lord can make even youthful teachers channels for the revealing of His grace, if they will consecrate themselves to Him (*Counsels to Parents, Teachers, and Students*, p. 152).

The teacher should bring true self-respect into all that he does. He should not allow himself to be quick-tempered. He should not punish harshly children that are in need of reform. Let him understand that self must be kept in subjection. He should never forget that over him is a divine Teacher, whose pupil he is, and under whose control he is ever to be. As the teacher humbles the heart before God, it will be softened and subdued by the thought of his own shortcomings. He will realize something of the meaning of the words, "You, that were sometime alienated and enemies in your mind by wicked works, yet now hath He reconciled in the body of His flesh through death, to present you holy and unblamable and unreprovable in His sight." Colossians 1:21, 22 (*Counsels to Parents, Teachers, and Students*, p. 152).

The best education that can be given to children and youth is that which bears the closest relation to the future, immortal life. This kind of education should be given by godly parents, by devoted teachers, and by the church, to the end that the youth in turn may become zealous missionaries for either home or foreign fields. They are to be earnestly instructed in the truths of the Bible, that they may become pillars in the church, champions for truth, rooted and grounded in the faith. They are to know whereof they believe, and to have such an experience in divine things that they will never become betrayers of sacred trusts (*Fundamentals of Christian Education*, p. 231).

By the blessing of the Lord the work has been started, and now the help of every one is needed. The students must be taught how to begin. The educators must be men and women who have had experience, and who will lead the students in the right way at every step they advance. Teach Bible manners; teach purity of thought the strictest integrity. This is the most valuable instruction that can be given. Keep Jesus, the Pattern, ever before your students by your example. This will act a prominent part in restoring the moral image of God in those under your charge. Teachers, you have no time, no duty to teach students the forms and ceremonies of this age of corruption, when everything is perverted to outward appearance and display. This must never find a place in our school. This reform is not to be brought in as essential (*Spaulding and Magan Collection*, p. 51).

Principal and teachers should have a living connection with God and should stand firmly and fearlessly as witnesses for Him. Never from cowardice or worldly policy let the word of God be placed in the background. Students will be profited intellectually, as well as morally and spiritually, by its study (*Counsels to Parents, Teachers, and Students*, p. 89).

"When the enemy begins to work, we need not allow our feelings to control, and resort to strange fire. We need not become combative. By doing this, we may thus betray the cause at the very point where victory is ours. If we let go our hold of Jesus, and trust in ourselves, it may take months, or perhaps years, to counteract that one wrong move. Unless we are converted, and become as little children, we shall never see the kingdom of God. These are the lessons we need to bring into our schools. The students do not need science as much as they need these principles. Teach them how to advance the truth as it is in Jesus (*Spaulding and Magan Collection*, p. 25).

Every teacher needs Christ abiding in his heart by faith, and to possess a true, self-denying, self-sacrificing spirit for Christ's sake. One may have sufficient education and knowledge in science to instruct; but has it been ascertained that he has tact and wisdom to deal with human minds? If instructors have not the love of Christ abiding in the heart, they are not fit to be brought into connection with children, and to bear the grave responsibilities placed upon them, of educating these children and youth. They lack the higher education and training in themselves, and they know not how to deal with human minds. There is the spirit of their own insubordinate, natural hearts that is striving for the control, and to subject the plastic minds and characters of children to such a discipline, is to leave scars and bruises upon the mind that will never be effaced (*Christian Education*, p. 144).

No limit can be set to our influence. One thoughtless act may prove the ruin of many souls. The course of every worker in our college is making impressions upon the minds of the young, and these are borne away to be reproduced in others. It should be the teacher's aim to prepare every youth under his care to be a blessing to the world. This object should never be lost sight of. There are some who profess to be working for Christ, yet who occasionally go over to the side of Satan and do his work. Can the Saviour pronounce these good and faithful servants? Are they, as watchmen, giving the trumpet a certain sound? (*Counsels to Parents, Teachers, and Students*, p. 96).

When the word of God is laid aside for books that lead away from God, and that confuse the understanding regarding the principles of the kingdom of heaven, the education given is a perversion of the name. Unless the student has pure mental food, thoroughly winnowed from the so-called "higher education," which is mingled with infidel sentiments, he cannot truly know God. Only those who co-operate with heaven in the plan of salvation can know what true education in its simplicity means (*Counsels to Parents, Teachers, and Students*, p. 15).

Prophecy and history should form a part of the studies in our schools, and all who accept positions as educators, should prize more and more the revealed will of God. They should, in simplicity, instruct the students. They should unfold the Scriptures, and show by their own life and character the preciousness of Bible religion and the beauty of holiness; but never, for one moment, let the impression be left upon any one that it would be for his profit to hide his faith and doctrines from the unbelieving people of the world, fearing that he might not be so highly honored if his principles were known (*Christian Education*, p. 212).

There is a great work to be done in our college, a work which demands the co-operation of every teacher; and it is displeasing to God for one to discourage another. But nearly all seem to forget that Satan is an accuser of the brethren, and they unite with the enemy in his work. While professed Christians are contending, Satan is laying his snares for the inexperienced feet of children and youth. Those who have had a religious experience should seek to shield the young from his devices. They should never forget that they themselves were once enchanted with the pleasures of sin. We need the mercy and forbearance of God every hour, and how unbecoming for us to be impatient with the errors of the inexperienced youth! So long as God bears with them, dare we, fellow sinners, cast them off? (*Counsels to Parents, Teachers, and Students*, p. 96).

Well balanced minds and symmetrical characters are required as teachers in every line. Give not this work into the hands of young women and young men who know not how to deal with human minds. They know so little of the controlling power of grace upon their own hearts and characters that they have to unlearn, and learn entirely new lessons in Christian experience. They have never learned to keep their own soul and character under discipline to Jesus Christ, and bring even the thoughts into captivity to Jesus Christ. There are all kinds of characters to deal with in the children and youth. Their minds are impressible. Anything like a hasty, passionate exhibition on the part of the teacher may cut off her influence for good over the students whom she is having the name of educating. And will this education be for the present and future eternal good of the children and youth? There is the correct influence to be exerted upon them for their spiritual good. Instruction is to be constantly given to encourage the children in the formation of correct habits in speech, in voice, in deportment (*Christian Education*, p. 151).

The study of Latin and Greek is of far less consequence to ourselves, to the world, and to God, than the thorough study and use of the whole human machinery. It is a sin to study books to the neglect of how to become familiar with the various branches of usefulness in practical life. With some, close application to books is a dissipation. The physical machinery being untaxed leads to a great amount of activity in the brain. This becomes the devil's workshop. never can that life that is ignorant of the house we live in be an all-round life (*Spaulding and Magan Collection*, p. 97).

A return to simpler methods will be appreciated by the children and youth. Work in the garden and field will be an agreeable change from the wearisome routine of abstract lessons to which the young minds should never be confined. To the nervous child or youth, who finds lessons from books exhausting and hard to remember, it will be especially valuable. There is health and happiness for him in the study of nature; and the impressions made will not fade out of his mind, for they will be associated with objects that are continually before his eyes (*Counsels to Parents, Teachers, and Students*, p. 187).

The hand was made to do all kinds of work, and students who think that education consists only in book study never make a right use of the fingers and hands. Students should be thoroughly taught to do this very work that thousands of hands are never educated to do. The powers thus developed and cultivated can be most usefully employed (*Spaulding and Magan Collection*, p. 97).

Well-balanced minds and symmetrical characters are required of teachers in every line. The work of teaching should not be given into the hands of young men and women who do not know how to deal with human minds, who have never learned to keep themselves under discipline to Jesus Christ, to bring even the thoughts into captivity to Him. They know so little about the controlling power of grace upon their own hearts and characters that they have much to unlearn, and must learn entirely new lessons in Christian experience (*Counsels to Parents, Teachers, and Students*, p. 191).

I have seen that danger attends every new phase of experience in the church, because some hear things with such a strong spirit. While some teachers may be strong and efficient in teaching in the lines of Bible doctrines, they will not all be men who have a knowledge of practical life, and can advise perplexed minds with surety and safety. They do not discern the perplexing situation that must necessarily come to every family who shall make a change. Therefore, let all be careful what they say; if they know not the mind of God in some matters, let them never speak from a guess or suppose so. If they know nothing definite, let them say so, and let the individual rely wholly upon God. Let there be much praying done, and even with fasting, that not one shall move in darkness, but move in the light as God is in the light (*Country Living*, p. 26).

Education

What book can begin to compare with the Bible? It is essential, for every child, for youth, and for those of mature age to understand, for it is the Word of God, the Word to guide all the human family to heaven. Then why does not the Word from God contain the chief elements which constitute education? Uninspired authors are placed in the hands of children and youth in our schools as a lesson book - books from which they are to be educated. They are kept before the youth, taking up their precious time in studying those things which they can never use. Many books have been introduced into the schools which should never have been placed there. These books do not in any sense voice the words of John, "Behold the Lamb of God that taketh away the sin of the world." The whole line of studies in our schools should be to prepare the people for the future immortal life (*Spaulding and Magan Collection*, p. 11).

In the school of Christ, students are never graduated. Among the pupils are both old and young. Those who give heed to the instructions of the divine Teacher constantly advance in wisdom, refinement, and nobility of soul, and thus they are prepared to enter that higher school where advancement will continue throughout eternity (*Counsels to Parents, Teachers, and Students*, p. 51).

Again, as to making public to the school the errors of students I have been brought in to see and hear some of these exposures, and then have been shown the after influence. It has been harmful in every respect, and has no beneficial influence upon the school. Had those who had acted a part in these things had the spirit and wisdom of Christ, they would have seen a way to remedy the existing difficulties more after the likeness of Jesus Christ. It never helps a student to be humiliated before the whole school. It creates a wound that mortifies. It heals nothing, cures nothing (*Spaulding and Magan Collection*, p. 143).

The present showing is sufficient to prove to all who have the true missionary spirit that the "regular lines" may prove a failure and a snare. God helping his people, the circle of kings who dared to take such great responsibilities shall never again exercise their unsanctified power in the so-called "regular lines". Too much power has been invested in unrevived, unreformed human agencies. Let not selfishness and covetousness be allowed to outline the work which must be done to fulfill the grand, noble commission which Christ has given to every disciple. He, our Lord and Master, has given us an example, in his life, of self-sacrifice, of the way in which we must work to advance the kingdom of God (*Spaulding and Magan Collection*, p. 175).

Parents who have never felt the care which they should feel for the souls of their children, and who have never given them proper restraint and instruction, are the very ones who manifest the most bitter opposition when their children are restrained, reproved, or corrected at school. Some of these children are a disgrace to the church and a disgrace to the name of Adventists (*Child Guidance*, p. 325).

Teachers are not to allow themselves to be quick-tempered. They should not manifest temper. They should not punish harshly the children that are in need of reform. Let the teachers first know and understand that self must be kept in subjection. Think of the boundless love Christ has bestowed on human beings. Never forget that over you there is a divine Teacher, whose subject you are, and under whose control you are ever to be. Humble the heart before God. It will be softened and subdued by the thought of the riches God has bestowed on his children. You will realize something of the meaning of the words, "You, that were sometimes alienated and enemies in your mind by wicked works, yet now hath he reconciled in the body of his flesh through death, to present you holy and unblameable and unreproveable in his sight." (*Spaulding and Magan Collection*, p. 184).

The value of song as a means of education should never be lost sight of... Let there be singing in the school, and the pupils will be drawn closer to God, to their teachers, and to one another (*Messages to Young People*, p. 292).

Never give up the school work in a place where a church school has been established, unless God plainly directs that this should be done. With God's help, the teacher may do a grand, saving work in changing the order of things. If the teacher works patiently, earnestly, perseveringly, in Christ's lines, the reformatory work done in the school will extend to the homes of the children, creating a purer, more refined, more Christlike atmosphere. This is indeed missionary work of the highest order. Teachers who do this work are doing God service for this life and for the life eternal (*Spaulding and Magan Collection*, p. 184).

In the school, as well as in the home, the question of discipline should be understood. We should hope that in the schoolroom there would never be occasion to use the rod. But if in a school there are those who stubbornly resist all counsel and entreaty, all prayers and burden of soul in their behalf, then it is necessary to make them understand that they must obey (*Child Guidance*, p. 323).

Students, I want to tell you, I thank God that you have advanced as you have in your studies, that there are those today who, as these brethren shall leave the school, can accompany them and carry on their education right where they shall go. How carry it on? By using the very education they have to the very best account, and be going into the houses as evangelists, Bible workers. When teaching the Scriptures, you will find that there is a knowledge that comes to you which you never thought of. Words will come, ideas will come, sentiments will come. You can begin to work for the ignorant, those who need your help, and you have an Educator right by your side; that is, the precious Jesus. The angels of God will help you in education. You remember how it was with Daniel. You know all about how he gave God the glory. He gave him glory for the work that he had done for him. He and his three companions were taken away from their country, from their parents, from their educators, at a very young age. They were so kind, respectful, and polite in all their manners, that the one who had charge of them fell in love with them (*Spaulding and Magan Collection*, p. 358).

The schoolwork in a place where a church school has been established should never be given up unless God plainly directs that this should be done. Adverse influences may seem to conspire against the school, but with God's help the teacher can do a grand, saving work in changing the order of things (*Child Guidance* p. 309).

Very many youth who have gone through a college course have not obtained that true education that they can put to practical use. They may have the name of having a collegiate education, but in reality they are only educated dunces (*Fundamentals of Christian Education*, p. 44).

Let the teacher bring love and peace and cheerfulness into this work. Let him not allow himself to become angry or provoked. The Lord is looking upon him with intense interest, to see if he is being educated by the great Teacher. The child who loses his self-control is far more excusable than the teacher who allows himself to become angry and impatient. When a teacher has a reproof to give, let him give it in a soft, gentle voice. Let him be careful not to make the child stubborn by speaking to him harshly. Let him follow every correction with drops of the oil of kindness. His heart should be softened by love and kindness. He should never forget that he is dealing with Christ in the person of one of Christ's little children (*Spaulding and Magan Collection*, p. 294).

The teacher should not be left to carry the burden of his work alone. He needs the sympathy, the kindness, the co-operation, and the love of every church member. The parents should encourage the teacher by showing that they appreciate his efforts. Never should they say or do anything that will encourage insubordination in their children (*Child Guidance*, p. 324).

Parents, when the church school teacher tries to train and discipline your children that they may gain eternal life, do not in their presence criticize his actions, even though you may think him too severe. If you desire them to give their hearts to the Saviour, co-operate with the teacher's efforts for their salvation. How much better it is for children, instead of hearing criticism, to hear from the lips of their mother words of commendation regarding the work of the teacher. Such words make lasting impressions and influence the children to respect the teacher (*Child Guidance*, p. 325).

Never rest satisfied with a low standard. In attending school, be sure that you have in view a noble, holy object. Go because you desire to fit yourselves for service in some part of the Lord's vineyard. Do all that you can to attain this object. You can do more for yourselves than anyone can do for you. And if you do all that you can for yourselves, what a burden you will lift from the principal and the teachers! (*Counsels to Parents, Teachers, and Students*, p. 218).

To know God is eternal life. Are you teaching this to your children, or are you teaching them to meet the world's standard? Are you getting ready for the home that God is preparing for you? Teach your children of the Saviour's life, death, and resurrection. Teach them to study the Bible. Teach them to form characters that will live through the eternal ages. We must pray as we never have before that God will keep and bless our children (*Child Guidance*, p. 494).

The great educating book is the Bible, and yet it is little read or practiced. O that every individual would seek to make of himself all that he could, improving his opportunities to the very best of his ability, purposing to use every power which God has given him, not simply to advance his temporal affairs, but to advance his spiritual interests. O that all might search diligently to know what is truth, to study earnestly that they might have correct language and cultivated voices, that they might present the truth in all its elevated and ennobling beauty. Let no one imagine that he will drift into some position of usefulness. If men would be used to work for God, let them put to the stretch their powers, and concentrate their minds in earnest application. It is Satan that would keep men in ignorance and inefficiency, that they may be developed in a one-sided way which they may never be able to correct. He would have men exercise one set of faculties to the exclusion of the exercise of another set, so that the mind will lose its vigor, and when there is a real necessity, be unable to rise to the emergency. God wants men to do their best, and while Satan is pulling the mind in one direction, Jesus is drawing it in another (*Christian Education*, p. 137).

Upon fathers and mothers devolves the responsibility of giving a Christian education to the children entrusted to them. They are never to neglect their children. In no case are they to let any line of business so absorb mind and time and talents that their children, who should be led into harmony with God, are allowed to drift until they are separated far from Him. They are not to allow their children to slip out of their grasp into the hands of unbelievers. They are to do all in their power to keep them from imbibing the spirit of the world. They are to train them to become helpers together with God. They are God's human hand, fitting themselves and their children for an endless life in the heavenly home (*Spaulding and Magan Collection*, p. 242).

Never has the world's need for teaching and healing been greater than it is today. The world is full of those who need to be ministered unto—the weak, the helpless, the ignorant, the degraded. The continual transgression of man for nearly six thousand years has brought sickness, pain, and death as its fruit. Multitudes are perishing for lack of knowledge (*Counsels to Parents, Teachers, and Students*, p. 467).

In education the work of climbing must begin at the lowest round of the ladder. The common branches should be fully and prayerfully taught. Many who feel that they have finished their education are faulty in spelling and in writing, and can neither read nor speak correctly. Not a few who study the classics and other higher branches of learning, and who reach certain standards, finally fail because they have neglected to do thorough work in the common branches. They have never obtained a good knowledge of the English language. They need to go back and begin to climb from the first round of the ladder (*Counsels to Parents, Teachers, and Students*, p. 215).

Great care should be shown in regard to making public the errors of students. To make public exposure of wrong is harmful in every respect to the wrongdoer and has no beneficial influence upon the school. It never helps a student to humiliate him before his fellow students. This heals nothing, cures nothing, but makes a wound that mortifies (*Counsels to Parents, Teachers, and Students*, p. 267).

Never think that you have learned enough, and that you may now relax your efforts. The cultivated mind is the measure of the man. Your education should continue during your lifetime; every day you should be learning, and putting to practical use the knowledge gained (*Messages to Young People*, p. 193).

Many a student has so long taxed the mind to learn that which his reason tells him will never be of any use, that his mental powers have become weakened and incapable of vigorous exertion and persevering effort to comprehend those things which are of vital importance. The money expended in his education, which perhaps was provided as the result of great sacrifice on the part of his parents, is well-nigh wasted; and a misapprehension as to what is of importance leads to a mistake in his lifework (*Counsels to Parents, Teachers, and Students* p. 392)

Chapter 5

Faith & Prayer

And it shall come to pass, that before they call, I will answer; and while they are yet speaking, I will hear (Isaiah 65:24).

Prayer is the opening of the heart to God as to a friend. Not that it is necessary in order to make known to God what we are, but in order to enable us to receive Him. Prayer does not bring God down to us, but brings us up to Him (*Steps to Christ*, p. 93).

Prayer is not intended to work any change in God; it brings us into harmony with God. It does not take the place of duty. Prayer offered ever so often and ever so earnestly will never be accepted by God in the place of our tithe. Prayer will not pay our debts to God (*Counsels on Stewardship*, p. 99).

The Bible should never be studied without prayer. The Holy Spirit alone can cause us to feel the importance of those things easy to be understood, or prevent us from wresting truths difficult of comprehension. It is the office of heavenly angels to prepare the heart so to comprehend God's word that we shall be charmed with its beauty, admonished by its warnings, or animated and strengthened by its promises. We should make the psalmist's petition our own, "Open Thou mine eyes, that I may behold wondrous things out of Thy law." Temptations often appear irresistible because, through neglect of prayer and the study of the Bible, the tempted one cannot readily remember God's promises and meet Satan with the Scripture weapons. But angels are round about those who are willing to be taught in divine things; and in the time of great necessity, they will bring to their remembrance the very truths which are needed (*Counsels on Stewardship*, p. 38).

The workers should keep the soul constantly uplifted to God in prayer. They are never alone. If they have faith in God, if they realize that to them is committed the work of giving to the people light on Bible subjects, they constantly enjoy the companionship of Christ (*Colporteur Ministry*, p. 81).

You can never be successful in elevating yourself, unless your will is on the side of Christ, co-operating with the Spirit of God. Do not feel that you cannot; but say, "I can, I will." And God has pledged his Holy Spirit to help you in every decided effort (*Christian Temperance and Bible Hygiene*, p. 148).

Never should the Bible be studied without prayer. Before opening its pages, we should ask for the enlightenment of the Holy Spirit, and it will be given. When Nathanael came to Jesus, the Saviour exclaimed, "Behold an Israelite indeed, in whom is no guile." (John 1:47.) Nathanael said,

"Whence knowest thou me?" Jesus answered, "Before that Philip called thee, when thou wast under the fig-tree, I saw thee." And Jesus will see us also in the secret places of prayer, if we will seek him for light, that we may know what is truth. Angels from the world of light will be with those who in humility of heart seek for divine guidance (*Christian Education*, p. 59).

Every sincere prayer that is offered is mingled with the efficacy of Christ's blood. If the answer is deferred, it is because God desires us to show a holy boldness in claiming the pledged word of God. He is faithful who hath promised. He will never forsake the soul who is wholly surrendered to Him (*In Heavenly Places*, p. 74).

Likewise the Spirit also helpeth our infirmities: for we know not what we should pray for as we ought: but the Spirit itself maketh intercession for us with groanings which cannot be uttered (Romans 8:26).

Make your requests known to your Maker. Never is one repulsed who comes to Him with a contrite heart. Not one sincere prayer is lost. Amid the anthems of the celestial choir, God hears the cries of the weakest human being. We pour out our heart's desire in our closets, we breathe a prayer as we walk by the way, and our words reach the throne of the Monarch of the universe. They may be inaudible to any human ear, but they cannot die away into silence, nor can they be lost through the activities of business that are going on. Nothing can drown the soul's desire. It rises above the din of the street, above the confusion of the multitude, to the heavenly courts. It is God to whom we are speaking, and our prayer is heard. You who feel the most unworthy, fear not to commit your case to God (*In Heavenly Places*, p. 82).

How complete this prayer is! There is no limit to the blessings that it is our privilege to receive. We may be "filled with the knowledge of his will." The Holy Ghost would never have inspired Paul to offer this prayer in behalf of his brethren if it had not been possible for them to receive an answer from God in accordance with the request (*In Heavenly Places*, p. 158).

We must pray more, and talk less (*Last Day Events,* p. 195).

Keep looking unto Jesus, offering up silent prayers in faith, taking hold of His strength, whether you have any manifest feeling or not. Go right forward as if every prayer offered was lodged in the throne of God and responded to by the One whose promises never fail. Go right along, singing and making melody to God in your hearts, even when depressed by a sense of weight and sadness. I tell you as one who knows, light will come, joy will be ours, and the mists and clouds will be rolled back. And we pass from the oppressive power of the shadow and darkness into the clear sunshine of His presence (*Mind, Character and Personality*, Volume 2, p. 538).

When you receive help and comfort, sing to the praise of God. Talk with God. Thus you will become a friend of God. You will rely on Him. You will obtain a faith that will trust whether you feel like trusting or not. Remember that feeling is not an evidence that you are a Christian. Implicit faith in God shows that you are His child. Trust in God. He will never disappoint you. He says, "I will not leave you comfortless: I will come to you. Yet a little while, and the world seeth Me no more; but ye see Me: because I live, ye shall live also" (John 14:18, 19). We do not see Christ in person. It is by faith that we behold Him. Our faith grasps His promises. Thus it was that Enoch walked with God (*Mind, Character and Personality*, Volume 2, p. 538).

Faith is the first round in the ladder of advancement. Without faith it is impossible to please God. But many stop on this round and never ascend higher. They seem to think that when they have professed Christ, when their names are on the church record, their work is completed. Faith is essential; but the Inspired Word says, "Add to your faith, virtue." Those who are seeking for eternal life and a home in the kingdom of God must lay for their character building the foundation of virtue. Jesus must be the chief cornerstone. The things that defile the soul must be banished from the mind and life. When temptations are presented, they must be resisted in the strength of Christ. The virtue of the spotless Lamb of God must be woven into the character till the soul can stand in its integrity... Joseph is an example of how the youth may stand unspotted, amid the evil of the world, and add to their faith, virtue (*My Life Today*, p. 96).

Pray without ceasing (1 Thessalonians 5:17).

There are conditions to the fulfillment of God's promises, and prayer can never take the place of duty. "If ye love Me," Christ says, "Keep My commandments." "He that hath My commandments, and keepeth them, he it is that loveth Me; and he that loveth Me shall be loved of My Father, and I will love him, and will manifest Myself to him." John 14:15, 21. Those who bring their petitions to God, claiming His promise while they do not comply with the conditions, insult Jehovah. They bring the name of Christ as their authority for the fulfillment of the promise, but they do not those things that would show faith in Christ and love for Him (*Christ Object Lessons*, p. 143).

The enemy has great power over minds that are not thoroughly fortified by prayer and established in Bible truth (*Counsels to Writers and Editors*, p. 46).

By your own example teach your children to pray with clear, distinct voice. Teach them to lift their heads from the chair and never to cover their faces with their hands. Thus they can offer their simple prayers, repeating the Lord's prayer in concert (*Child Guidance*, p. 522).

We must pray more and in faith. We must not pray and then run away as though afraid we should receive an answer. God will not mock us. He will answer if we watch unto prayer, if we believe we receive the things we ask for, and keep believing and never lose patience in believing. This is watching unto prayer. We guard the prayer of faith with expectancy and hope. We must wall it in with assurance and be not faithless, but believing. The fervent prayer of the righteous is never lost. The answer may not come according as we expected, but it will come, because God's word is pledged (*Our High Calling*, p. 134).

Never should a worker encourage one who is in need of instruction and help to go first to human agencies for an understanding of his duty. It is our privilege as laborers to pray together and to counsel together; but we are individually to seek God to know what he would have us do. When the Lord impresses the mind of one of his servants that he is to go to a certain place to labor, that man is not under obligation to go to a human being to know if it is right for him to do this (*Spaulding and Magan Collection*, p. 415).

We should pray to God much more than we do. There is great strength and blessing in praying together in our families, with and for our children. When my children have done wrong, and I have talked with them kindly and then prayed with them, I have never found it necessary after that to punish them. Their hearts would melt in tenderness before the Holy Spirit that came in answer to prayer (*Child Guidance*, p. 525).

This is the way I did with my children, and before I would get through, they would be weeping, and they would say, "Won't you pray for us?" Well, I never refused to pray for them. I knelt by their side and prayed with them. Then I have gone away and have pleaded with God until the sun was up in the heavens, the whole night long, that the spell of the enemy might be broken, and I have had the victory. Although it cost me a night's labor, yet I felt richly paid when my children would hang about my neck and say, "Oh, Mother, we are so glad that you did not let us go when we wanted to. Now we see that it would have been wrong." (*Adventist Home*, p. 528).

Let all who are afflicted or unjustly used, cry to God. Turn away from those whose hearts are as steel, and make your requests known to your Maker. Never is one repulsed who comes to Him with a contrite heart. Not one sincere prayer is lost. Amid the anthems of the celestial choir, God hears the cries of the weakest human being. We pour out our heart's desire in our closets, we breathe a prayer as we walk by the way, and our words reach the throne of the Monarch of the universe. They may be inaudible to any human ear, but they cannot die away into silence, nor can they be lost through the activities of business that are going on. Nothing can drown the soul's desire. It rises above the din of the street, above the confusion of the multitude, to the heavenly courts. It is God to whom we are speaking, and our prayer is heard (*Christ Object Lessons*, p. 174).

Feeling and faith are as distinct from each other as the east is from the west. Faith is not dependent on feeling. Daily we should dedicate ourselves to God, and believe that Christ understands and accepts the sacrifice, without examining ourselves to see if we have that degree of feeling that we think should correspond with our faith. Have we not the assurance that our heavenly Father is more willing to give the Holy Spirit to them that ask Him in faith than parents are to give good gifts to their children? We should go forward as if to every prayer that we send to the throne of God we heard the response from the One whose promises never fail. Even when depressed by sadness it is our privilege to make melody in our hearts to God. When we do this the mists and clouds will be rolled back and we will pass from the shadow and darkness into the clear sunshine of His presence (*Our High Calling*, p. 120).

Never allow your children to suppose that they are not children of God until they are old enough to be baptized. Baptism does not make children Christians; neither does it convert them; it is but an outward sign, showing that they are sensible that they should be children of God by acknowledging that they believe in Jesus Christ as their Saviour and will henceforth live for Christ (*Child Guidance*, p. 499).

Bring earnestness and fervency into your prayers, and into your Bible readings, and into your preaching, that you may leave the impression that the sacred truths you are presenting to others are to you a living reality. Whatever you do for Jesus, seek with all your powers to do it with earnestness. Never feel that you have attained to the highest point, and can therefore rise no higher... Set your mind to task, that you may present the truth in a manner to interest them. Seize the most interesting portions of Scripture that you can bring before them, come right to the point, and seek to fasten their attention, and instruct them in the ways of the Lord (*Christian Service*, p. 144).

He will regard the prayer of the destitute, and not despise their prayer (Psalm 102:17).

The strength acquired in prayer to God will prepare us for our daily duties. The temptations to which we are daily exposed make prayer a necessity. In order that we may be kept by the power of God through faith, the desires of the mind should be continually ascending in silent prayer. When we are surrounded by influences calculated to lead us away from God, our petitions for help and strength must be unwearied. Unless this is so, we shall never be successful in breaking down pride and overcoming the power of temptation to sinful indulgences which keep us from the Saviour. The light of truth, sanctifying the life, will discover to the receiver the sinful passions of his heart which are striving for the mastery, and which make it necessary for him to stretch every nerve and exert all his powers to resist Satan that he may conquer through the merits of Christ (*Messages to Young People*, p. 248).

Neglect of prayer leads men to rely on their own strength and opens the door to temptation. In many cases the imagination is captivated by scientific research, and men are flattered through the consciousness of their own powers. The sciences which treat of the human mind are very much exalted. They are good in their place, but they are seized upon by Satan as his powerful agents to deceive and destroy souls. His arts are accepted as from heaven, and he thus receives the worship which suits him well. The world, which is supposed to be benefited so much by phrenology and animal magnetism, never was so corrupt as now. Through these sciences, virtue is destroyed and the foundations of spiritualism are laid (*Selected Messages*, Volume 2, pp. 351, 352).

The path of men who are placed as leaders is not an easy one. But they are to see in every difficulty a call to prayer. Never are they to fail of consulting the great Source of all wisdom. Strengthened and enlightened by the Master Worker, they will be enabled to stand firm against unholy influences and to discern right from wrong, good from evil. They will approve that which God approves, and will strive earnestly against the introduction of wrong principles into His cause. The wisdom that Solomon desired above riches, honor, or long life, God gave him. His petition for a quick mind, a large heart, and a tender spirit was granted (*Conflict and Courage*, p. 190).

Some think it a mark of humility to pray to God in a common manner... They profane His name by needlessly and irreverently mingling with their prayers the words, "God Almighty"—awful, sacred words, which should never pass the lips except in subdued tones and with a feeling of awe (*Faith I Live By*, p. 41).

Many, many confessions should never be spoken in the hearing of mortals; for the result is that which the limited judgment of finite beings does not anticipate... God will be better glorified if we confess the secret, inbred corruption of the heart to Jesus alone than if we open its recesses to finite, erring man, who cannot judge righteously unless his heart is constantly imbued with the Spirit of God... Do not pour into human ears the story which God alone should hear (*Faith I Live By*, p. 128).

Confess your faults one to another, and pray one for another, that ye may be healed. The effectual fervent prayer of a righteous man availeth much (James 5:16).

To hallow the name of the Lord requires that the words in which we speak of the Supreme Being be uttered with reverence. "Holy and reverend is his name" (Psalms 111:9). We are never in any manner to treat lightly the titles or appellations of the Deity. In prayer we enter the audience chamber of the Most High; and we should come before Him with holy awe. The angels veil their faces in His presence. The cherubim and the bright and holy seraphim approach His throne with solemn reverence. How much more should we, finite, sinful beings, come in a reverent manner before the Lord, our Maker! (*God's Amazing Grace*, p. 94).

No man is safe for a day or an hour without prayer. Especially should we entreat the Lord for wisdom to understand His Word. Here are revealed the wiles of the tempter, and the means by which he may be successfully resisted. Satan is an expert in quoting Scripture, placing his own interpretation upon passages, by which he hopes to cause us to stumble. We should study the Bible with humility of heart, never losing sight of our dependence upon God. While we must constantly guard against the devices of Satan, we should pray in faith continually, "Lead us not into temptation." (*Faith I Live By*, p. 331).

Some think it a mark of humility to pray to God in a common manner, as if talking with a human being. They profane His name by needlessly and irreverently mingling with their prayers the words, "God Almighty"—awful, sacred words, which should never pass the lips except in subdued tones and with a feeling of awe (*God's Amazing Grace*, p. 92).

Be careful for nothing; but in every thing by prayer and supplication with thanksgiving let your requests be made known unto God (Philippians 4:6).

Day after day is passing into eternity, bringing us nearer to the close of probation. As never before we must pray for the Holy Spirit to be more abundantly bestowed upon us, and we must look for its sanctifying influence to come upon the workers (*God's Amazing Grace*, p. 219).

Prayer is the opening of the heart to God as to a friend. The eye of faith will discern God very near, and the suppliant may obtain precious evidence of the divine love and care for him. But why is it that so many prayers are never answered? David says, "I cried unto Him with my mouth, and he was extolled with my tongue. If I regard iniquity in my heart, the Lord will not hear me." (Psalms 66:17, 18.) By another prophet the Lord gives us the promise, "Ye shall seek me, and find me, when ye shall search for me with all your heart." (Jeremiah 29:13.) Again, he speaks of some who "have not cried unto me with their heart." (Hosea 7:14.) Such petitions are prayers of form, lip-service only, which the Lord does not accept (*Gospel Workers*, 1915, p. 257).

If we confess our sins, he is faithful and just to forgive us our sins, and to cleanse us from all unrighteousness (1 John 1:9).

Communion with God imparts to the soul an intimate knowledge of his will. But many who profess the faith know not what true conversion is. They have no experience in communion with the Father through Jesus Christ, and have never felt the power of divine grace to sanctify the heart. Praying and sinning, sinning and praying, their lives are full of malice, deceit, envy, jealousy, and self-love. The prayers of this class are an abomination to God. True prayer engages the energies of the soul, and affects the life. He who thus pours out his wants before God feels the emptiness of everything else under heaven. "All my desire is before thee," said David, "and my groaning is not hid from thee." "My soul thirsteth for God, for the living God: when shall I come and appear before God?" "When I remember these things, I pour out my soul in me" (Psalms 38:9; 42:2, 4) (*Gospel Workers*, 1892, p. 36).

And when thou prayest, thou shalt not be as the hypocrites are: for they love to pray standing in the synagogues and in the corners of the streets, that they may be seen of men. Verily I say unto you, They have their reward. But thou, when thou prayest, enter into thy closet, and when thou hast shut thy door, pray to thy Father which is in secret; and thy Father which seeth in secret shall reward thee openly. But when ye pray, use not vain repetitions, as the heathen do: for they think that they shall be heard for their much speaking. Be not ye therefore like unto them: for your Father knoweth what things ye have need of, before ye ask him (Matthew 6:5–8).

The Christian minister should never enter the desk until he has first sought God in his closet, and has come into close connection with him. He may, with humility, lift his thirsty soul to God, and be refreshed with the dew of grace before he shall speak to the people. With an unction of the Holy Spirit upon him, giving him a burden for souls, he will not dismiss a congregation without presenting before them Jesus Christ, the sinner's only refuge, making earnest appeals that will reach their hearts. He should feel that he may never meet these hearers again until the great day of God (*Gospel Workers*, 1892, p. 41).

Those who exercise but little faith now, are in the greatest danger of falling under the power of Satanic delusions and the decree to compel the conscience. And even if they endure the test, they will be plunged into deeper distress and anguish in the time of trouble, because they have never made it a habit to trust in God. The lessons of faith which they have neglected, they will be forced to learn under a terrible pressure of discouragement (*Great Controversy*, p. 621).

And whatsoever ye shall ask in my name, that will I do, that the Father may be glorified in the Son. If ye shall ask any thing in my name, I will do it (John 14:13, 14).

No man is safe for a day or an hour without prayer. Especially should we entreat the Lord for wisdom to understand His word. Here are revealed the wiles of the tempter and the means by which he may be successfully resisted. Satan is an expert in quoting Scripture, placing his own interpretation upon passages, by which he hopes to cause us to stumble. We should study the Bible with humility of heart, never losing sight of our dependence upon God. While we must constantly guard against the devices of Satan, we should pray in faith continually: "Lead us not into temptation." (*Great Controversy*, p. 530).

"Holy and reverend is His name." We are never in any manner to treat lightly the titles or appellations of the Deity. In prayer we enter the audience chamber of the Most High, and we should come before Him with holy awe. The angels veil their faces in His presence. The cherubim and the bright and holy seraphim approach His throne with solemn reverence. How much more should we, finite, sinful beings, come in a reverent manner before the Lord, our Maker! (*My Life Today*, p. 282).

Let our young men institute a warfare against every habit that has the least danger of leading the soul from duty and devotion. Let them have stated seasons for prayer, never neglecting them if it can possibly be avoided. If they go out to battle with their vicious habits indulged as before they professed fellowship with Christ, they will soon fall an easy prey to Satan's devices. But armed with the Word of God, having it treasured in heart and mind, they will come forth unharmed by all the assaults of the foes of God or man (*My Life Today*, p. 315).

Take time to pray, to search the Scriptures, to put self under discipline to Jesus Christ. Live in contact with the living Christ, and as soon as you do this, He will take hold of you and hold you firmly by a strong hand that will never let go (*Our High Calling*, p. 101).

Chapter 6

Relationships

Great care should be taken by Christian youth in the formation of friendships and in the choice of companions. Take heed, lest what you now think to be pure gold turns out to be base metal. Worldly associations tend to place obstructions in the way of your service to God, and many souls are ruined by unhappy unions, either business or matrimonial, with those who can never elevate of ennoble (*Adventist Home*, p. 44).

Where no counsel is, the people fall: but in the multitude of counsellors there is safety (Proverbs 11:14).

Wherever there is an impulse of love and sympathy, wherever the heart reaches out to bless and uplift others, there is revealed the working of God's Holy Spirit. In the depths of heathenism, men who have had no knowledge of the written law of God, who have never even heard the name of Christ, have been kind to His servants, protecting them at the risk of their own lives. Their acts show the working of a divine power. The Holy Spirit has implanted the grace of Christ in the heart of the savage, quickening his sympathies contrary to his nature, contrary to his education. The "Light which lighteth every man that cometh into the world" (John 1:9), is shining in his soul; and this light, if heeded, will guide his feet to the kingdom of God (*Christ Object Lessons*, p. 385).

Everyone will find companions or make them. And just in proportion to the strength of the friendship will be the amount of influence which friends will exert over one another for good or for evil. All will have associates and will influence and be influenced in their turn (*Adventist Home*, p. 455).

Now I beseech you, brethren, mark them which cause divisions and offences contrary to the doctrine which ye have learned; and avoid them (Romans 6:17).

Shun those who are irreverent. Shun one who is a lover of idleness; shun the one who is a scoffer of hallowed things. Avoid the society of one who uses profane language, or is addicted to the use of even one glass of liquor. Listen not to the proposals of a man who has no realization of his responsibility to God. The pure truth which sanctifies the soul will give you courage to cut yourself loose from the most pleasing acquaintance whom you know does not love and fear God, and knows nothing of the principles of true righteousness. We may always bear with a friend's infirmities and with his ignorance, but never with his vices (*Adventist Home*, p. 47).

He that walketh with wise men shall be wise: but a companion of fools shall be destroyed (Proverbs 13:20).

Thy brother, sick in spirit, needs thee, as thou thyself hast needed a brother's love. He needs the experience of one who has been as weak as he, one who can sympathize with him and help him. The knowledge of our own weakness should help us to help another in his bitter need (*Christ Object Lessons*, p. 387).

They should be taught that the gospel of Christ tolerates no spirit of caste, that it gives no place to unkind judgment of others, which tends directly to self-exaltation. The religion of Jesus never degrades the receiver, nor makes him coarse and rough; nor does it make him unkind in thought and feeling toward those for whom Christ died (*Christian Education*, p. 201).

The world is not to be our criterion. We are not to associate with the ungodly and partake of their spirit, for they will lead the heart away from God to the worship of false gods. The steadfast soul, firm in the faith, can do much good; he can impart blessings of the highest order to those with whom he associates, for the law of the Lord is in his heart. But we cannot willingly associate with those who are trampling upon the law of God, and preserve our faith pure and untarnished. We shall catch the spirit, and unless we separate from them, we shall be bound up with them at last, to share their doom (*Adventist Home*, p. 459).

Iron sharpeneth iron; so a man sharpeneth the countenance of his friend (Proverbs 27:17).

Our great adversary has agents that are constantly hunting for an opportunity to destroy souls, as a lion hunts his prey. Shun them, young man; for, while they appear to be your friends, they will slyly introduce evil ways and practices. They flatter you with their lips, and offer to help and guide you; but their steps take hold on hell. If you listen to their counsel, it may be the turning point in your life. One safeguard removed from conscience, the indulgence of one evil habit, a single neglect of the high claims of duty, may be the beginning of a course of deception that will pass you into the ranks of those who are serving Satan, while you are all the time professing to love God and His cause. A moment of thoughtlessness, a single misstep, may turn the whole current of your lives in the wrong direction. And you may never know what caused your ruin until the sentence is pronounced: "Depart from Me, ye that work iniquity." (*Colporteur Ministry*, p. 52).

If we place ourselves among associates whose influence has a tendency to make us forgetful of the high claims the Lord has upon us, we invite temptation and become too weak in moral power to resist it. We come to partake of the spirit and cherish the ideas of our associates and to place sacred and eternal things lower than the ideas of our friends. We are, in short, leavened just as the enemy of all righteousness designed we should be (*Adventist Home*, p. 459).

Be ye not unequally yoked together with unbelievers: for what fellowship hath righteousness with unrighteousness? and what communion hath light with darkness? (2 Corinthians 6:14).).

Absolutely Positively

Those with whom we associate day by day need our help, our guidance. They may be in such a condition of mind that a word spoken in season will be as a nail in a sure place. Tomorrow some of these souls may be where we can never reach them again. What is our influence over these fellow travelers? (*Conflict and Courage*, p. 241).

The righteous is more excellent than his neighbour: but the way of the wicked seduceth them (Proverbs 12:26).

It has been truly said, "Show me your company, and I will show you your character." The youth fail to realize how sensibly both their character and their reputation are affected by their choice of associates. One seeks the company of those whose tastes and habits and practices are congenial. He who prefers the society of the ignorant and vicious to that of the wise and good shows that his own character is defective. His tastes and habits may at first be altogether dissimilar to the tastes and habits of those whose company he seeks; but as he mingles with this class, his thoughts and feelings change; he sacrifices right principles and insensibly yet unavoidably sinks to the level of his companions. As a stream always partakes of the property of the soil through which it runs, so the principles and habits of youth invariably become tinctured with the character of the company in which they mingle (*Adventist Home*, p. 456).

Live up strictly to the convictions of your own enlightened mind. Be not led into indulgence by the entreaties of friends. Live the reform at home; and when you go abroad, carry it with you. Live it, and at proper times, in proper places, and in a proper manner, talk its principles. Never let the opposition or the kind entreaties of friends gain ground on you. Ever hold on your way, and by all proper means labor to impress those around you with the importance of the subject (*Counsels on Health*, p. 447).

It is wrong for Christians to associate with those whose morals are loose. An intimate, daily intercourse which occupies time without contributing in any degree to the strength of the intellect or morals is dangerous. If the moral atmosphere surrounding persons is not pure and sanctified, but is tainted with corruption, those who breathe this atmosphere will find that it operates almost insensibly upon the intellect and heart to poison and to ruin. It is dangerous to be conversant with those whose minds naturally take a low level. Gradually and imperceptibly those who are naturally conscientious and love purity will come to the same level and partake of and sympathize with the imbecility and moral barrenness with which they are so constantly brought in contact (*Adventist Home*, p. 462).

Now we command you, brethren, in the name of our Lord Jesus Christ, that ye withdraw yourselves from every brother that walketh disorderly, and not after the tradition which he received of us (2 Thessalonians, p. 36).

Never entertain the thought that you can be Christians and yet withdraw within yourselves. Each one is a part of the great web of humanity, and the nature and quality of your experience will be largely determined by the experiences of those with whom you associate... Then let us not forsake the assembling of ourselves together (*Faith I Live By*, p. 246).

Christian sociability is altogether too little cultivated by God's people... Those who shut themselves up within themselves, who are unwilling to be drawn upon to bless others by friendly associations, lose many blessings; for by mutual contact minds receive polish and refinement; by social intercourse acquaintances are formed and friendships contracted which result in a unity of heart and an atmosphere of love which is pleasing in the sight of heaven (*Adventist Home*, p. 457).

We should have the love of Christ in the heart to such a degree that our interest in others will be impartial and sincere. Our affections should take a wide range, and not center simply upon a few who flatter us by special confidences. The tendency of such friendships is to lead us to neglect those who are in greater need of love than those upon whom we bestow our attentions (*Our High Calling*, p. 259).

Young friends, do not spend an hour in the company of those who would unfit you for the pure and sacred work of God. Do nothing before strangers that you would not do before your father and mother, or that you would be ashamed of before Christ and the holy angels (*Adventist Home*, p. 463).

The divine love emanating from Christ never destroys human love, but includes it. By it human love is refined and purified, elevated and ennobled. Human love can never bear its precious fruit until it is united with the divine nature and trained to grow heavenward (*Faith I Live By*, p. 255).

Students should be taught that they are not independent atoms, but that each one is a thread which is to unite with other threads in composing a fabric. In no department can this instruction be more effectually given than in the school home. Here students are daily surrounded by opportunities which, if improved, will greatly aid in developing the social traits of their characters. It lies in their own power so to improve their time and opportunities as to develop a character that will make them happy and useful. Those who shut themselves up within themselves, who are unwilling to be drawn upon to bless others by friendly associations, lose many blessings; for by mutual contact minds receive polish and refinement; by social intercourse acquaintances are formed and friendships contracted which result in a unity of heart and an atmosphere of love which is pleasing in the sight of heaven (*Messages to Young People*, p. 405).

Our own human affections and sympathies are not to wane away and become extinct, but through living connection with God our love is to deepen, our interest to become more intense, our efforts more successful in promoting the happiness of those around us... Souls about us are perishing for sympathy which is never expressed (*Healthful Living*, p. 274).

Those who possess large affections are under obligation to God to bestow them, not merely on their friends, but on all who need their help. Social advantages are talents and are to be used for the benefit of all within reach of our influence (*Mind, Character and Personality*, Volume 2, p. 621).

Absolutely Positively

If the youth could be persuaded to associate with the pure, the thoughtful, and the amiable, the effect would be most salutary. If choice is made of companions who fear the Lord, the influence will lead to truth, to duty, and to holiness. A truly Christian life is a power for good. But, on the other hand, those who associate with men and women of questionable morals, of bad principles and practices, will soon be walking in the same path. The tendencies of the natural heart are downward. He who associates with the skeptic will soon become skeptical; he who chooses the companionship of the vile will most assuredly become vile. To walk in the counsel of the ungodly is the first step toward standing in the way of sinners and sitting in the seat of the scornful (*Adventist Home*, p. 456).

Christ did not refuse to mingle with others in friendly intercourse. When invited to a feast by Pharisee or publican, He accepted the invitation. On such occasions every word that He uttered was a savor of life unto life to His hearers; for He made the dinner hour an occasion of imparting many precious lessons adapted to their needs. Christ thus taught His disciples how to conduct themselves when in the company of those who were not religious as well as of those who were (*Messages to Young People*, p. 406).

Chapter 7

The Bible

Every word of God is pure: he is a shield unto them that put their trust in him (Proverbs 30:5).

No soul can prosper without time to pray, to search the Scriptures; and all should, as far as possible, have the privilege of attending public worship. All need to keep the oil of grace in their vessels with their lamps. Above all others, the workers who are thrown into the society of worldlings need to have Jesus held up before them, that they may behold the Lamb of God that taketh away the sin of the world. The godless element to which they are exposed makes it essential that personal labor should be bestowed upon them. Who could be closely related to these patients, and hear them talk, and breathe in the atmosphere that surrounds their souls, without running some risk? Counteracting influences should always be exerted, lest, through the tempting allurements of Satan, the worldly element shall steal away hearts from God. Never let the worldly class be honored and great deference be paid to them above those who love God and are seeking to do His will (*Counsels on Health*, p. 422).

For the word of God is quick, and powerful, and sharper than any two edged sword, piercing even to the dividing asunder of soul and spirit, and of the joints and marrow, and is a discerner of the thoughts and intents of the heart (Hebrews 4:12) .

When a doctrine is presented that does not meet our minds, we should go to the word of God, seek the Lord in prayer, and give no place for the enemy to come in with suspicion and prejudice. We should never permit the spirit to be manifested that arraigned the priests and rulers against the Redeemer of the world. They complained that He disturbed the people, and they wished He would let them alone; for He caused perplexity and dissension. The Lord sends light to us to prove what manner of spirit we are of. We are not to deceive ourselves (*Counsels to Writers and Editors*, p. 43).

Our faith, our example, must be held more sacred than they have been held in the past. The word of God must be studied as never before; for it is the precious offering that we must present to men, in order that they may learn the way of peace, and obtain that life which measures with the life of God. Human wisdom so highly exalted among men sinks into insignificance before that wisdom which points out the way cast up for the ransomed of the Lord to walk in. The Bible alone affords the means of distinguishing the path of life from the broad road that leads to perdition and death (*Christian Education*, p. 98).

Health, truth, and happiness can never be advanced without an intelligent knowledge of, and full obedience to, the law of God and perfect faith in Jesus Christ. The Lord uses no other medium through which to reach the human heart. Many professed Christians acknowledge that in the use of tobacco they are indulging a filthy, expensive, and hurtful practice. But they excuse themselves by saying that the habit is formed and they cannot overcome it. In this acknowledgment they yield homage to Satan, saying by their actions, if not in words, that, although God is powerful, Satan has greater power. By profession they say, We are the servants of Jesus Christ, while their works say that they yield subjection to Satan's sway because it costs them the least inconvenience. Is this overcoming as Christ overcame? Or is it being overcome by temptation? And the above apology is urged by men in the ministry, who profess to be Christ's ambassadors (*Confrontation.* p. 76).

True religion brings man into harmony with the laws of God, physical, mental, and moral. It teaches self-control, serenity, temperance. Religion ennobles the mind, refines the taste, and sanctifies the judgment. It makes the soul a partaker of the purity of heaven (*Christian Education*, p. 68).

God has bountifully provided for the sustenance and happiness of all His creatures; if His laws were never violated, if all acted in harmony with the divine will, health, peace, and happiness, instead of misery and continual evil, would be the result (*Counsels on Diets and Foods*, p. 20).

Children are in need of having a steady, firm, living principle of righteousness exercised over them and practiced before them. Be sure you let the true light shine before your pupils. The light of heaven is wanted. Never let the world have the impression that your spirit and taste and longings are of no higher and purer order than that of worldlings. If you in your actions leave this impression upon them, you let a false, deceptive light lead them to ruin. The trumpet must give a certain sound. There is a broad, clear, and deep line drawn by the eternal God between the righteous and unrighteous, the godly and the ungodly; between those who are obedient to God's commandments and those who are disobedient. *Christian Education*, p. 155).

While there is need of thorough investigation of the word of God, that precious truth may be discovered and brought to light, we should be guarded, that the spirit of controversy does not control in our discussions of the Sabbath school lesson. In bringing out points upon which there may be a difference of opinion, the grace of Christ should be manifested by those who are seeking for an understanding of the word of God. There should be liberty given for a frank investigation of truth, that each may know for himself what is the truth. Among the pupils of the Sabbath school there should be a spirit of investigation, that those who are old enough to discern evidence may be encouraged to search for fresh rays of light, and to appreciate all that God may send to His people. The light which God will send to His people will never appear unless there is a diligent searching of the word of truth (*Counsels on Stewardship*, p. 27).

We should exert all the powers of the mind in the study of the Scriptures, and should task the understanding to comprehend, as far as mortals can, the deep things of God; yet we must not forget that the docility and submission of a child is the true spirit of the learner. Scriptural difficulties can never be mastered by the same methods that are employed in grappling with philosophical problems. We should not engage in the study of the Bible with that self-reliance with which so many enter the domains of science, but with a prayerful dependence upon God, and a sincere desire to learn His will. We must come with a humble and teachable spirit to obtain knowledge from the great I am. Otherwise, evil angels will so blind our minds and harden our hearts that we shall not be impressed by the truth (*Counsels on Stewardship*, p. 37).

Thy word is a lamp unto my feet, and a light unto my path (Psalms 119:105).

Take time to study the Bible, the Book of books. There never was a time when it was so important that the followers of Christ should study the Bible as now. Deceptive influences are upon all sides, and it is essential that you counsel with Jesus, your best friend. The wayfaring man may find the way of life through faith and obedience, through abiding in the sunshine of Christ's righteousness. But how shall we understand what is meant by these terms, if we do not understand the Bible? In the Word of God duty is made plain, and everything relating to the religious life is presented in a definite way. The whole plan of salvation is delineated, and the helps to the soul are pointed out. The way in which the believer may be complete in Christ is unfolded (*Sons and Daughters of God*, p. 78).

God will flash the knowledge obtained by diligent searching of the Scriptures, into their memory at the very time when it is needed. But if they neglect to fill their minds with the gems of truth, if they do not acquaint themselves with the words of Christ, if they have never tasted the power of His grace in trial, then they cannot expect that the Holy Spirit will bring His words to their remembrance. They are to serve God daily with their undivided affections, and then trust Him (*Counsels on Stewardship*, p. 41).

There is need of a much closer study of the word of God; especially should Daniel and the Revelation have attention as never before in the history of our work. We may have less to say in some lines, in regard to the Roman power and the papacy, but we should call attention to what the prophets and apostles have written under the inspiration of the Spirit of God. The Holy Spirit has so shaped matters, both in the giving of the prophecy, and in the events portrayed, as to teach that the human agent is to be kept out of sight, hid in Christ, and the Lord God of heaven and His law are to be exalted (*Counsels to Writers and Editors*, p. 65).

A great work is to be accomplished by the setting forth of the saving truths of the Bible. This is the means ordained of God to stem the tide of moral corruption in the earth. Christ gave His life to make it possible for man to be restored to the image of God. It is the power of His grace that draws men together in obedience to the truth. Those who would experience more of the sanctification of the truth in their own souls should present this truth to those who are ignorant of it. Never will they find a more elevating, ennobling work (*Counsels to Parents, Teachers, and Students*, p. 249).

The Bible should not be brought into our schools to be sandwiched in between infidelity. The Bible must be made the ground-work and subject matter of education. It is true that we know much more of the Word of the living God than we knew in the past, but there is still much more to be learned. It should be used as the Word of the living God, and esteemed as first and last and best in everything. Then will be seen true spiritual growth (*Gospel Medical Messenger*, December 3, 1913).

Absolutely Positively

If the teachers in our schools would search the Scriptures for the purpose of securing a better understanding for themselves, opening their hearts to the light given in the word, they would be taught of God. They would love and practice the truth, and would labor to bring in less of the theories and sentiments of men who have never had a connection with God, and more of the knowledge that endures. They would feel a deep soul hunger for the wisdom that comes from above (*Counsels to Parents, Teachers, and Students*, p. 391).

Our salvation depends upon our knowledge of God's will as it is contained in His word. Never cease asking and searching for Truth. You need to know your duty. You need to know what you must do to be saved. And it is God's will that you shall know what He has said to you. But you must exercise faith. As you search the Scriptures, you must believe that God is, and that He rewards those who diligently seek Him (*Messages to Young People*, p. 260).

But though we, or an angel from heaven, preach any other gospel unto you than that which we have preached unto you, let him be accursed. As we said before, so say I now again, if any man preach any other gospel unto you than that ye have received, let him be accursed (Galatians 1:8-9).

We are to regard the Bible as God's disclosure to us of eternal things—the things of most consequence for us to know. By the world it is thrown aside as if the perusal of it were finished, but a thousand years of research would not exhaust the hidden treasure it contains. Eternity alone will disclose the wisdom of this Book, for it is the wisdom of an infinite mind. Shall we, then, cultivate a deep hunger for the productions of human authors and disregard the word of God? It is this longing for something they never ought to crave that makes men substitute for true knowledge that which can never make them wise unto salvation. Let not man's assertions be regarded as truth when they are contrary to the word of God (*Counsels to Parents, Teachers, and Students*, p. 443).

For I testify unto every man that heareth the words of the prophecy of this book, If any man shall add unto these things, God shall add unto him the plagues that are written in this book: And if any man shall take away from the words of the book of this prophecy, God shall take away his part out of the book of life, and out of the holy city, and from the things which are written in this book (Revelation 22:18, 19).

The young man who makes the Bible his guide need not mistake the path of duty and of safety. That Book will teach him to preserve his integrity of character, to be truthful, to practice no deception. It will teach him that he must never transgress God's law in order to accomplish a desired object, even though to obey involves a sacrifice. It will teach him that the blessing of heaven will not rest upon him if he departs from the path of right doing; that although men may appear to prosper in disobedience, they will surely reap the fruit of their sowing (*Counsels to Parents, Teachers, and Students*, p. 449).

We should reverence God's word. For the printed volume we should show respect, never putting it to common uses, or handling it carelessly. And never should Scripture be quoted in a jest, or paraphrased to point a witty saying. "Every word of God is pure;" "as silver tried in a furnace of earth, purified seven times." Proverbs 30:5; Psalm 12:6 (*Education*, p. 244).

What book can begin to compare with the Bible? It is essential for every child, for youth, and for those of mature age to understand; for it is the word of God, the word to guide all the human family to heaven. Then why does not the word from God contain the chief elements which constitute education? Uninspired authors are placed in the hands of children and youth in our schools as lesson books—books from which they are to be educated. They are kept before the youth, taking up their precious time in studying those things which they can never use. Many books have been introduced into the schools which should never have been placed there. These books do not in any sense voice the words of John, "Behold the Lamb of God, which taketh away the sin of the world." The whole line of study in our schools should be to prepare a people for the future, immortal life (*Fundamentals of Christian Education*, p. 383).

The grass withereth, the flower fadeth: but the word of our God shall stand for ever (Isaiah 40:8).

There is necessity for every family to make the Bible the book of their study. Christ's sayings are pure gold, without one particle of dross, unless men, with their human understanding, shall try to put it there, and make falsehood appear as a portion of truth. To those who have received the false interpretation of the word, when they search the Scriptures with the determined effort to obtain the very marrow of truth contained in them, the Holy Spirit opens the eyes of their understanding, and the truths of the word are to them as a new revelation. Their hearts are quickened to a new and living faith, and they behold wondrous things out of His law. The teachings of Christ have a breadth and depth to many which they have never understood before (*Fundamentals of Christian Education*, p. 386).

In its wide range of style and subjects the Bible has something to interest every mind and appeal to every heart. In its pages are found history the most ancient; biography the truest to life; principles of government for the control of the state, for the regulation of the household—principles that human wisdom has never equaled. It contains philosophy the most profound, poetry the sweetest and the most sublime, the most impassioned and the most pathetic. Immeasurably superior in value to the productions of any human author are the Bible writings, even when thus considered; but of infinitely wider scope, of infinitely greater value, are they when viewed in their relation to the grand central thought. Viewed in the light of this thought, every topic has a new significance. In the most simply stated truths are involved principles that are as high as heaven and that compass eternity (*Lift Him Up*, p. 122).

The moral law was never a type or a shadow. It existed before man's creation, and will endure as long as God's throne remains. God could not change nor alter one precept of His law in order to save man; for the law is the foundation of His government. It is unchangeable, unalterable, infinite, and eternal. In order for man to be saved, and for the honor of the law to be maintained, it was necessary for the Son of God to offer Himself as a sacrifice for sin. He who knew no sin became sin for us, He died for us on Calvary. His death shows the wonderful love of God for man, and the immutability of His law (*God's Amazing Grace*, p. 80).

He that rejecteth me, and receiveth not my words, hath one that judgeth him: the word that I have spoken, the same shall judge him in the last day (John 12:48).

As an educating power the Bible is without a rival. Nothing will so impart vigor to all the faculties as requiring students to grasp the stupendous truths of revelation. The mind gradually adapts itself to the subjects upon which it is allowed to dwell. If occupied with commonplace matters only, to the exclusion of grand and lofty themes, it will become dwarfed and enfeebled. If never required to grapple with difficult problems or put to the stretch to comprehend important truths, it will after a time almost lose the power of growth (*Mind, Character and Personality*, Volume 1, p. 91).

The law of God was written with His own finger on tables of stone, thus showing that it could never be changed or abrogated. It is to be preserved through the eternal ages, immutable as the principles of His government... Christ gave His life to make it possible for man to be restored to the image of God. It is the power of His grace that draws men together in obedience to the truth (*God's Amazing Grace*, p. 158).

Men of ability have devoted a lifetime of study and prayer to the searching of the Scriptures, and yet there are many portions of the Bible that have not been fully explored. Some passages of Scripture will never be perfectly comprehended until in the future life Christ shall explain them. There are mysteries to be unraveled, statements that human minds cannot harmonize. And the enemy will seek to arouse argument upon these points, which might better remain undiscussed (*Gospel Workers*, 1915, p. 312).

Being born again, not of corruptible seed, but of incorruptible, by the word of God, which liveth and abideth for ever. For all flesh is as grass, and all the glory of man as the flower of grass. The grass withereth, and the flower thereof falleth away: But the word of the Lord endureth for ever. And this is the word which by the gospel is preached unto you (1 Peter 1:23–25).

Without Bible history, geology can prove nothing. Relics found in the earth do give evidence of a state of things differing in many respects from the present. But the time of their existence, and how long a period these things have been in the earth, are only to be understood by Bible history... When men leave the Word of God in regard to the history of Creation, and seek to account for God's creative works upon natural principles, they are upon a boundless ocean of uncertainty. Just how God accomplished the work of Creation in six literal days He has never revealed to mortals. His creative works are just as incomprehensible as His existence (*Lift Him Up*, p. 52).

All scripture is given by inspiration of God, and is profitable for doctrine, for reproof, for correction, for instruction in righteousness (2 Timothy 3:16).

Scientific research will open to the minds of the really wise vast fields of thought and information. They will see God in His works, and will praise Him. He will be to them first and best, and the mind will be centered upon Him. Skeptics, who read the Bible for the sake of caviling, through ignorance claim to find decided contradictions between science and revelation. But man's measurement of God will never be correct. The mind unenlightened by God's Spirit will ever be in darkness in regard to His power (*Lift Him Up*, p. 61).

The human mind becomes dwarfed and enfeebled when dealing with common-place matters only, never rising above the level of time and sense to grasp the mysteries of the unseen. The understanding is gradually brought to the level of the things with which it is constantly familiar. The mind will contract its powers and lose its ability, if it is not exercised to acquire additional knowledge, and put to the stretch to comprehend the revelations of divine power in nature and in the Sacred Word (*Testimonies for the Church*, Volume 4, p. 546).

Open the Bible to our youth, draw their attention to its hidden treasures, teach them to search for its jewels of truth, and they will gain a strength of intellect such as the study of all that philosophy embraces could not impart. The grand subjects upon which the Bible treats, the dignified simplicity of it inspired utterances, the elevated themes which it presents to the mind, the light, sharp and clear, from the throne of God, enlightening the understanding, will develop the powers of the mind to an extent that can scarcely be comprehended, and never fully explained (*Messages to Young People*, p. 254).

The moral law was never a type or a shadow. It existed before man's creation, and will endure as long as God's throne remains. God could not change nor alter one precept of His law in order to save men; for the law is the foundation of His government. It is unchangeable, unalterable, infinite, and eternal. In order for man to be saved, and for the honor of the law to be maintained, it was necessary for the Son of God to offer Himself as a sacrifice for sin. He who knew no sin became sin for us. He died for us on Calvary. His death shows the wonderful love of God for man, and the immutability of His law (*Lift Him Up*, p. 147).

In your study of the word, lay at the door of investigation your preconceived opinions and your hereditary and cultivated ideas. You will never reach the truth if you study the Scriptures to vindicate your own ideas. Leave these at the door, and with a contrite heart go in to hear what the Lord has to say to you. As the humble seeker for truth sits at Christ's feet, and learns of Him, the word gives him understanding. To those who are too wise in their own conceit to study the Bible, Christ says, You must become meek and lowly in heart if you desire to become wise unto salvation (*Messages to Young People*, p. 260).

A familiar acquaintance with the Scriptures sharpens the discerning powers and fortifies the soul against the attacks of Satan. The Bible is the sword of the Spirit, which will never fail to vanquish the adversary. It is the only true guide in all matters of faith and practice. The reason why Satan has so great control over the minds and hearts of men is that they have not made the Word of God the man of their counsel, and all their ways have not been tried by the true test. The Bible will show us what course we must pursue to become heirs of glory (*Mind, Character and Personality*, Volume 1, p. 89).

Let it be made plain that the way of God's commandments is the way of life. God has established the laws of nature, but His laws are not arbitrary exactions. Every "Thou shalt not," whether in physical or in moral law, implies a promise. If we obey it, blessing will attend our steps. God never forces us to do right, but He seeks to save us from the evil and lead us to the good (*Ministry of Healing*, p. 114).

A familiar acquaintance with the Scriptures sharpens the discerning powers, and fortifies the soul against the attacks of Satan. The Bible is the sword of the Spirit, which will never fail to vanquish the adversary. It is the only true guide in all matters of faith and practice. The reason why Satan has so great control over the minds and hearts of men is that they have not made the Word of God the man of their counsel, and all their ways have not been tried by the true test. The Bible will show us what course we must pursue to become heirs of glory (*Our High Calling*, p. 31).

If Adam had not transgressed the law of God, the ceremonial law would never have been instituted. The gospel of good news was first given to Adam in the declaration made to him that the seed of the woman should bruise the serpent's head; and it was handed down through successive generations to Noah, Abraham, and Moses. The knowledge of God's law, and the plan of salvation were imparted to Adam and Eve by Christ Himself. They carefully treasured the important lesson, and transmitted it by word of mouth, to their children, and children's children. Thus the knowledge of God's law was preserved (*Selected Messages*, volume 1, p 230).

Chapter 8

Communication

A lack of courtesy, a moment of petulance, a single rough, thoughtless word, will mar your reputation, and may close the door to hearts so that you can never reach them (*Adventist Home*, p. 38).

Never be like a chestnut bur. In the home do not allow yourself to use harsh, rasping words. You should invite the heavenly Guest to come into your home, at the same time making it possible for Him and the heavenly angels to abide with you. You should receive the righteousness of Christ, the sanctification of the Spirit of God, the beauty of holiness, that you may reveal to those around you the Light of life (*Child Guidance*, p. 95).

Never talk unless you have something to say—something which will add to the general information of those with whom you converse. Children, let your aim be to be right, just right. Let not others who love not God be your patterns, but imitate the life of Christ (*An Appeal to the Youth*, p. 79).

Parents, be cheerful, not common and cheap, but be thankful and obedient and submissive to your heavenly Father. You are not at liberty to act out your feelings if things should arise that irritate. Winning love is to be like deep waters, ever flowing forth in the management of your children. They are the lambs of the flock of God. Bring your little ones to Christ (*Adventist Home*, p. 432).

Let not one word of fretfulness, harshness, or passion escape your lips. The grace of Christ awaits your demand. His Spirit will take control of your heart and conscience, presiding over your words and deeds. Never forfeit your self-respect by hasty, thoughtless words. See that your words are pure, your conversation holy. Give your children an example of that which you wish them to be... Let there be peace, pleasant words, and cheerful countenances (*Child Guidance*, p. 219).

Parents should keep the atmosphere of the home pure and fragrant with kind words, with tender sympathy and love; but at the same time they are to be firm and unyielding in principle. If you are firm with your children, they may think that you do not love them. This you may expect, but never manifest harshness. Justice and mercy must clasp hands; there must be no wavering or impulsive movements (*Adventist Home*, p. 434).

Keep thy tongue from evil, and thy lips from speaking guile (Psalm 34:13).

Remember that you are never on vantage ground when you are ruffled and when you carry the burden of setting right every soul who comes near you. If you yield to the temptation to criticize others, to point out their faults, to tear down what they are doing, you may be sure that you will fail to act your own part nobly and well (*My Life Today*, p. 335).

Let us guard against speaking words that discourage. Let us resolve never to engage in evil speaking and backbiting. Let us refuse to serve Satan by implanting seeds of doubt. Let us guard against cherishing unbelief, or expressing it to others. Many, many times I have wished that there might be circulated a pledge containing a solemn promise to speak only those words that are pleasing to God. There is a great need for such a pledge as there is for one against the use of intoxicating liquor. Let us begin to discipline the tongue, remembering always that we can do this only be disciplining the mind, for "out of the abundance of the heart the mouth speaketh." Matthew 12:34 (*Our High Calling*, p. 291).

Do you never manifest rudeness, unkindness, and impoliteness in the family circle? If you do manifest unkindness at your home, no matter how high may be your profession, you are breaking God's commandments (*Mind, Character and Personality*, volume 1, p. 157).

He that keepeth his mouth keepeth his life: but he that openeth wide his lips shall have destruction (Proverbs 13:3).

Let us remember that there is need of sanctified pens and sanctified tongues. When we as a people live as God would be pleased to have us live, we shall see the deep movings of His Spirit. Much will then be done for those who have never heard the truth (*My Life Today*, p. 265).

When you are tempted to speak unadvisedly, be on guard. If some one else approaches you with words of criticism regarding one of God's children, turn a deaf ear to every such word. If you are spoken to harshly, never retaliate. Utter not a word. When under provocation, remember that "silence in eloquence." Silence is the greatest rebuke that you can possibly give to a faultfinder or one whose temper is irritated (*Our High Calling*, p. 293).

Let the words of my mouth, and the meditation of my heart, be acceptable in thy sight, O LORD, my strength, and my redeemer (Psalms 19:14).

Never speak disparagingly of ministers regardless of their origin. Our ministers in responsible places are men whom God has accepted. No matter what their origin, no matter what their former position, whether they followed the plow, worked at the carpenter's trade, or enjoyed the discipline of a college; if God has accepted them, let every man beware of casting the slightest reflection upon them (*Pastoral Ministry* p. 57).

The language of the meek is never that of boasting. Like the child Samuel, they pray, "Speak, Lord; for thy servant heareth" (1 Samuel 3:9) (*Reflecting Christ*, p. 264).

Allow nothing like strife or dissension to come into the home. Speak gently. Never raise your voice to harshness. Keep yourselves calm. Put away faultfinding and all untruthfulness. Tell the children that you want to help them to prepare for a holy heaven, where all is peace, where not one jarring note is heard. Be patient with them in their trials, which may look small to you but which are large to them (*Adventist Home*, p. 436).

God requires parents, by self-control, by an example of solid character building, to disseminate light within the immediate circle of their own little flock. No trifling, common conversation is to be indulged. God looks into every secret thing of life. By some a constant battle is maintained for self-control. Daily they strive silently and prayerfully against harshness of speech and temper. These strivings may never be appreciated by human beings. They may get no praise from human lips for keeping back the hasty words which sought for utterance. The world will never see these conquests, and if it could, it would only despise the conquerors. But in heaven's record they are registered as overcomers. There is One who witnesses every secret combat and every silent victory, and He says, "He that is slow to anger is better than the mighty; and he that ruleth his spirit than he that taketh a city." (*Adventist Home*, p. 443).

Never let your children have the semblance of an excuse for saying, Mother does not tell the truth. Father does not tell the truth. When you are tried in the heavenly courts, shall the record be made against your name, A deceiver? Shall your offspring be perverted by the example of those who ought to guide them in the way of truth? Instead of this, shall not the converting power of God enter the hearts of mothers and fathers? Shall not the Holy Spirit of God be allowed to make its mark upon their children? (*Child Guidance*, p. 150).

It would be well for every man to sign a pledge to speak kindly in his home, to let the law of love rule his speech. Parents, never speak hastily. If your children do wrong, correct them, but let your words be full of tenderness and love. Every time you scold, you lose a precious opportunity of giving a lesson in forbearance and patience. Let love be the most prominent feature in your correction of wrong (*Adventist Home*, p. 440).

Parents, never prevaricate; never tell an untruth in precept or in example. If you want your child to be truthful, be truthful yourself. Be straight and undeviating. Even a slight prevarication should not be allowed. Because mothers are accustomed to prevaricate and be untruthful, the child follows her example (*Child Guidance*, p. 151).

Be careful that you are not rude to your children… Require obedience, and do not allow yourself to speak carelessly to your children, because your manners and your words are their lesson book. Help them gently, tenderly over this period of their life. Let the sunshine of your presence make sunshine in their hearts. These growing boys and girls feel very sensitive, and by roughness you may mar their whole life. Be careful, mothers; never scold, for that never helps (*Child Guidance*, p. 216).

A talebearer revealeth secrets: but he that is of a faithful spirit concealeth the matter (Proverbs 11:13).

Absolutely Positively

Harsh, angry words are not of heavenly origin. Scolding and fretting never help. Instead, they stir up the worst feelings of the human heart. When your children do wrong and are filled with rebellion, and you are tempted to speak and act harshly, wait before you correct them. Give them an opportunity to think, and allow your temper to cool (*Child Guidance*, p. 246).

Praise the children when they do well, for judicious commendation is as great a help to them as it is to those older in years and understanding. Never be cross-grained in the sanctuary of the home. Be kind and tenderhearted, showing Christian politeness, thanking and commending your children for the help they give you (*Child Guidance* p. 260).

Be pleasant. Never speak loud, passionate words. In restraining and disciplining your children, be firm, but kind. Encourage them to do their duty as members of the family firm. Express your appreciation of the efforts they put forth to restrain their inclinations to do wrong (*Child Guidance*, p. 260).

Christ is ready to teach the father and the mother to be true educators. Those who learn in His school … will never speak in a harsh, unsympathetic tone; for words spoken in this manner grate upon the ear, wear upon the nerves, cause mental suffering, and create a state of mind that makes it impossible to curb the temper of the child to whom such words are spoken. This is often the reason why children speak disrespectfully to parents (*Child Guidance*, p. 282).

Of all the people in the world, reformers should be the most unselfish, the most kind, the most courteous. In their lives should be seen the true goodness of unselfish deeds. The worker who manifests a lack of courtesy, who shows impatience at the ignorance or waywardness of others, who speaks hastily or acts thoughtlessly, may close the door to hearts so that he can never reach them (*Counsels on Diets and Foods*, p. 460).

Sharp words and continual censure bewilder the child, but never reform him. Keep back that pettish word; keep your own spirit under discipline to Jesus Christ; then you will learn how to pity and sympathize with those brought under your influence (*Counsels on Stewardship*, p. 124).

They (parents) are not authorized to fret and scold and ridicule. They should never taunt their children with perverse traits of character, which they themselves have transmitted to them. This mode of discipline will never cure the evil. Parents, bring the precepts of God's Word to admonish and reprove your wayward children. Show them a "Thus saith the Lord" for your requirements. A reproof which comes as the word of God is far more effective than one falling in harsh, angry tones from the lips of parents (*Child Guidance*, p. 282).

All whose hearts are in sympathy with the heart of Infinite Love will seek to reclaim, and not to condemn. Christ dwelling in the soul is a spring that never runs dry. Where He abides, there will be an overflowing of beneficence (*Evangelism* p. 174).

We may never know until the judgment the influence of a kind, considerate course of action to the inconsistent, the unreasonable, and unworthy (*Christian Leadership*, p. 7).

He that goeth about as a talebearer revealeth secrets: therefore meddle not with him that flattereth with his lips (Proverbs 20:19).

The harmony of the domestic circle is often broken by a hasty word and abusive language. How much better were it left unsaid. One smile of pleasure, one peaceful, approving word spoken in the spirit of meekness, would be a power to soothe, to comfort, and to bless.. Many excuse their hasty words and passionate tempers by saying: "I am sensitive; I have a hasty temper." This will never heal the wounds made by hasty, passionate words... The natural man must die, and the new man, Christ Jesus, take possession of the soul... You may show by your life what the power and grace of God can do in transforming the natural man into a spiritual man in Christ Jesus (*God's Amazing Grace*, p. 226).

Be sure to maintain the dignity of the work by a well-ordered life and godly conversation. Never be afraid of raising the standard too high... All coarseness and roughness must be put away from us. Courtesy, refinement, Christian politeness, must be cherished. Guard against being abrupt and blunt. Do not regard such peculiarities as virtues; for God does not so regard them. Endeavor not to offend any unnecessarily (*Christian Service*, p. 226).

The most careful attention to the outward proprieties of life is not sufficient to shut out all fretfulness, harsh judgment, and unbecoming speech. True refinement will never be revealed so long as self is considered as the supreme object. Love must dwell in the heart. A thoroughgoing Christian draws his motives of action from his deep heart-love for his Master. Up through the roots of his affection for Christ springs an unselfish interest in his brethren. Love imparts to its possessor grace, propriety, and comeliness of deportment. It illuminates the countenance and subdues the voice; it refines and elevates the entire being (*Gospel Workers*, 1915, p. 123).

In the work of soul-winning, great tact and wisdom are needed. The Saviour never suppressed the truth, but He uttered it always in love. In His intercourse with others, He exercised the greatest tact, and He was always kind and thoughtful. He was never rude, never needlessly spoke a severe word, never gave unnecessary pain to a sensitive soul. He did not censure human weakness. He fearlessly denounced hypocrisy, unbelief, and iniquity, but tears were in His voice as He uttered His scathing rebukes. He never made truth cruel, but ever manifested a deep tenderness for humanity. Every soul was precious in His sight. He bore Himself with divine dignity; yet He bowed with the tenderest compassion and regard to every member of the family of God. He saw in all, souls whom it was His mission to save (*Christian Service*, p. 231).

Never search for words that will give the impression that you are learned. The greater your simplicity, the better will your words be understood (*Evangelism*, p. 482).

Christ is ready to teach the father and the mother to be true educators. Those who learn in His school... will never speak in a harsh, unsympathetic tone; for words spoken in this manner grate upon the ear, wear upon the nerves, cause mental suffering, and create a state of mind that makes it impossible to curb the temper of the child to whom such words are spoken. This is often the reason why children speak disrespectfully to parents (*Child Guidance*, p. 282).

When you speak, let every word be full and well rounded, every sentence clear and distinct to the very last word. Many as they approach the end of a sentence lower the tone of the voice, speaking so indistinctly that the force of the thought is destroyed. Words that are worth speaking at all are worth speaking in a clear, distinct voice, with emphasis and expression (*Colporteur Ministry*, p. 71).

Harsh dealing will never help the youth to see his errors, or aid him to reform. Let the rules and regulations of the school be carried out in the Spirit of Jesus, and when reproof must be given, let this disagreeable work be done with sorrow blended with love. Do not feel that it is your work to openly rebuke the pupil, and thus humiliate him before the whole school. This will not be a proper example to set before the children, for it will be as seed that will bear a like harvest. Never publish the errors of any pupil outside the circle in which they must be known; for, if this is done, sympathy will be created for the wrongdoer, by leaving an impression on the mind that he has been dealt with unjustly. By exposing the wrongdoer, he may be thrown upon Satan's battlefield, and from that moment go steadily downward. Christ bears long with us, and we must be Christlike. He does not cut us off because of our errors, but reproves in tenderness, and by love draws us close to Himself (*Counsels on Stewardship*, p. 172).

After the family then comes the church. The influence of the family is to be such that it will be a help and a blessing in the church. Never speak a word of complaint or faultfinding. There are churches in which the spirituality has been almost killed, because the spirit of backbiting has been allowed to enter. Why do we speak words of blame and censure? To be silent is the strongest rebuke that you can give to one who is speaking harsh, discourteous words to you. Keep perfectly silent. Often silence is eloquence (*Child Guidance*, p. 551).

In dealing with the erring, harsh measures should not be resorted to; milder means will effect far more. Make use of the milder means most perseveringly, and even if they do not succeed, wait patiently; never hurry the matter of cutting off a member from the church. Pray for him, and see if God will not move upon the heart of the erring. Discipline has been largely perverted. Those who have had very defective characters themselves have been very forward in disciplining others, and thus all discipline has been brought into contempt. Passion, prejudice, and partiality, I am sorry to say, have had abundant room for exhibition, and proper discipline has been strangely neglected. If those who deal with the erring had hearts full of the milk of human kindness, what a different spirit would prevail in our churches. May the Lord open the eyes and soften the hearts of those who have a harsh, unforgiving, unrelenting spirit toward those whom they think in error. Such men dishonor their office and dishonor God. They grieve the hearts of his children, and compel them to cry unto God in their distress. The Lord will surely hear their cry, and will judge for these things (*Christian Leadership*, p. 65).

But I say unto you, That every idle word that men shall speak, they shall give account thereof in the day of judgment (Matthew 12:36

Let us not disourage one another. Let us take hold unitedly to make every line of the Lord's work a success. If someone comes to you and talks discouragingly about the work in one or another of our institutions, telling you that they are extravagant beyond measure, say to them, "I am sorry if that is so, but let us help them out if they are in difficulty." If you will speak thus you may avoid much of the evil that might result were you to withdraw your sympathy, and should you refuse to help those who, possibly, may have been misrepresented. Let us never discourage even those who have done wrong, by treating them as if they had committed against us an unpardonable sin. Let us rather encourage them in every way possible, and if we see that they are lifting hard in a worthy enterprise, let us lift with them (*Counsels on Health*, p. 243).

We are not called upon to enter into controversy with those who hold false theories. Controversy is unprofitable. Christ never entered into it. "It is written," is the weapon used by the world's Redeemer. Let us keep close to the word. Let us allow the Lord Jesus and His messengers to testify. We know that their testimony is true (*Medical Missionary*, p. 97).

Those who indulge in such language will experience shame, loss of self-respect, loss of self-confidence, and will have bitter remorse and regret that they allowed themselves to lose self-control and speak in this way. How much better would it be if words of this character were never spoken. How much better to have the oil of grace in the heart, to be able to pass by all provocation, and bear all things with Christlike meekness and forbearance (*Messages to Young People*, p. 327).

We need to beware of self-pity. Never indulge the feeling that you are not esteemed as you should be, that your efforts are not appreciated, that your work is too difficult. Let the memory of what Christ has endured for us silence every murmuring thought. We are treated better than was our Lord. "Seekest thou great things for thyself? seek them not" (Jeremiah 45:5) (*Mind, Character and Personality*, volume 1, p. 259).

Heaven sees in the child the undeveloped man or woman, with capabilities and powers that, if correctly guided and developed with heavenly wisdom, will become the human agencies through whom the divine influences can cooperate to be laborers together with God. Sharp words and continual censure bewilder the child but never reform him. Keep back that pettish word; keep your own spirit under discipline to Jesus Christ; then will you learn how to pity and sympathize with those brought under your influence. Do not exhibit impatience and harshness, for if these children did not need educating, they would not need the advantages of the school. They are to be patiently, kindly, and in love brought up the ladder of progress, climbing step by step in obtaining knowledge (*Mind, Character and Personality*, volume 1, p. 356).

Jesus never suppressed one word of the truth; but he uttered it always in love. He exercised the greatest tact, and thoughtful, kind attention in his intercourse with the people. He was never rude, never needlessly spoke a severe word, never gave needless pain to a sensitive soul. He did not censure human weakness. He fearlessly denounced hypocrisy, unbelief, and iniquity, but tears were in his voice as he uttered his scathing rebukes. He wept over Jerusalem, the city he loved, that refused to receive him, the way, the truth, and the life. They had rejected him, the Saviour; but he regarded them with pitying tenderness, and sorrow so deep that it broke his heart. His life was one of self-denial and thoughtful care for others. He never made truth cruel, but manifested a wonderful tenderness for humanity. Every soul was precious in his eyes. He always bore himself with divine dignity; yet he bowed with the tenderest compassion and regard to every member of the family of God. He saw in all, fallen souls whom it was his mission to save (*Gospel Workers*, 1892, p. 391).

The words of a man's mouth are as deep waters, and the wellspring of wisdom as a flowing brook (Proverbs 18:4).

Never are we to be cold and unsympathetic, especially when dealing with the poor. Courtesy, sympathy, and compassion are to be shown to all. Partiality for the wealthy is displeasing to God. Jesus is slighted when His needy children are slighted. They are not rich in this world's goods, but they are dear to His heart of love. God recognizes no distinction of rank. With Him there is no caste. In His sight, men are simply men, good or bad. In the day of final reckoning, position, rank, or wealth will not alter by a hairsbreadth the case of anyone. By the all-seeing God, men will be judged by what they are in purity, in nobility, in love for Christ. *Counsels on Stewardship*, p. 162).

What harm is wrought in the family circle by the utterance of impatient words; for the impatient utterance of one leads another to retort in the same spirit and manner. Then come words of retaliation, words of self-justification, and it is by such words that a heavy, galling yoke is manufactured for your neck; for all these bitter words will come back in a baleful harvest to your soul (*Sons and Daughters of God*, p. 142).

Let no corrupt communication proceed out of your mouth, but that which is good to the use of edifying, that it may minister grace unto the hearers (Ephesians 4:29).

Reverence should be shown also for the name of God. Never should that name be spoken lightly or thoughtlessly. Even in prayer its frequent or needless repetition should be avoided. "Holy and reverend is His name." Psalm 111:9. Angels, as they speak it, veil their faces. With what reverence should we, who are fallen and sinful, take it upon your lips! (*Education*, p. 243).

It should be our aim to bring all the pleasantness possible into our lives, and to do all the kindness possible to those around us. Kind words are never lost. Jesus records them as if spoken to Himself. Sow the seeds of kindness, of love, and of tenderness, and they will blossom and bear fruit (*Our High Calling*, p. 293).

Let every minister learn to wear the gospel shoes. He who is shod with the preparation of the gospel of peace will walk as Christ walked. He will be able to speak right words, and to speak them in love. He will not try to drive home God's message of truth. He will deal tenderly with every heart, realizing that the Spirit will impress the truth on those who are susceptible to divine impressions. Never will he be vehement in his manner. Every word spoken will have a softening, subduing influence (*Evangelism*, p. 174).

Hearts that are filled with the love of Christ can never get very far apart. Religion is love, and a Christian home is one where love reigns and finds expression in words and acts of thoughtful kindness and gentle courtesy (*Faith I Live By*, p. 255).

In all your transactions with your fellow men, never forget that you are dealing with God's property. Be kind; be pitiful; be courteous. Respect God's purchased possession. Treat one another with tenderness and courtesy. Exert every God-given faculty to become examples to others (*God's Amazing Grace*, p. 65).

Speak not evil one of another, brethren. He that speaketh evil of his brother, and judgeth his brother, speaketh evil of the law, and judgeth the law: but if thou judge the law, thou art not a doer of the law, but a judge (James 4:11).

Remember that a revengeful speech never makes one feel that he has gained a victory. Let Christ speak through you. Do not lose the blessing that comes from thinking no evil (*Mind, Character and Personality*, volume 2, p. 529).

Come close to the great heart of pitying love, and let the current of that divine compassion flow into your heart and from you to the hearts of others. Let the tenderness and mercy that Jesus has revealed in His own precious life be an example to us of the manner in which we should treat our fellow beings, especially those who are our brethren in Christ... Never, never become heartless, cold, unsympathetic, and censorious. Never lose an opportunity to say a word to encourage and inspire hope. We cannot tell how far-reaching may be our tender words of kindness, our Christlike efforts to lighten some burden. The erring can be restored in no other way than in the spirit of meekness, gentleness, and tender love (*God's Amazing Grace*, p. 234).

The servants of God should manifest a tender, compassionate spirit, and show to all that they are not actuated by any personal motives in their dealings with the people, and that they do not take delight in giving messages of wrath in the name of the Lord. But they must never flinch from pointing out the sins that are corrupting the professed people of God, nor cease striving to influence them to turn from their errors and obey the Lord (*Gospel Workers*, 1892, p. 86).

The religion of Jesus Christ never degrades; it never makes men and women coarse and rough. Incorrect speech, wrong habits, must be overcome. God would have every man correct in speech, correct in habits, possessing knowledge that will give him a standing place among men. I present this matter as the Lord has presented it to me. Let us determine to put ourselves to the task of learning in the school of Christ (*Medical Missionary*, p. 200).

Cultivate the habit of speaking well of others. Dwell upon the good qualities of those with whom you associate, and see as little as possible of their errors and failings. When tempted to complain of what some one has said or done, praise something in that person's life or character. Cultivate thankfulness. Praise God for His wonderful love in giving Christ to die for us. It never pays to think of our grievances. God calls upon us to think of His mercy and His matchless love, that we may be inspired with praise (*Gospel Workers*, 1915, p. 479).

Never let your tongue and voice be employed in discovering and dilating upon the defects of your brethren, for the record of heaven identifies Christ's interests with those He has purchased with His own blood. "Inasmuch as ye have done it unto one of the least of these my brethren," He says, "ye have done it unto me" (Matthew 25:40). We are to learn to be loyal to one another, to be true as steel in the defense of our brethren. Look to your own defects. You had better discover one of your own faults than ten of your brother's. Remember that Christ has prayed for these, His brethren, that they all might be one as He is one with the Father. Seek to the uttermost of your capabilities to be in harmony with your brethren to the extent of Christ's measurement, as He is one with the Father (*In Heavenly Places*, p. 178).

Courtesy is one of the graces of the Spirit. It is an attribute of Heaven. The angels never fly into a passion, never are envious or selfish. No harsh or unkind words escape their lips. If we are to be the companions of angels, we too must be refined and courteous (*In Heavenly Places*, p. 180).

Never prevaricate; never tell an untruth in precept or in example... Be straight and undeviating. Even a slight prevarication should not be allowed (*My Life Today*, p. 331).

Preach in your lives the practical godliness of the faith that you believe. Let it be seen that the truth never degrades the receiver, making him rough and coarse, or fretful and impatient. Make apparent to all your patience, your kindness, your long-suffering, gentleness, compassion, and true goodness; for these graces are the expression of the character of the God whom you serve (*Evangelism*, p. 400).

When you speak, let every word be full and well rounded, every sentence clear and distinct, to the very last word. Many as they approach the end of a sentence lower the tone of the voice, speaking so indistinctly that the force of the thought is destroyed. Words that are worth speaking at all are worth speaking in a clear, distinct voice, with emphasis and expression (*Gospel Workers*, 1915, p. 88).

Never speak disparagingly of any man, for he may be great in the sight of the Lord, while those who feel great may be lightly esteemed of God because of the perversity of their hearts. Our only safety is to lie low at the foot of the cross, be little in our own eyes, and trust in God; for He alone has power to make us great (*Maranatha*, p. 228).

If you do not feel light-hearted and joyous, do not talk of your feelings. Cast no shadow upon the lives of others. A cold, sunless religion never draws souls to Christ. It drives them away from Him, into the nets that Satan has spread for the feet of the straying. Instead of thinking of your discouragements, think of the power you can claim in Christ's name. Let your imagination take hold upon things unseen. Let your thoughts be directed to the evidences of the great love of God for you. Faith can endure trial, resist temptation, bear up under disappointment. Jesus lives as our advocate. All is ours that His mediation secures (*Gospel Workers*, 1915, p. 478).

The witness borne concerning Jesus was, "never man spake like this man" (John 7:46). The reason that Christ spoke as no other man spoke was that He lived as no other man lived. If He had not lived as He did, He could not have spoken as He did. His words bore with them convincing power, because they came from a heart pure and holy, burdened with love and sympathy, beneficence and truth (*In Heavenly Places*, p. 237).

Show that you reverence your faith, speaking reverently of sacred things. Never allow one expression of lightness and trifling to escape your lips when quoting Scripture. As you take the Bible in your hands, remember that you are on holy ground (*My Life Today*, p. 283).

This place should not be filled by a man who has an irritable temper,—a sharp combativeness. Care must be taken that the religion of Christ be not made repulsive by harshness or impatience. The servant of God should seek, by meekness, gentleness, and love, rightly to represent our holy faith. While the cross must never be concealed, he should present also the Saviour's matchless love. The worker must be imbued with the spirit of Jesus, and then the treasures of the soul will be presented in words that will find their way to the hearts of those who hear. The religion of Christ, exemplified in the daily life of his followers, will exert a tenfold greater influence than the most eloquent sermons (*Testimonies for the Church*, Volume. 4, p. 547).

Never be sour and harsh at any time. Abstain from frowns and contempt, however much you may feel them. You should win respect by being respectful and courteous. Treat every one with civility; they are the purchase of the blood of Christ. If you seek to imitate Christ in your character, the impression upon the people will not be made by you, but by the angels of God that stand right by your side; they will touch the hearts of those to whom you speak (*In Heavenly Places*, p. 296).

Remember that you cannot read hearts. You do not know the motives which prompted the actions that to you look wrong. There are many who have not received a right education; their characters are warped, they are hard and gnarled and seem to be crooked in every way. But the grace of Christ can transform them. Never cast them aside, never drive them to discouragement or despair by saying, "You have disappointed me, and I will not try to help you." A few words spoken hastily under provocation—just what we think they deserve—may cut the cords of influence that should have bound their hearts to ours (*Mind, Character and Personality*, volume 2, p. 755).

If impatient words are spoken to you, never reply in the same spirit. Remember that "a soft answer turneth away wrath." Proverbs 15:1. And there is wonderful power in silence. Words spoken in reply to one who is angry sometimes serve only to exasperate. But anger met with silence, in a tender, forbearing spirit, quickly dies away (*Ministry of Healing*, p. 486).

Even so the tongue is a little member, and boasteth great things. Behold, how great a matter a little fire kindleth! And the tongue is a fire, a world of iniquity: so is the tongue among our members, that it defileth the whole body, and setteth on fire the course of nature; and it is set on fire of hell. For every kind of beasts, and of birds, and of serpents, and of things in the sea, is tamed, and hath been tamed of mankind: But the tongue can no man tame; it is an unruly evil, full of deadly poison. Therewith bless we God, even the Father; and therewith curse we men, which are made after the similitude of God. Out of the same mouth proceedeth blessing and cursing. My brethren, these things ought not so to be (James 3:5–10).

Cultivate the habit of speaking well of others. Dwell upon the good qualities of those with whom you associate, and see as little as possible of their errors and failings. When tempted to complain of what someone has said or done, praise something in that person's life or character. Cultivate thankfulness. Praise God for His wonderful love in giving Christ to die for us. It never pays to think of our grievances. God calls upon us to think of His mercy and His matchless love, that we may be inspired with praise (*Ministry of Healing*, p. 492).

The language of the meek is never that of boasting. Like the child Samuel, they pray, "Speak, Lord, for Thy servant heareth." When Joshua was placed in the highest position of honor, as commander of Israel, he bade defiance to all the enemies of God. His heart was filled with noble thoughts of his great mission. Yet upon the intimation of a message from Heaven, he placed himself in the position of a little child to be directed. "What saith my Lord unto His servant?" was his response (*My Life Today*, p. 253).

Christ never flattered men. He never spoke that which would exalt their fancies and imaginations, nor did He praise them for their clever inventions; but deep, unprejudiced thinkers received His teaching and found that it tested their wisdom. They marveled at the spiritual truth expressed in the simplest language (*Mind, Character and Personality*, Volume 2, p. 587).

He that hath knowledge spareth his words: and a man of understanding is of an excellent spirit. Even a fool, when he holdeth his peace, is counted wise: and he that shutteth his lips is esteemed a man of understanding (Proverbs 17:27–28).

Never should we lose control of ourselves. Let us ever keep before us the perfect Pattern. It is a sin to speak impatiently and fretfully or to feel angry—even though we do not speak. We are to walk worthy, giving a right representation of Christ. The speaking of an angry word is like flint striking flint: it at once kindles wrathful feelings (*Child Guidance*, p. 95).

Angels hear the words that are spoken in the home. Therefore, never scold; but let the influence of your words be such that it will ascend to heaven as fragrant incense (*Adventist Home*, p. 434).

Wherefore, my beloved brethren, let every man be swift to hear, slow to speak, slow to wrath (James 1:19).

If parents desire their children to be pleasant, they should never speak to them in a scolding manner. The mother often allows herself to become irritable and nervous. Often she snatches at the child and speaks in a harsh manner. If a child is treated in a quiet, kind manner, it will do much to preserve in him a pleasant temper (*Child Guidance*, p. 286).

Never allow an indistinct utterance to pass unnoticed. Let the speech be as perfect as possible. Accept nothing else. By cultivating the voice a grand work will be done, not only in learning how to breathe, inhaling the pure, life-giving air and exhaling by speaking in loud, clear tones, but also in the preservation of life (*Spaulding and Magan Collection*, p. 200).

Among the members of many families there is practiced the habit of saying loose, careless things; and the habit of tantalizing, of speaking harsh words, becomes stronger and stronger as it is indulged, and thus many objectionable words are spoken that are after Satan's order and not after the order of God... Burning words of passion should never be spoken, for in the sight of God and holy angels they are as a species of swearing (*Adventist Home* p. 439).

Chapter 9

Family

Especially dreadful is the thought of a child turning in hatred upon a mother who has become old and feeble, upon whom has come those infirmities of disposition attendant upon second childhood. How patiently, how tenderly, should children bear with such a mother! Tender words which will not irritate the spirit should be spoken. A true Christian will never be unkind, never under any circumstances be neglectful of his father or mother, but will heed the command, "Honour thy father and thy mother." God has said, "Thou shalt rise up before the hoary head, and honour the face of the old man." (*Adventist Home*, p. 362).

My Dear Willie: I have just finished a letter to your brothers, and will now write you a few lines. I was glad to hear that you loved to visit grandpa and grandma White. Tell them that we have not forgotten them. We wish them to have a special care for their health. We hope they are well and happy. You must do your part to make them happy. They love you, Willie, very much, because you are not mischievous, and do not make them trouble by disarranging grandfather's tools. You should never grieve them by being noisy, for this often annoys aged people (*An Appeal to the Youth*, p. 71).

To the man who is a husband and a father, I would say, Be sure that a pure, holy atmosphere surrounds your soul… You are to learn daily of Christ. Never, never are you to show a tyrannical spirit in the home. The man who does this is working in partnership with satanic agencies. Bring your will into submission to the will of God. Do all in your power to make the life of your wife pleasant and happy. Take the word of God as the man of your counsel. In the home live out the teachings of the word. Then you will live them out in the church and will take them with you to your place of business. The principles of heaven will ennoble all your transactions. Angels of God will cooperate with you, helping you to reveal Christ to the world (*Adventist Home*, p. 213).

Never raise your hand to give them a blow unless you can with a clear conscience bow before God and ask His blessing upon the correction you are about to give. Encourage love in the hearts of your children. Present before them high and correct motives for self-restraint. Do not give them the impression that they must submit to control because it is your arbitrary will, because they are weak, and you are strong, because you are the father, they the children. If you wish to ruin your family, continue to govern by brute force, and you will surely succeed (*Child Guidance*, p. 252).

The power of a mother's prayers cannot be too highly estimated. She who kneels beside her son and daughter through the vicissitudes of childhood, through the perils of youth, will never know till the judgment the influence of her prayers upon the life of her children. If she is connected by faith with the Son of God, the mother's tender hand may hold back her son from the power of temptation, may restrain her daughter from indulging in sin. When passion is warring for the mastery, the power of love, the restraining, earnest, determined influence of the mother, may balance the soul on the side of right (*Adventist Home*, p. 266).

Parents have not given their children the right education. Frequently they manifest the same imperfections which are seen in the children. They eat improperly, and this calls their nervous energies to the stomach, and they have no vitality to expand in other directions. They cannot properly control their children because of their own impatience; neither can they teach them the right way. Perhaps they take hold of them roughly and give them an impatient blow. I have said that to shake a child would shake two evil spirits in, while it would shake one out. If a child is wrong, to shake it only makes it worse. It will not subdue it (*Child Guidance*, p. 252).

When you take up your duties as a parent in the strength of God, with a firm determination never to relax your efforts nor to leave your post of duty in striving to make your children what God would have them, then God looks down upon you with approbation. He knows that you are doing the best you can, and He will increase your power. He will Himself do the part of the work that the mother or father cannot do; He will work with the wise, patient, well-directed efforts of the God-fearing mother. Parents, God does not propose to do the work that He has left for you to do in your home. You must not give up to indolence and be slothful servants, if you would have your children saved from the perils that surround them in the world (*Adventist Home*, p. 207).

It will pay to manifest affection in your association with your children. Do not repel them by lack of sympathy in their childish sports, joys, and griefs. Never let a frown gather upon your brow, or a harsh word escape your lips (*Child Guidance*, p. 264).

If you fail in everything else, be thorough, be efficient, here. If your children come forth from the home training pure and virtuous, if they fill the least and lowest place in God's great plan of good for the world, your life can never be called a failure and can never be reviewed with remorse (*Adventist Home*, p. 267).

The will of the parents must be under the discipline of Christ. Molded and controlled by God's pure Holy Spirit, they may establish unquestioned dominion over the children. But if the parents are severe and exacting in their discipline, they do a work which they themselves can never undo. By their arbitrary course of action, they stir up a sense of injustice (*Child Guidance*, p. 281).

Patiently, lovingly, as faithful stewards of the manifold grace of Christ, parents are to do their appointed work. It is expected of them that they will be found faithful. Everything is to be done in faith. Constantly they must pray that God will impart His grace to their children. Never must they become weary, impatient, or fretful in their work. They must cling closely to their children and to God. If parents work in patience and love, earnestly endeavoring to help their children to reach the highest standard of purity and modesty, they will succeed (*Adventist Home*, p. 208).

Absolutely Positively

Allow the children under your care to have an individuality, as well as yourselves. Ever try to lead them, but never drive them (*Child Guidance*, p. 210).

Few parents begin early enough to teach their children to obey. The child is usually allowed to get two or three years the start of its parents, who forbear to discipline it, thinking it too young to learn to obey. But all this time self is growing strong in the little being, and every day makes harder the parent's task of gaining control. At a very early age children can comprehend what is plainly and simply told them, and by kind and judicious management can be taught to obey. Never should they be allowed to show their parents disrespect. Self-will should never be permitted to go unrebuked. The future well-being of the child requires kindly, loving, but firm discipline (*Counsels to Parents, Teachers, and Students*, p. 111).

Let not the mother gather to herself so many cares that she cannot give time to the spiritual needs of her family. Let parents seek God for guidance in their work. On their knees before Him they will gain a true understanding of their great responsibilities, and there they can commit their children to One who will never err in counsel and instruction (*Adventist Home*, p. 321).

The father of the righteous shall greatly rejoice: and he that begetteth a wise child shall have joy of him (Proverbs 23:24).

Our obligation to our parents never ceases. Our love for them, and theirs for us, is not measured by years or distance, and our responsibility can never be set aside (*Adventist Home*, p. 360).

The work of wise parents will never be appreciated by the world, but when the judgment shall sit and the books shall be opened, their work will appear as God views it and will be rewarded before men and angels. It will be seen that one child who has been brought up in a faithful way has been a light in the world. It cost tears and anxiety and sleepless nights to oversee the character building of this child, but the work was done wisely, and the parents hear the "Well done" of the Master (*Adventist Home*, p. 536).

When parents do not maintain their authority, when the children go to school, they have no particular respect for the teachers or principal of the school. The reverence and respect that they should have, they were never taught to have at home. Father and mother were on the same level with the children (*Child Guidance*, p. 98).

It will pay to manifest affection in your association with your children. Do not repel them by lack of sympathy in their childish sports, joys, and griefs. Never let a frown gather upon your brow or a harsh word escape your lips. God writes all these words in His book of records (*Adventist Home*, p. 309).

Never should they [the children] be allowed to show their parents disrespect. Self-will should never be permitted to go unrebuked. The future well-being of the child requires kindly, loving, but firm discipline (*Child Guidance*, p. 83).

It is impossible to depict the evil that results from leaving a child to its own will. Some who go astray because of neglect in childhood will later, through the inculcation of practical lessons, come to their senses; but many are lost forever because in childhood and youth they received only a partial, one-sided culture. The child who is spoiled has a heavy burden to carry throughout his life. In trial, in disappointment, in temptation, he will follow his undisciplined, misdirected will. Children who have never learned to obey will have weak, impulsive characters. They seek to rule, but have not learned to submit. They are without moral strength to restrain their wayward tempers, to correct their wrong habits, or to subdue their uncontrolled wills. The blunders of untrained, undisciplined childhood become the inheritance of manhood and womanhood. The perverted intellect can scarcely discern between the true and the false (*Counsels to Parents, Teachers, and Students*, p. 112).

The mother should enter upon her work with courage and energy, relying constantly upon divine aid in all her efforts. She should never rest satisfied until she sees in her children a gradual elevation of character, until they have a higher object in life than merely to seek their own pleasure (*Adventist Home*, p. 265).

The youth should not be left to learn good and evil indiscriminately, the parents thinking that at some future time the good will predominate and the evil lose its influence. The evil will increase faster than the good. It is possible that the evil which children learn may be eradicated after many years, but who would trust to this? Whatever else they neglect, parents should never leave their children free to wander in the paths of sin (*Counsels to Parents, Teachers, and Students*, p. 119).

Children, obey your parents in the Lord: for this is right. Honour thy father and mother; which is the first commandment with promise; That it may be well with thee, and thou mayest live long on the earth (Ephesians 6:1–3).

Mothers should guard against training their children to be dependent and self-absorbed. Never give them cause to think that they are the center and that everything must revolve around them. Some parents give much time and attention to amusing their children; but children should be trained to amuse themselves, to exercise their own ingenuity and skill. Thus they will learn to be content with simple pleasures. They should be taught to bear bravely their little disappointments and trials. Instead of calling attention to every trifling pain or hurt, divert their minds; teach them to pass lightly over little annoyances and discomforts (*Counsels to Parents, Teachers, and Students*, p. 123).

Children who have lost the one in whose breasts maternal love has flowed have met with a loss that can never be supplied. But when one ventures to stand in the place of mother to the little stricken flock, a double care and burden rests upon her to be even more loving if possible, more forbearing of censure and threatening than their own mother could have been, and in this way supply the loss which the little flock have sustained (*Adventist Home*, p. 272).

There is a sacred circle around every family which should be preserved. No other one has any right in that sacred circle. The husband and wife should be all to each other. The wife should have no secrets to keep from her husband and let others know, and the husband should have no secrets to keep from his wife to relate to others. The heart of his wife should be the grave for the faults of the husband, and the heart of the husband the grave for his wife's faults. Never should either party indulge in a joke at the expense of the other's feelings. Never should either the husband or wife in sport or in any other manner complain of each other to others, for frequently indulging in this foolish and what may seem perfectly harmless joking will end in trial with each other and perhaps estrangement. I have been shown that there should be a sacred shield around every family (*Adventist Home*, p. 177).

Be firm, be decided in carrying out Bible instruction, but be free from all passion. Bear in mind that when you become harsh and unreasonable before your little ones, you teach them to be the same. God requires you to educate your children, bringing into your discipline all the generalship of a wise teacher who is under the control of God. If the converting power of God is exercised in your home, you yourselves will be constant learners. You will represent the character of Christ, and your efforts in this direction will please God. Never neglect the work that should be done for the younger members of the Lord's family. You are, parents, the light of your home. Then let your light shine forth in pleasant words, in soothing tones of the voice. Take all the sting out of them by prayer to God for self-control. And angels will be in your home, for they will observe your light. The discipline you give your children will go forth in strong, clear currents from your correctly managed home to the world (*Child Guidance*, p. 240).

If parents would educate their children to be pleasant, they should never speak in a scolding manner to them. Educate yourself to carry a pleasant countenance, and bring all the sweetness and melody possible into your voice. The angels of God are ever near your little ones, and your harsh loud tones of fretfulness are not pleasant to their ears (*Adventist Home*, p. 432).

Parents should devise ways and means for keeping their children usefully busy. Let the children be given little pieces of land to cultivate, that they may have something to give as a freewill offering. Parents must never forget that they must work earnestly for themselves and their little ones, if they with them are gathered into the ark of safety. We are still in the enemy's country. Let parents strive to reach a higher standard, and to carry their children with them. Let them cast off the works of darkness and put on the armor of light (*Spaulding and Magan Collection*, p. 185).

Let us put away the spirit of murmuring and complaining, remembering that by cherishing such a spirit we are disrespectful to God. We are living in his dwelling-place; we are members of His family - His by creation and by redemption. Every one is to cherish feelings of respect and tenderness for those with who he associates. In our relations with one another we should be careful never to mar and scar the life and the spirit of others. When in life and character we show the miracle-working power of God, the world will take knowledge of us, that we have been with Jesus and learned of Him (*Spaulding and Magan Collection*, p. 241).

Give some of your leisure hours to your children; associate with them in their work and in their sports, and win their confidence. Cultivate their friendship. Give them responsibilities to bear, small at first, and larger as they grow older. Let them see that you think they help you. Never, never let them hear you say, "They hinder me more than they help me." *(Counsels to Parents, Teachers, and Students*, p. 124).

Let it be your study to select and make your homes as far from Sodom and Gomorrah as you can. Keep out of the large cities. If possible make your homes in the quiet retirement of the country, even if you can never become wealthy by so doing. Locate where there is the best influence (*Adventist Home*, p. 139).

The Lord is calling for men and women to guard their own houses and families, and instead of watching their fellow-workers, regarding with jealousy their outgoing and incoming, to turn their attention to self. The Lord has a report to make of every soul who would restrict the liberty of another. There is a Watcher who is taking the measure of character, and who will judge accordingly. The jealousy revealed by some who claim to be in the truth, plainly reveals that unless their hearts are changed they will never be overcomers. Unless they respond to the subduing, sanctifying influences of the grace of God, they will never wear the crown of life (*Spaulding and Magan Collection*, p. 424).

The home of our first parents was to be a pattern for other homes as their children should go forth to occupy the earth. That home, beautified by the hand of God Himself, was not a gorgeous palace. Men, in their pride, delight in magnificent and costly edifices, and glory in the works of their own hands: but God placed Adam in a garden. This was his dwelling. The blue heavens were its dome; the earth, with its delicate flowers and carpet of living green, was its floor; and the leafy branches of the goodly trees were its canopy. Its walls were hung with the most magnificent adornings—the handiwork of the great Master Artist. In the surroundings of the holy pair was a lesson for all time—that true happiness is found, not in the indulgence of pride and luxury, but in communion with God through His created works (*Adventist Home*, p. 132).

The mother should enter upon her work with courage and energy, relying constantly upon divine aid in all her efforts. She should never rest satisfied until she sees in her children a gradual elevation of character, until they have a higher object in life than merely to seek their own pleasure (*Adventist Home*, p. 265).

A Christian father is the house-band of his family, binding them close to the throne of God. Never is his interest in his children to flag. The father who has a family of boys should not leave these restless boys wholly to the care of the mother. This is too heavy a burden for her. He should make himself their companion and friend. He should exert himself to keep them from evil associates. It may be hard for the mother to exercise self-control. If the husband sees that his wife's weakness is endangering the safety of the children, he should take more of the burden upon himself, doing all in his power to lead his boys to God (*Mind, Character and Personality*, volume 1, p. 166).

Parents, your sons and daughters are not properly guarded. They should never be permitted to go and come when they please, without your knowledge and consent. The unbounded freedom granted to children at this age has proved the ruin of thousands. How many are allowed to be in the streets at night, and parents are content to be ignorant of the associates of their children. Too often companions are chosen whose influence tends only to demoralize (*Adventist Home*, p. 466).

As a people who have had great light, we are to be uplifting in our habits, in our words, in our domestic life and association. Give the Word its honored position as a guide in the home. Let it be regarded as the counselor in every difficulty, the standard of every practice. Will my brethren and sisters be convinced that there can never be true prosperity to any soul in the family circle unless the truth of God, the wisdom of righteousness, presides? Every effort should be made by fathers and mothers to bring their own minds up from the lazy habit of regarding the service of God as a burden. The power of the truth must be a sanctifying agency in the home (*Child Guidance*, p. 509).

Prayerfully, unitedly, the father and the mother should bear the grave responsibility of guiding their children aright. Whatever else they neglect, they should never leave their children free to wander in paths of sin. Many parents allow children to go and do as they please, amusing themselves and choosing evil associates. In the judgment such parents will learn that their children have lost heaven because they have not been kept under home restraint (*Adventist Home*, p. 468).

One that ruleth well his own house, having his children in subjection with all gravity; (For if a man know not how to rule his own house, how shall he take care of the church of God?) (1 Timothy 3:4–5).

Among the first tasks of the mother is the restraining of passion in her little ones. Children should not be allowed to manifest anger; they should not be permitted to throw themselves upon the floor, striking and crying because something has been denied them which was not for their best good. I have been distressed as I have seen how many parents indulge their children in the display of angry passions. Mothers seem to look upon these outbursts of anger as something that must be endured, and appear indifferent to the child's behavior. But if an evil is permitted once, it will be repeated, and its repetition will result in habit, and so the child's character will receive an evil mold (*Child Guidance*, p. 92).

Fathers and mothers too often leave their children to choose for themselves their amusements, their companions, and their occupation. The result is such as might reasonably be expected. Leave a field uncultivated, and it will grow up to thorns and briers. You will never see a lovely flower or a choice shrub peering above the unsightly, poisonous weeds. The worthless bramble will grow luxuriantly without thought or care, while plants that are valued for use or beauty require thorough culture. Thus it is with our youth. If right habits are formed and right principles established, there is earnest work to be done. If wrong habits are corrected, diligence and perseverance are required to accomplish the task (*Adventist Home*, p. 468).

Let us teach the little ones to help us while their hands are small and their strength is slight. Let us impress upon their minds the fact that labor is noble, that it was ordained to man of heaven, that it was enjoined upon Adam in Eden, as an essential to the healthy development of mind and body.

Let us teach them that innocent pleasure is never half so satisfying as when it follows active industry (*Child Guidance*, p. 127).

Too few realize the importance of retaining, as far as possible, their own youthful feelings, and not becoming harsh and unsympathizing in their nature. God would be pleased to have parents mingle the graceful simplicity of a child with the strength, wisdom, and maturity of manhood and womanhood. Some never had a genuine childhood. They never enjoyed the freedom, simplicity, and freshness of budding life. They were scolded and snubbed, reproved and beaten, until the innocence and trustful frankness of the child was exchanged for fear, envy, jealousy, and deceitfulness. Such seldom have the characteristics that will make the childhood of their own dear ones happy (*Child Guidance*, p. 212).

If your children are disobedient, they should be corrected... Before correcting them, go by yourself, and ask the Lord to soften and subdue the hearts of your children and to give you wisdom in dealing with them. Never in a single instance have I known this method to fail. You cannot make a child understand spiritual things when the heart is stirred with passion (*Child Guidance*, p. 244).

The family firm must be well organized. Together the father and mother must consider their responsibilities, and with a clear comprehension undertake their task. There is to be no variance. The father and mother should never in the presence of their children criticize each other's plans and judgment (*Adventist Home*, p. 314).

Lo, children are an heritage of the LORD: and the fruit of the womb is his reward. As arrows are in the hand of a mighty man; so are children of the youth. Happy is the man that hath his quiver full of them: they shall not be ashamed, but they shall speak with the enemies in the gate (Psalms 127:3–5).

Do not depend upon the teachers of the Sabbath school to do your work of training your children in the way they should go. The Sabbath school is a great blessing; it may help you in your work, but it can never take your place. God has given to all fathers and mothers the responsibility of bringing their children to Jesus, teaching them how to pray and believe in the word of God (*Adventist Home*, p. 189).

Instruct them patiently. Sometimes they will have to be punished, but never do it in such a way that they will feel that they have been punished in anger. By such a course you only work a greater evil. Many unhappy differences in the family circle might be avoided if parents would obey the counsel of the Lord in the training of their children (*Child Guidance*, p. 244).

Children who dishonor and disobey their parents, and disregard their advice and instructions, can have no part in the earth made new. The purified new earth will be no place for the rebellious, the disobedient, the ungrateful son or daughter. Unless such learn obedience and submission here, they will never learn it; the peace of the ransomed will not be marred by disobedient, unruly, unsubmissive children. No commandment breaker can inherit the kingdom of heaven (*Adventist Home*, p. 294).

You should correct your children in love. Do not let them have their own way until you get angry, and then punish them. Such correction only helps on the evil, instead of remedying it (*Child Guidance*, p. 245).

He knew that these children would listen to His counsel and accept Him as their Redeemer, while those who were worldly-wise and hardhearted would be less likely to follow Him and find a place in the kingdom of God. These little ones, by coming to Christ and receiving His advice and benediction, had His image and His gracious words stamped upon their plastic minds, never to be effaced. We should learn a lesson from this act of Christ, that the hearts of the young are most susceptible to the teachings of Christianity, easy to influence toward piety and virtue, and strong to retain the impressions received (*Adventist Home*, p. 275).

If parents would place themselves in the position of the teachers, and see how difficult it must necessarily be to manage and discipline a school of hundreds of students of every grade and class of minds, they might upon reflection see things differently. They should consider that some children have never been disciplined at home (*Christian Education*, p. 237).

A Christian father is the house-band of his family, binding them close to the throne of God. Never is his interest in his children to flag. The father who has a family of boys should not leave these restless boys wholly to the care of the mother.. He should make himself their companion and friend. He should exert himself to keep them from evil associates... He should take more of the burden upon himself, doing all in his power to lead his boys to God (*Faith I Live By*, p. 265).

Never should parents cause their children pain by harshness or unreasonable exactions. Harshness drives souls into Satan's net (*Adventist Home*, p. 307).

Our youth profess to be among those who keep the commandments of God, and yet many of them neglect and break the fifth commandment; and the rich blessing promised to those who observe this precept, and honor father and mother, cannot be fulfilled to them. Unless they repent of their sin, and reform their practices and character through the grace of Christ, they will never enter into the new earth, upon which they may live eternally. Those who do not respect and love their parents will not respect and honor God. Those who fail to bear the test, who fail to honor their God-fearing parents, fail to obey God, and therefore cannot expect to come into the land of promise (*Messages to Young People*, p. 331).

Children have active minds, and they need to be employed in lifting the burdens of practical life... They should never be left to pick up their own employment. Parents should control this matter themselves (*Adventist Home*, p. 282).

The home that is beautified by love, sympathy, and tenderness is a place that angels love to visit and where God is glorified. The influence of a carefully guarded Christian home in the years of childhood and youth is the surest safeguard against the corruptions of the world. In the atmosphere of such a home the children will learn to love both their earthly parents and their heavenly Father

(*Mind, Character and Personality*, volume 1, p. 216).

He [Christ] identified Himself with the lowly, the needy, and the afflicted. He took little children in His arms and descended to the level of the young. His large heart of love could comprehend their trials and necessities, and He enjoyed their happiness. His spirit, wearied with the bustle and confusion of the crowded city, tired of association with crafty and hypocritical men, found rest and peace in the society of innocent children. His presence never repulsed them. The Majesty of heaven condescended to answer their questions and simplified His important lessons to meet their childish understanding. He planted in their young, expanding minds the seeds of truth that would spring up and produce a plentiful harvest in their riper years. He [Christ] knew that these children would listen to His counsel and accept Him as their Redeemer, while those who were worldly-wise and hardhearted would be less likely to follow Him and find a place in the kingdom of God. These little ones, by coming to Christ and receiving His advice and benediction, had His image and His gracious words stamped upon their plastic minds, never to be effaced. We should learn a lesson from this act of Christ, that the hearts of the young are most susceptible to the teachings of Christianity, easy to influence toward piety and virtue, and strong to retain the impressions received (*Adventist Home*, p. 275).

God calls upon you to teach them to prepare to be members of the royal family, children of the heavenly King. Co-operate with God by working diligently for their salvation. If they err, do not scold them. Never taunt them with being baptized and yet doing wrong. Remember that they have much to learn in regard to the duties of a child of God (*Child Guidance*, p. 500).

He who has a family of boys must understand that, whatever his calling, he is never to neglect the souls placed in his care. He has brought these children into the world and has made himself responsible to God to do everything in his power to keep them from unsanctified associations, from evil companionship. He should not leave his restless boys wholly to the care of the mother. This is too heavy a burden for her. He must arrange matters for the best interests of the mother and the children. It may be very hard for the mother to exercise self-control and to manage wisely in the training of her children. If this is the case, the father should take more of the burden upon his soul. He should be determined to make the most decided efforts to save his children (*Adventist Home*, p. 220).

Never give your child a passionate blow, unless you want him to learn to fight and quarrel. As parents you stand in the place of God to your children, and you are to be on guard (*Child Guidance*, p. 251).

Fathers, spend as much time as possible with your children. Seek to become acquainted with their various dispositions, that you may know how to train them in harmony with the word of God. Never should a word of discouragement pass your lips. Do not bring darkness into the home. Be pleasant, kind, and affectionate toward your children, but not foolishly indulgent. Let them bear their little disappointments, as every one must. Do not encourage them to come to you with their petty complaints of one another. Teach them to bear with one another and to seek to maintain each other's confidence and respect (*Adventist Home*, p. 222).

While we are not to indulge blind affection, neither are we to manifest undue severity. Children cannot be brought to the Lord by force. They can be led, but not driven (*Counsels to Parents, Teachers, and Students*, p. 114).

Too often the parents are not united in their family government. The father, who is with his children but little, and is ignorant of their peculiarities of disposition and temperament, is harsh and severe. He does not control his temper, but corrects in passion. The child knows this, and instead of being subdued, the punishment fills him with anger. The mother allows misdemeanors to pass at one time for which she will severely punish at another. The children never know just what to expect, and are tempted to see how far they can transgress with impunity. Thus are sown seeds of evil that spring up and bear fruit (*Adventist Home*, p. 314).

Children's children are the crown of old men; and the glory of children are their fathers (Proverbs 17:6).

The mother may ask, "Shall I never punish my child?" Whipping may be necessary when other resorts fail; yet she should not use the rod if it is possible to avoid doing so. But if milder measures prove insufficient, punishment that will bring the child to its senses should in love be administered. Frequently one such correction will be enough for a lifetime, to show the child that he does not hold the lines of control (*Counsels to Parents, Teachers, and Students*, p. 116).

Let the father seek to lighten the mother's task… Let him point them to the beautiful flowers, the lofty trees, in whose very leaves they can trace the work and love of God. He should teach them that the God who made all these things loves the beautiful and the good. Christ pointed His disciples to the lilies of the field and the birds of the air, showing how God cares for them and presenting this as evidence that He will care for man, who is of higher consequence than birds or flowers. Tell the children that however much time may be wasted in attempts at display, our appearance can never compare, for grace and beauty, with that of the simplest flowers of the field. Thus their minds may be drawn from the artificial to the natural. They may learn that God has given them all these beautiful things to enjoy, and that He wants them to give Him the heart's best and holiest affections (*Adventist Home*, p. 222).

And these words, which I command thee this day, shall be in thine heart: And thou shalt teach them diligently unto thy children, and shalt talk of them when thou sittest in thine house, and when thou walkest by the way, and when thou liest down, and when thou risest up. And thou shalt bind them for a sign upon thine hand, and they shall be as frontlets between thine eyes. And thou shalt write them upon the posts of thy house, and on thy gates (Deuteronomy 6:6–9

Never correct your child in anger. An exhibition of passion on your part will not cure your child's evil temper. That is the time of all times when you should act with humility and patience and prayer. Then is the time to kneel down with the children and ask the Lord for pardon. Before you cause your child physical pain, you will, if you are a Christian father or mother, reveal the love you have for your erring little one. As you bow before God with your child you will present before the sympathizing Redeemer His own words, "Suffer the little children to come unto Me, and forbid them not: for of such is the kingdom of God." Mark 10:14. That prayer will bring angels to your side. Your child will not forget these experiences, and the blessing of God will rest upon such instruction, leading him to Christ (*Counsels to Parents, Teachers, and Students*, p. 117).

Her work [the Christian mother's], if done faithfully in God, will be immortalized. The votaries of fashion will never see or understand the immortal beauty of that Christian mother's work, and will sneer at her old-fashioned notions and her plain, unadorned dress; while the Majesty of heaven will write the name of that faithful mother in the book of immortal fame (*Adventist Home*, p. 238).

A good man leaveth an inheritance to his children's children: and the wealth of the sinner is laid up for the just (Proverbs 13:22).

The Lord has not called you to neglect your home and your husband and children. He never works in this way; and He never will... never for a moment suppose that God has given you a work that will necessitate a separation from your precious little flock. Do not leave them to become demoralized by improper associations and to harden their hearts against their mother. This is letting your light shine in a wrong way, altogether; you are making it more difficult for your children to become what God would have them and win heaven at last. God cares for them, and so must you if you claim to be His child (*Adventist Home*, p. 246).

Never let your child hear you say, "I cannot do anything with you." As long as we may have access to the throne of God, we as parents should be ashamed to utter any such word. Cry unto Jesus, and He will help you to bring your little ones to Him (*Child Guidance*, p. 238).

Never act from impulse in governing children. Let authority and affection be blended. Cherish and cultivate all that is good and lovely, and lead them to desire the higher good by revealing Christ to them. While you deny them those things that would be an injury to them, let them see that you love them and want to make them happy. The more unlovely they are, the greater pains you should take to reveal your love for them. When the child has confidence that you want to make him happy, love will break every barrier down. This is the principle of the Saviour's dealing with man; it is the principle that must be brought into the church (*Adventist Home*, p. 198).

Parents should never hurry their children out of their childhood. Let the lessons given them be of that character which will inspire their hearts with noble purposes; but let them be children and grow up with that simple trust, candor, and truthfulness which will prepare them to enter the kingdom of heaven (*Child Guidance*, p. 204).

Our business in this world... is to see what virtues we can teach our children and our families to possess, that they shall have an influence upon other families, and thus we can be an educating power although we never enter into the desk. A well-ordered, a well-disciplined family in the sight of

Absolutely Positively

God is more precious than fine gold, even than the golden wedge of Ophir (*Adventist Home*, p. 32).

Parents should never lose sight of their own responsibility for the future happiness of their children. Isaac's deference to his father's judgment was the result of the training that had taught him to love a life of obedience (*Adventist Home*, p. 74).

Parents, take your children with you into your religious exercises. Throw around them the arms of your faith, and consecrate them to Christ. Do not allow anything to cause you to throw off your responsibility to train them aright; do not let any worldly interest induce you to leave them behind. Never let your Christian life isolate them from you. Bring them with you to the Lord; educate their minds to become familiar with divine truth. Let them associate with those that love God. Bring them to the people of God as children whom you are seeking to help to build characters fit for eternity (*Adventist Home*, p. 321).

Never forget that you are to make the home bright and happy for yourselves and your children by cherishing the Saviour's attributes. If you bring Christ into the home, you will know good from evil. You will be able to help your children to be trees of righteousness, bearing the fruit of the Spirit (*Adventist Home*, p. 17).

As united rulers of the home kingdom, let father and mother show kindness and courtesy to each other. Never should their deportment militate against the precepts they seek to inculcate. They must maintain purity of heart and life if they would have their children pure. They must train and discipline self if they would have their children subject to discipline. They must set before their children an example worthy of imitation. Should they be remiss in this respect, what will they answer if the children entrusted to them stand before the bar of heaven as witnesses to their neglect? How terrible will be their realization of loss and failure as they face the Judge of all the earth! *(Counsels to Parents, Teachers, and Students*, p. 128).

Children of two to four years of age should not be encouraged to think that they must have everything that they ask for. Parents should teach them lessons of self-denial and never treat them in such a way as to make them think they are the center, and that everything revolves about them (*Child Guidance*, p. 132).

The wife and mother who nobly overcomes difficulties under which others sink for want of patience and fortitude to persevere not only becomes strong herself in doing her duty, but her experience in overcoming temptations and obstacles qualifies her to be an efficient help to others, both by words and example. Many who do well under favorable circumstances seem to undergo a transformation of character under adversity and trial; they deteriorate in proportion to their troubles. God never designed that we should be the sport of circumstances (*Adventist Home*, p. 248).

Be careful how you relinquish the government of your children to others. No one can properly relieve you of your God-given responsibility. Many children have been utterly ruined by the interference of relatives or friends in their home government. Mothers should never allow their sisters or mothers to interfere with the wise management of their children. Though the mother may have received the very best training at the hands of her mother, yet, in nine cases out of ten, as a grandmother she would spoil her daughter's children, by indulgence and injudicious praise. All the patient effort of the mother may be undone by this course of treatment. It is proverbial that grandparents, as a rule, are unfit to bring up their grandchildren. Men and women should pay all the respect and deference due to their parents; but in the matter of the management of their own children, they should allow no interference, but hold the reins of government in their own hands (*Child Guidance*, p. 288).

And, ye fathers, provoke not your children to wrath: but bring them up in the nurture and admonition of the Lord (Ephesians 6:4).

Parents are not authorized to fret and scold and ridicule. They should never taunt their children with perverse traits of character, which they themselves have transmitted to them. This mode of discipline will never cure the evil. Parents, bring the precepts of God's Word to admonish and reprove your wayward children. Show them a "Thus saith the Lord" for your requirements. A reproof which comes as the word of God is far more effective than one falling in harsh, angry tones from the lips of parents (*Child Guidance*, p. 282).

It is the cry of many mothers: "I have no time to be with my children." Then for Christ's sake spend less time on your dress. Neglect if you will to adorn your apparel. Neglect to receive and make calls. Neglect to cook an endless variety of dishes. But never, never neglect your children. What is the chaff to the wheat? Let nothing interpose between you and the best interests of your children (*Adventist Home* p. 191).

Chapter 10

God

For this God is our God for ever and ever: he will be our guide even unto death. (Psalms 48:14).

The whole universe will have become witnesses to the nature and results of sin. And its utter extermination, which in the beginning would have brought fear to angels and dishonor to God, will now vindicate his love and establish his honor before a universe of beings who delight to do his will, and in whose heart is his law. Never will evil again be manifest... The law of God, which Satan has reproached as the yoke of bondage, will be honored as the law of liberty. A tested and proved creation will never again be turned from allegiance to Him whose character has been fully manifested before them as fathomless love and infinite wisdom (*The Great Controversy*, p. 504).

For God is not the author of confusion, but of peace, as in all churches of the saints. (1 Corinthians 14:33)

Christ Jesus is represented as continually standing at the altar, momentarily offering up the sacrifice for the sins of the world. He is a minister of the true tabernacle which the Lord pitched and not man. The typical shadows of the Jewish tabernacle no longer possess any virtue. A daily and yearly typical atonement is no longer to be made, but the atoning sacrifice through a mediator is essential because of the constant commission of sin. Jesus is officiating in the presence of God, offering up His shed blood, as it had been a lamb slain (*God's Amazing Grace*, p. 154).

Let us never lose sight of the fact that Jesus is a well-spring of joy. He does not delight in the misery of human beings, but loves to see them happy (*Counsels to Parents, Teachers, and Students*, p. 55).

For the LORD thy God is a consuming fire, even a jealous God (Deuteronomy 4:24).

The divine Teacher bears with the erring through all their perversity. His love does not grow cold; His efforts to win them do not cease. With outstretched arms He waits to welcome again and again the erring, the rebellious, and even the apostate. His heart is touched with the helplessness of the little child subject to rough usage. The cry of human suffering never reaches His ear in vain. Though all are precious in His sight, the rough, sullen, stubborn dispositions draw most heavily upon His sympathy and love; for He traces from cause to effect. The one who is most easily tempted, and is most inclined to err, is the special object of his solicitude (*Counsels on Stewardship*, p. 178).

For the LORD your God is he that goeth with you, to fight for you against your enemies, to save you (Deuteronomy 20:4).

The Lord is our helper... No one ever trusted God in vain. He never disappoints those who put their dependence on Him. If we would only do the work that the Lord would have us do, walking in the footsteps of Jesus, our hearts would become sacred harps, every chord of which would send forth praise and thanksgiving to the One sent by God to take away the sin of the world (*Conflict and Courage*, p. 218).

O Lord GOD, thou hast begun to shew thy servant thy greatness, and thy mighty hand: for what God is there in heaven or in earth, that can do according to thy works, and according to thy might? (Deuteronomy 3:24).

In the courts above, Christ is pleading for His church, pleading for those for whom He has paid the redemption price of His blood. Centuries, ages, can never lessen the efficacy of His atoning sacrifice. Neither life nor death, height nor depth, can separate us from the love of God which is in Christ Jesus; not because we hold Him so firmly, but because He holds us so fast (*Acts of the Apostles*, p. 552).

Through all our trials we have a never-failing Helper. He does not leave us alone to struggle with temptation, to battle with evil, and be finally crushed with burdens and sorrow. Though now He is hidden from mortal sight, the ear of faith can hear His voice saying, Fear not; I am with you. "I am he that liveth, and was dead; and, behold, I am alive forevermore" (Revelation 1:18) (*God's Amazing Grace*, p. 77).

(For the LORD thy God is a merciful God;) he will not forsake thee, neither destroy thee, nor forget the covenant of thy fathers which he swear unto them (Deuteronomy 4:31).

Angels rejoice as they gaze upon this precious token of God's love to man. The world's Redeemer looks upon it; for it was through His instrumentality that this bow was made to appear in the heavens, as a token or covenant of promise to man. God Himself looks upon the bow in the clouds, and remembers His everlasting covenant between Himself and man... As we gaze upon the beautiful sight, we may be joyful in God, assured that He Himself is looking upon this token of His covenant, and that as He looks upon it He remembers the children of earth, to whom it was given. Their afflictions, perils, and trials are not hidden from Him. We may rejoice in hope, for the bow of God's covenant is over us. He never will forget the children of His care (*God's Amazing Grace*, p. 159).

God is our refuge and strength, a very present help in trouble. Therefore will not we fear, though the earth be removed, and though the mountains be carried into the midst of the sea (Psalms 46:1–2).

And we have known and believed the love that God hath to us. God is love; and he that dwelleth in love dwelleth in God, and God in him (1 John 4:16).

Let us never forget that Jesus loves us. He died for us, and now he lives to make intercession in our behalf. And the Father also loves us, and desires our happiness. "He that spared not his own Son, but delivered him up for us all, how shall he not with him also freely give us all things?" (Romans 8:32.) Brethren, you should set an example of faith, confidence, and love, to the churches over which the Lord has made you overseers. Will you do your work with fidelity, in the fear of God? Will you feel that you must avail yourselves of every opportunity to obtain grace and power from on high, that you may render to God the very best service possible? (*Gospel Workers*, 1892, p. 423).

Understand therefore this day, that the LORD thy God is he which goeth over before thee; as a consuming fire he shall destroy them, and he shall bring them down before thy face: so shalt thou drive them out, and destroy them quickly, as the LORD hath said unto thee (Deuteronomy 9:3).

Look constantly to Jesus. Take all your troubles to Him. He will never misunderstand you. He is the refuge of His people. Under the shadow of His protection they can pass unharmed. Believe in Him and trust in Him. He will not give you up to the spoiler (*In Heavenly Places*, p. 176).

In God is my salvation and my glory: the rock of my strength, and my refuge, is in God. Trust in him at all times; ye people, pour out your heart before him: God is a refuge for us. Selah (Psalms 62:7–8).

This is Jesus, the life of every grace, the life of every promise, the life of every ordinance, the life of every blessing. Jesus is the substance, the glory and fragrance, the very life itself. "He that followeth Me shall not walk in darkness, but shall have the light of life" (John 8:12). Then the royal path cast up for the ransomed to walk in is not discouraging darkness. Our pilgrimage would indeed be lonely and painful were it not for Jesus. "I will not," He says, "leave you comfortless" (John 14:18). Then let us gather every registered promise. Let us repeat them by day and meditate upon them in the night season, and be happy (*Mind, Character and Personality*, Volume 2, p. 643).

For the LORD your God is God of gods, and Lord of lords, a great God, a mighty, and a terrible, which regardeth not persons, nor taketh reward (Deuteronomy 10:17).

Since God is infinite, and in Him are all the treasures of wisdom, we may to all eternity be ever searching, ever learning, yet never exhaust the riches of His wisdom, His goodness, or His power (*My Life Today*, p. 360).

And the LORD descended in the cloud, and stood with him there, and proclaimed the name of the LORD. And the LORD passed by before him, and proclaimed, The LORD, The LORD God, merciful and gracious, longsuffering, and abundant in goodness and truth, Keeping mercy for thousands, forgiving iniquity and transgression and sin, and that will by no means clear the guilty; visiting the iniquity of the fathers upon the children, and upon the children's children, unto the third and to the fourth generation (Exodus 34:5–7).

God is our tender, pitiful Father, and every believing child is the object of His special care (*Faith I Live By*, p. 38).

God is not a man, that he should lie; neither the son of man, that he should repent: hath he said, and shall he not do it? or hath he spoken, and shall he not make it good? (Numbers 23:19).

God is a Spirit; yet He is a personal being; for so He has revealed Himself (*Faith I Live By*, p. 40).

For who is God, save the LORD? and who is a rock, save our God? God is my strength and power: and he maketh my way perfect. He maketh my feet like hinds' feet: and setteth me upon my high places (2 Samuel 22:32–34

We need to realize that the Holy Spirit…is as much a person as God is a person … (*Faith I Live By*, p. 52).

For if ye turn again unto the LORD, your brethren and your children shall find compassion before them that lead them captive, so that they shall come again into this land: for the LORD your God is gracious and merciful, and will not turn away his face from you, if ye return unto him (2 Chronicles 30:9)

The hour and place of prayer and the services of public worship the child should be taught to regard as sacred because God is there. And as reverence is manifested in attitude and demeanor, the feeling that inspires it will be deepened (*Child Guidance*, p. 539).

The hand of our God is upon all them for good that seek him; but his power and his wrath is against all them that forsake him (Ezra 8:22).

God is the fountain of life, and we can have life only as we are in communion with Him. Separated from God, existence may be ours for a little time, but we do not possess life… Only through the surrender of our will to God is it possible for Him to impart life to us. Only by receiving His life through self-surrender is it possible, said Jesus, for these hidden sins … to be overcome. It is possible that you ma34y bury them in your hearts and conceal them from human eyes, but how will you stand in God's presence? … To sin, wherever found, God is a consuming fire (*Reflecting Christ*, p. 377).

Behold, God is mine helper: the Lord is with them that uphold my soul (Psalms 54:4).

Those who reject the truth of the Bible do it under a pretense of loving Jesus. Those who love Jesus will reveal that love by being obedient children. They will be doers of the Word and not hearers only. They will not be continually pleading, "All that we have to do is to believe in Jesus." This is true in the fullest sense, but they do not comprehend, they do not take it in its fullest sense. To believe in Jesus is to take Him as your Redeemer, as your Pattern. All who love Jesus must follow His example. They must connect themselves with Jesus as closely as the branch is connected with the living vine. They are abiding in Jesus and Jesus is abiding in them and they are doers of His Word, partakers of His divine nature (*This Day With God*, p. 299).

For the LORD God is a sun and shield: the LORD will give grace and glory: no good thing will he withhold from them that walk uprightly. O LORD of hosts, blessed is the man that trusteth in thee (Psalms 84:11–12).

Some who come to God by repentance and confession, and even believe that their sins are forgiven, still fail of claiming, as they should, the promises of God. They do not see that Jesus is an ever-present Saviour; and they are not ready to commit the keeping of their souls to him, relying upon him to perfect the work of grace begun in their hearts. While they think they are committing themselves to God, there is a great deal of self-dependence. There are conscientious souls that trust partly to God, and partly to themselves. They do not look to God, to be kept by his power, but depend upon watchfulness against temptation, and the performance of certain duties for acceptance with him. There are no victories in this kind of faith. Such persons toil to no purpose; their souls are in continual bondage, and they find no rest until their burdens are laid at the feet of Jesus (*Gospel Workers*, 1892, p. 414).

Gracious is the LORD, and righteous; yea, our God is merciful (Psalms 116:5).

Come to Jesus, and receive rest and peace. You may have the blessing even now. Satan suggests that you are helpless, and cannot bless yourself. It is true; you are helpless. But lift up Jesus before him: "I have a risen Saviour. In him I trust, and he will never suffer me to be confounded. In his name I triumph. He is my righteousness, and my crown of rejoicing." Let no one here feel that his case is hopeless; for it is not. You may see that you are sinful and undone; but it is just on this account that you need a Saviour. If you have sins to confess, lose no time. These moments are golden. "If we confess our sins, he is faithful and just to forgive us our sins, and to cleanse us from all unrighteousness." (1 John 1:9.) Those who hunger and thirst after righteousness will be filled; for Jesus has promised it. Precious Saviour! his arms are open to receive us, and his great heart of love is waiting to bless us (*Gospel Workers*, 1892, p. 413).

For the wages of sin is death; but the gift of God is eternal life through Jesus Christ our Lord (Romans 6:23).

We are wanting in simple faith; we need to learn the art of trusting our very best Friend. Although we see him not, Jesus is watching over us with tender compassion; and he is touched with the feeling of our infirmities. No one in his great need ever looked to him in faith and was disappointed. Brethren, do not express doubt; do not let your lips utter one complaining, repining word. Begin now to fix your minds more firmly upon Jesus and heavenly things, remembering that by beholding we become changed into the same image (*Gospel Workers*, 1892, p. 422).

Our Saviour is a Saviour for the perfection of the whole man. He is not the God of part of the being only. The grace of Christ works to the disciplining of the whole human fabric. He made all. He has redeemed all. He has made the mind, the strength, the body as well as the soul, partaker of the divine nature, and all is His purchased possession. He must be served with the whole mind, heart, soul, and strength. Then the Lord will be glorified in His saints in even the common, temporal things with which they are connected. "Holiness unto the Lord" will be the inscription placed upon them (*That I May Know Him*, p. 331).

This then is the message which we have heard of him, and declare unto you, that God is light, and in him is no darkness at all (1 John 1:5).

Chapter 11

Stewardship

Time is money, and many are wasting precious time which might be used in useful labor, working with their hands the thing that is good. The Lord will never say, "Well done, thou good and faithful servant," to the man who has not taxed the physical powers which have been lent him of God as precious talents by which to gather means, wherewith the needy may be supplied, and offerings may be made to God (*Counsels on Stewardship*, p. 288).

Habits of self-indulgence or a want of tact and skill on the part of the wife and mother may be a constant drain upon the treasury; and yet that mother may think she is doing her best because she has never been taught to restrict her wants or the wants of her children and has never acquired skill and tact in household matters. Hence one family may require for its support twice the amount that would suffice for another family of the same size (*Adventist Home*, p. 374).

Labour not to be rich: cease from thine own wisdom. Wilt thou set thine eyes upon that which is not? for riches certainly make themselves wings; they fly away as an eagle toward heaven (Proverbs 23:4–5).

In every business transaction be rigidly honest. However tempted, never deceive or prevaricate in the least matter. At times a natural impulse may bring temptation to diverge from the straightforward path of honesty, but do not vary one hairsbreadth. If in any matter you make a statement as to what you will do, and afterward find that you have favored others to your own loss, do not vary a hairsbreadth from principle. Carry out your agreement. By seeking to change your plans you would show that you could not be depended on. And should you draw back in little transactions, you would draw back in larger ones. Under such circumstances some are tempted to deceive, saying, I was not understood. My words have been taken to mean more than I intended. The fact is, they meant just what they said, but lost the good impulse, and then wanted to draw back from their agreement, lest it prove a loss to them. The Lord requires us to do justice, to love mercy, and truth, and righteousness (*Child Guidance*, p. 154).

Worldlings spend upon dress large sums of money that ought to be used to feed and clothe those suffering from hunger and cold. Many for whom Christ gave His life have barely sufficient of the cheapest, most common clothing, while others spend thousands of dollars in the efforts to satisfy the never-ending demands of fashion (*Counsels on Stewardship*, p. 301).

Rob not the poor, because he is poor: neither oppress the afflicted in the gate (Proverbs 22:22)

There are men who do not move wisely. They are anxious to make a large appearance. They think that outward display will give them influence. In their work, they do not first sit down and count the cost, to see whether they are able to finish what they have begun. Thus they show their weakness. They show that they have much to learn in regard to the necessity of moving carefully and guardedly. In their self-confidence they make many mistakes. Thus some have received harm from which they will never recover (*Counsels on Stewardship*, p. 273).

In every business transaction a Christian will be just what he wants his brethren to think he is. His course of action is guided by underlying principles. He does not scheme; therefore he has nothing to conceal, nothing to gloss over. He may be criticized, he may be tested, but his unbending integrity will shine forth like pure gold. He is a blessing to all connected with him, for his word is trustworthy. He is a man who will not take advantage of his neighbor. He is a friend and benefactor to all, and his fellow men put confidence in his counsel … A truly honest man will never take advantage of weakness and incompetency in order to fill his own purse (*Child Guidance*, p. 153).

Charge them that are rich in this world, that they be not highminded, nor trust in uncertain riches, but in the living God, who giveth us richly all things to enjoy; That they do good, that they be rich in good works, ready to distribute, willing to communicate; Laying up in store for themselves a good foundation against the time to come, that they may lay hold on eternal life (1 Timothy 6:17–19).

We can every one of us do something, if we will only take the position that God would have us. Every move that you make to enlighten others, brings you nearer in harmony with the God of heaven. If you sit down and look at yourself and say, "I can barely support my family," you will never do anything; but if you say, "I will do something for the truth, I will see it advance, I will do what I can," God will open ways so that you can do something. You should invest in the cause of truth so that you will feel that you are a part of it (*Counsels on Stewardship*, p. 304).

If there be among you a poor man of one of thy brethren within any of thy gates in thy land which the LORD thy God giveth thee, thou shalt not harden thine heart, nor shut thine hand from thy poor brother (Deuteronomy 15:7).

The only plan which the gospel has marked out for sustaining the work of God is one that leaves the support of His cause to the honor of men. With an eye single to the glory of God, men are to give to God the proportion which He has required. Viewing the cross of Calvary, looking upon the world's Redeemer, who for our sake became poor, that we through His poverty might be made rich, we shall feel that we are not to lay up for ourselves treasures on the earth, but to lay up treasures in the bank of heaven, which will never suspend payment nor fail. The Lord has given Jesus to our world, and the question is, What can we give back to God in gifts and offerings to show our appreciation of His love? "Freely ye have received, freely give." (*Counsels on Stewardship*, p. 287).

He that trusteth in his riches shall fall; but the righteous shall flourish as a branch (Proverbs 11:28).

Absolutely Positively

Be determined never to incur another debt. Deny yourself a thousand things rather than run in debt. This has been the curse of your life, getting into debt. Avoid it as you would the smallpox (*Counsels on Stewardship*, p. 257).

Let the proper estimate be placed upon the publications, and then let all in our offices study to economize in every possible way, even though considerable inconvenience is caused in consequence. Stop every leak. Mind the little things. It is the little losses that tell heavily in the end. Look after the littles, gather up the fragments, that nothing be lost; for many who look after the larger matters have never learned to guard and save the trifles. Waste not the minutes, for they mar the hours. Persevering diligence, work done in faith, will always be crowned with success. Some men think it beneath their dignity to look after small things. They consider it the evidence of a narrow mind and small spirit to be careful of the littles. Watch the little outgoes; save the little incomes. The smallest leak has sunk many a ship. No derision or jesting should keep us from saving the littles. Nothing that would serve the purpose should be left to go to waste. A lack of economy will bring debt upon our institutions. Much money may be received, but it will be lost in the little wastes of every branch of the work. Economy is not stinginess (*The Publishing Ministry*, p. 331).

He that loveth silver shall not be satisfied with silver; nor he that loveth abundance with increase: this is also vanity (Ecclesiastes 5:10).

God help the managers of our schools never to allow the outgo to exceed the income, if the school has to be closed. There has not been the talent that is needed in the management of our schools financially. These things God will require of the managers. Every needless, expensive habit is to be laid aside, every unnecessary indulgence cut away. When the principles so manifestly indicated by the word of God to all schools, are taken hold of as earnestly as they should be, the debts will not accumulate (*Counsels on Stewardship*, p. 271).

You might today have had a capital of means to use in case of emergency and to aid the cause of God, if you had economized as you should. Every week a portion of your wages should be reserved and in no case touched unless suffering actual want, or to render back to the Giver in offerings to God... (*Selected Messages*, Volume 2, p. 329).

Honour the LORD with thy substance, and with the first fruits of all thine increase: (Proverbs 3:9).

The precious grace of God is made secondary to matters of no real importance; and many, while collecting material for enjoyment, lose the capacity for happiness. They find that their possessions fail to give the satisfaction they had hoped to derive from them. This endless round of labor, this unceasing anxiety to embellish the home for visitors and strangers to admire, never pays for the time and means thus expended. It is placing upon the neck a yoke of bondage grievous to be borne (*Adventist Home*, p. 151).

Pharisaism in the Christian world today is not extinct. The Lord desires to break up the course of precision which has become so firmly established, which has hindered instead of advancing his work. He desires his people to remember that there is a large space over which the light of present truth is to be shed. Divine wisdom must have abundant room in which to work. It is to advance without asking permission or support from those who have taken to themselves a kingly power. In the past one set of men have tried to keep in their own hands the control of all the means coming from the churches, and have used this means in a most disproportionate manner, erecting expensive buildings where such large buildings were unnecessary and uncalled for, and leaving needy places without help or encouragement. They have taken upon themselves the grave responsibility of retarding the work where the work should have been advanced. It has been left to a few supposed kindly minds to say what fields should be worked and what fields should be left unworked. A few men have kept the truth in circumscribed channels, because to open new fields would call for money. Only in those places in which they were interested have they been willing to invest means. And at the same time, in a few places, five times as much money as was necessary has been invested in buildings. The same amount of money used in establishing plants in places where the truth has never been introduced would have brought many souls to a saving knowledge of Christ (*Spaulding and Magan Collection*, p. 174).

We are admonished to redeem the time. But time squandered can never be recovered. We cannot call back even one moment. The only way in which we can redeem our time is by making the most of that which remains, by being co-workers with God in His great plan of redemption (*Christ Object Lessons*, p. 342).

Time is money, and many are wasting precious time which might be used in useful labor, working with their hands the thing that is good. The Lord will never say, "Well done, thou good and faithful servant," to the man who has not taxed the physical powers which have been lent him of God as precious talents by which to gather means, wherewith the needy may be supplied, and offerings may be made to God. The rich are not to feel that they can be content in giving of their money merely. They have talents of ability, and they are to study to show themselves approved unto God, to be earnest spiritual agents in educating and training their children for fields of usefulness. Parents and children are not to regard themselves as their own, and feel that they can dispose of their time and property as shall please themselves. They are God's purchased possession, and the Lord calls for the profit of their physical powers, which are to be employed in bringing a revenue to the treasury of the Lord (*Review and Herald*, July 14, 1896).

Every moment is freighted with eternal consequences. We are to stand as minute men, ready for service at a moment's notice. The opportunity that is now ours to speak to some needy soul the word of life may never offer again. God may say to that one, "This night thy soul shall be required of thee," and through our neglect he may not be ready. (Luke 12:20.) In the great judgment day, how shall we render our account to God? (*Christ Object Lessons,* p. 343).

Bring ye all the tithes into the storehouse, that there may be meat in mine house, and prove me now herewith, saith the LORD of hosts, if I will not open you the windows of heaven, and pour you out a blessing, that there shall not be room enough to receive it (Malachi 3:10).

There are men in the ranks of Sabbathkeepers who are holding fast their earthly treasure. It is their god, their idol; and they love their money, their farms, their cattle, and their merchandise better than they love their Saviour, who for their sakes became poor, that they, through His poverty, might be made rich. They exalt their earthly treasures, considering them of greater value than the souls of men. Will such have the "Well done" spoken to them? No; never. The irrevocable sentence, "Depart," will fall upon their startled senses. Christ has no use for them. They have been slothful servants, hoarding the means God has given them, while their fellow men have perished in darkness and error (*Counsels on Stewardship*, p. 123).

Better is little with the fear of the LORD than great treasure and trouble therewith (Proverbs 15:16).

In the balances of the sanctuary, the gifts of the poor, made from love to Christ, are not estimated according to the amount given, but according to the love which prompts the sacrifice. The promises of Jesus will as surely be realized by the liberal poor man, who has but little to offer, but who gives that little freely, as by the wealthy man who gives of his abundance. The poor man makes a sacrifice of his little, which he really feels. He really denies himself of some things that he needs for his own comfort, while the wealthy man gives of his abundance, and feels no want, denies himself nothing that he really needs. Therefore there is a sacredness in the poor man's offering that is not found in the rich man's gift; for the rich give of their abundance. God's providence has arranged the entire plan of systematic benevolence for the benefit of man. His providence never stands still. If God's servants follow His opening providence, all will be active workers (*Counsels on Stewardship*, p. 180).

The holidays are approaching. In view of this fact, it will be well to consider how much money is expended yearly in making presents to those who have no need of them. The habits of custom are so strong that to withhold gifts from our friends on these occasions would seem to us almost a neglect of them. But let us remember that our kind heavenly Benefactor has claims upon us far superior to those of any earthly friends. Shall we not, during the coming holidays, present our offerings to God? Even the children may participate in this work. Clothing and other useful articles may be given to the worthy poor, and thus a work may be done for the Master (*Messages to Young People*, p. 311).

Punctuality and decision in the work and cause of God are highly essential. Delays are virtually defeats. Minutes are golden, and should be improved to the very best account. Earthly relations and personal interests should ever be secondary. Never should the cause of God be left to suffer in a single particular, because of our earthly friends or dearest relatives (*Gospel Workers*, 1892, p. 247).

Those who rightly value money are those who see its availability in bringing the truth before those who have never heard it, and by this means rescuing them from the power of the enemy. If one soul accepts the truth, his love for earthly things is dislodged. He sees the surpassing glory of heavenly things, appreciates the excellency of that which relates to everlasting life. He is charmed with the unseen and eternal. His grasp loosens from earthly things. He fastens his eye with admiration upon the invincible glories of the other world. He realizes that his trials are working out for him a far more exceeding and eternal weight of glory, and in comparison to the riches that are his to enjoy he counts them light afflictions which are but for a moment (*Our High Calling*, p. 340).

Let all who profess to believe the present truth calculate how much they spend yearly, and especially upon the recurrence of the annual holidays, for the gratification of selfish and unholy desires, how much in the indulgence of appetite, and how much to compete with others in unchristian display. Sum up the means thus spent all needlessly, and then estimate how much might be saved as consecrated gifts to God's cause without injury to soul or body (*Messages to Young People*, p. 312).

The bright morning hours are wasted by many in bed. These precious hours, once lost, are gone never to return; they are lost for time and for eternity. Only one hour lost each day, and what a waste of time in the course of a year! Let the slumberer think of this, and pause to consider how he will give an account to God for lost opportunities (*Gospel Workers*, 1915, p. 278).

Christ's own words make His meaning plain,—that in acts of charity the aim should not be to secure praise and honor from men. Real godliness never prompts an effort at display. Those who desire words of praise and flattery, and feed upon them as a sweet morsel, are Christians in name only (*Counsels on Stewardship*, p. 195).

The more means persons expend in dress, the less they can have to feed the hungry and clothe the naked; and the streams of beneficence, which should be constantly flowing, are dried up. Every dollar saved by denying one's self of useless ornaments may be given to the needy, or may be placed in the Lord's treasury to sustain the gospel, to send missionaries to foreign countries, to multiply publications to carry rays of light to souls in the darkness of error. Every dollar used unnecessarily deprives the spender of a precious opportunity to do good (*Counsels on Health*, p. 602).

On another visit I saw the coveted musical instrument in the house, and knew that some hundreds of dollars had been added to the burden of debt. I hardly know whom to blame most, the indulgent parents or the selfish children. Both are guilty before God. This one case will illustrate many. These young persons, although they profess to be Christians, have never taken the cross of Christ; for the very first lesson to be learned of Christ is the lesson of self-denial. Said our Saviour, "If any man will come after Me, let him deny himself, and take up his cross, and follow Me." In no way can we become disciples of Christ, except by complying with this condition (*Counsels on Stewardship*, p. 251).

But if any provide not for his own, and specially for those of his own house, he hath denied the faith, and is worse than an infidel (1 Timothy 5:8).

Our laborers must learn to exercise economy, not only in their efforts to advance the cause of truth, but in their own home expenses. They should locate their families where they can be cared for at as little expense as possible. Donations and bequests do not come to our people as they do to other denominations; and those who have not educated themselves to live within their means, will surely have to do this now, or engage in some other employment. Habits of self-indulgence, or a want of tact and skill on the part of the wife and mother, may be a constant drain upon the treasury; and yet that mother may think she is doing her best, because she has never been taught to restrict her wants or the wants of her children, and has never acquired skill and tact in household matters. Hence one family may require for its support twice the amount that would suffice for another family of the same size (*Gospel Workers*, 1915 p. 459).

Every week you should lay by in some secure place five or ten dollars not to be used up unless in case of sickness. With economy you may place something at interest. With wise management you can save something after paying your debts (*Selected Messages*, p. 329).

A truly honest man will never take advantage of weakness or incompetency in order to fill his own purse. He accepts a fair equivalent for that which he sells. If there are defects in the articles sold, he frankly tells his brother or his neighbor, although by so doing he may work against his own pecuniary interests (*Mind, Character and Personality*, volume 2, p. 438).

Chapter 12

Health & Healing

In almost every church there are young men and women who might receive education either as nurses or physicians. They will never have a more favorable opportunity than now. I would urge that this subject be considered prayerfully, that special effort be made to select those youth who give promise of usefulness and moral strength. Let these receive an education ... to go out as missionaries wherever the Lord may call them to labor. It should ever be kept before them that their work is not only to relieve physical suffering, but to minister to souls that are ready to perish. It is important that everyone who is to act as a medical missionary be skilled in ministering to the soul as well as to the body. He is to be an imitator of Christ, presenting to the sick and suffering the preciousness of pure and undefiled religion. While doing all in his power to relieve physical distress and to preserve this mortal life, he should point to the mercy and the love of Jesus, the Great Physician, who came that "whosoever believeth in Him should not perish, but have everlasting life." John 3:16 (*Counsels on Health*, p. 506).

We are health reformers. Physicians should have wisdom and experience, and be thorough health reformers. Then they will be constantly educating by precept and example their patients from drugs. For they well know that the use of drugs may produce for the time being favorable results, but will implant in the system that which will cause great difficulties hereafter, which they may never recover from during their lifetime. Nature must have a chance to do her work. Obstructions must be removed and opportunity given her to exert her healing forces, which she will surely do, if every abuse is removed from her and she has a fair chance (*Medical Missionary*, p. 224).

Many physicians in our world are of no benefit to the human family. The drug science has been exalted, but if every bottle that comes from every such institution were done away with, there would be fewer invalids in the world today. Drug medication should never have been introduced into our institutions. There was no need of this being so, and for this very reason the lord would have us establish an institution where he can come in and where his grace and power can be revealed. "I am the resurrection and the life," he declares (*Spaulding and Magan Collection*, p. 137).

Physicians should not allow their attention to be diverted from their work; neither should they confine themselves so closely to professional work that health will be injured. In the fear of God they should be wise in the use of strength that God has given them. Never should they disregard the means that God has provided for the preservation of health. It is their duty to bring under the control of reason every power that God has given them (*Counsels on Health*, p. 361).

Disease never comes without a cause. The way is prepared, and disease invited, by disregard of the laws of health. Many suffer in consequence of the transgression of their parents. While they are not responsible for what their parents have done, it is nevertheless their duty to ascertain what are and what are not violations of the laws of health. They should avoid the wrong habits of their parents, and by correct living, place themselves in better conditions (*Counsels on Diets and Foods*, p. 122).

For years I have from time to time been shown that the sick should be taught that it is wrong to suspend all physical labor in order to regain health. In thus doing the will becomes dormant, the blood moves sluggishly through the system and constantly grows more impure. Where the patient is in danger of imagining his case worse than it really is, indolence will be sure to produce the most unhappy results. Well-regulated labor gives the invalid the idea that he is not totally useless in the world, that he is at least of some benefit. This will afford him satisfaction, give him courage, and impart to him vigor, which vain mental amusements can never do (*Adventist Home*, p. 510).

Delicate treatments should not be given by male physicians to women in our institutions. Never should a lady patient be alone with a gentleman physician, either for special examination or for treatment. Let the physicians be faithful in preserving delicacy and modesty under all circumstances (*Counsels on Health*, p. 364).

The Lord has brought us into possession of our health institutions that we may learn to bring to the sick, in the most attractive way, truths of heavenly origin. We must never lose sight of the fact that these institutions are instrumentalities in the hands of God for bringing the light of truth to those who are in darkness (*Medical Missionary*, p. 194).

Henceforth medical missionary work is to be carried forward with an earnestness with which it has never yet been carried. This work is the door through which the truth is to find entrance to the large cities (*A Call to Medical Evangelism and Health Education*, p. 17).

When a physician sees that the ailment which has taken hold of the body is the result of improper eating and drinking, yet neglects to tell the patient that his suffering is caused by a wrong course of action, he is doing the human brotherhood an injury. Present the matter tenderly, but never keep silent as to the cause of the affliction (*Medical Missionary*, p. 49).

Nothing should be allowed to stand in the way of perfect, complete unity between the medical missionary workers, and the gospel ministry. God has not empowered Dr. Kellogg with spiritual grace to be lord over all our physicians and other medical missionaries. It is time that the teachings of the great Medical Missionary should be brought into the life-practice of our medical missionary workers. It is time that God's voice should be heard; for his words, spoken in truth, are spirit and life. He never makes a mistake (*Spaulding and Magan Collection*, p. 336).

Never, never should the physician feel that he may prevaricate. It is not always safe and best to lay before the invalid the full extent of his danger. The truth may not all be spoken on all occasions, but never speak a lie. If it is important for the good of the invalid not to alarm him lest such a course might prove fatal, do not lie to him (*Medical Missionary*, p. 38).

A merry heart doeth good like a medicine: but a broken spirit drieth the bones (Proverbs 17:22).

The physician should never lead his patients to fix their attention on him. He is to teach them to grasp with the hand of faith the outstretched hand of the Saviour. Then the mind will be illuminated with the light radiating from the Sun of Righteousness. What physicians attempt to do, Christ did in deed and in truth. They try to save life; He is life itself (*Counsels on Health*, p. 352).

It is not best to tell patients that flesh-meats shall never be used; but reason and conscience are to be awakened in regard to self-preservation and purity from every perverted appetite. They can learn to relish a diet that is healthful and abstemious, consisting of fruits, grains, and vegetables (*Medical Missionary*, p. 227).

The sympathy that Christ ever expressed for the physical needs of His hearers won many a response to the truths He sought to teach. Was not the gospel message of deepest importance to that company of five thousand people who for hours had followed Him and hung upon His words? Many had never before heard truths such as they listened to on that occasion. Yet Christ's desire to teach them spiritual truths did not make Him indifferent to their physical needs (*A Call to Medical Evangelism and Health Education*, p. 15).

It is the divine plan that we shall work as the disciples worked. Physical healing is bound up with the gospel commission. In the work of the gospel, teaching and healing are never to be separated (*Christian Service*, p. 133).

Christ has left us an example, that we should follow in His steps. He always drew near to the most needy, the most hopeless, and, attracted by His sympathy, they came close to Him. He assures every suffering, needy, sinful soul that he will never want for a great Physician to give him spiritual help. We stand too far away from suffering humanity. Let us draw nearer to Christ, that our souls may be filled with His grace, and with a desire to give this grace to others (*Evangelism*, p. 524).

Physicians must stand firmly under the banner of the third angel's message, fighting the good fight of faith perseveringly and successfully, relying not on their own wisdom, but on the wisdom of God, putting on the heavenly armor, the equipment of God's word, never forgetting that they have a Leader who never has been, and never can be, overcome by evil (*Medical Missionary*, p. 32).

A sound heart is the life of the flesh: but envy the rottenness of the bones (Proverbs 14:30).

Never is a physician to do his work in a coarse, careless, or haphazard way. The physician is constantly to study refinement. In every sense of the word, he is to be one that ministers—a servant entrusted by an absent Lord with the care of his fellow beings. The lax, loose way that some of our physicians have of working brings into disrepute the work that should be kept on an elevated platform before the world. When a physician does a weak, inefficient work, his fellow physicians are injured (*Medical Missionary*, p. 32).

Absolutely Positively

Unless the physicians can obtain the confidence of their patients, they can never help them (*Healthful Living*, p. 267).

The circulation of our health publications is a most important work. It is a work in which all who believe the special truths for this time should have a living interest. God desires that now, as never before, the minds of the people shall be deeply stirred to investigate the great temperance question and the principles underlying true health reform (*Colporteur Ministry*, p. 131).

The sick should not be compelled to wait when they need advice and relief. Never should the physician neglect his patients. He should have quick, penetrating judgment, and should carry into the sickroom a genial atmosphere. He should not be cold, reticent, or hesitating, but should cultivate those qualities which exert a soothing influence over the suffering ones. They want more than looks; they want kind, hopeful words. The doctor should be ready to give them cheerful, reassuring words, words spoken from the heart in wisdom, showing that he understands the cases of those under his care. This will inspire a restfulness and confidence, even at the first interview (*Medical Missionary*, p. 193).

The purest example of unselfishness is now to be shown by our medical missionary workers. With the knowledge and experience gained by practical work, they are to go out to give treatments to the sick. As they go from house to house, they will find access to many hearts. Many will be reached who otherwise would never have heard the gospel message (*A Call to Medical Evangelism and Health Education*, p. 11).

Never should familiarity with suffering cause the physician to become careless or unsympathetic. In cases of dangerous illness, the afflicted one feels that he is at the mercy of the physician. He looks to that physician as his only earthly hope, and the physician should ever point the trembling soul to One who is greater than himself, even the Son of God, who gave His life to save him from death, who pities the sufferer, and who by His divine power will give skill and wisdom to all who ask Him (*Counsels on Health*, p. 334).

Medicine deranges nature's fine machinery, and breaks down the constitution. It kills, but never cures (*Healthful Living*, p. 244).

When the leading physician passes by the spiritual part of the work, he is remiss in his duty, and gives a wrong example to the younger helpers who are learning to do the work of a Christian physician. These students neglect a part of the work that is most essential. This, I greatly fear, will result in a loss that can never be remedied (*Medical Missionary*, p. 189).

In almost every church there are young men and women who might receive an education either as physicians or nurses. They will never have a more favorable opportunity than now. I would urge that this subject be considered prayerfully, that special effort be made to select those youth who give promise of usefulness and moral strength. Let these receive an education at our Sanitarium at Battle Creek, to go out as missionaries wherever the Lord may call them to labor (*Healthful Living*, p. 249).

In all our medical institutions, patients should be systematically and carefully instructed how to prevent disease by a wise course of action. Through lectures and the consistent practice of the principles of healthful living on the part of consecrated physicians and nurses, the blinded understanding of many will be opened, and truths never before thought of will be fastened on the mind. Many of the patients will be led to keep the body in the most healthy condition possible, because it is the Lord's purchased possession (*Counsels on Health*, p. 470).

But when Jesus heard that, he said unto them, They that be whole need not a physician, but they that are sick. But go ye and learn what that meaneth, I will have mercy, and not sacrifice: for I am not come to call the righteous, but sinners to repentance (Matthew 9:12–13).

Often physicians and nurses are called upon during the Sabbath to minister to the sick, and sometimes it is impossible for them to take time for rest and for attending devotional services. The needs of suffering humanity are never to be neglected. The Saviour by His example has shown us that it is right to relieve suffering on the Sabbath. But unnecessary work, such as ordinary treatments and operations that can be postponed, should be deferred. Let the patients understand that physicians and helpers should have one day for rest. Let them understand that the workers fear God and desire to keep holy the day that He has set apart for His followers to observe as a sign between Him and them (*Counsels on Health*, p. 236).

Never entertain the thought that an honest, truthful physician cannot succeed. Such a sentiment dishonors the God of truth and righteousness. He can succeed; for he has God and heaven on his side. Let every bribe to dissimulate be sternly refused. Hold fast your integrity in the strength of the grace of Christ, and He will fulfill His word to you (*Medical Missionary*, p. 128).

Physicians should remember that they will often be required to perform the duties of a minister. Medical missionaries come under the head of evangelists. The workers should go forth two by two, that they may pray and consult together. Never should they be sent out alone. The Lord Jesus Christ sent forth His disciples two and two into all the cities of Israel. He gave them the commission, "Heal the sick that are therein, and say unto them, The kingdom of God is come nigh unto you." (*Evangelism*, p. 520).

The consciousness of right doing is the best medicine for diseased bodies and minds. The special blessing of God resting upon the receiver is health and strength. One whose mind is quiet and satisfied in God is on the highway to health. To have the consciousness that the eye of the Lord is upon us, and that His ear is open to our prayers, is a satisfaction indeed. To know that we have a never-failing Friend to whom we can confide all the secrets of the soul, is a happiness which words can never express. Those whose moral faculties are clouded by disease are not the ones to rightly represent the Christian life or the beauties of holiness. They are too often in the fire of fanaticism or the water of cold indifference or stolid gloom (*Counsels on Health*, p. 628).

You will never be ministers after the gospel order till you show a decided interest in medical missionary work, the gospel of healing and blessing and strengthening (*Evangelism*, p. 523).

Let the mind become intelligent, and the will be placed on the Lord's side, and there will be a wonderful improvement in the physical health. But this can never be accomplished in mere human strength (*Healthful Living*, p. 232).

Today we are combining the work of ministry and of healing as we have never done before. We are working to educate our people how to treat the body in sickness, how to regain health, and how to keep well when health is restored (*Medical Missionary*, p. 63).

Never should a physician neglect his patients (*Healthful Living*, p. 267).

When you understand physiology in its truest sense, your drug bills will be very much smaller, and finally you will cease to deal out drugs at all. The physician who depends upon drug medication in his practice shows that he does not understand the delicate machinery of the human organism. He is introducing into the system a seed crop that will never lose its destroying properties throughout the lifetime. I tell you this because I dare not withhold it. Christ paid too much for man's redemption to have his body so ruthlessly treated as it has been by drug medication (*Medical Missionary*, p. 229).

I was shown that physicians and helpers should be of the highest order, those who have an experimental knowledge of the truth, who will command respect, and whose word can be relied on. They should be persons who have not a diseased imagination, persons who have perfect self-control, who are not fitful or changeable, who are free from jealousy and evil surmising; persons who have a power of will that will not yield to slight indispositions, who are unprejudiced, who will think no evil, who think and move calmly, considerately, having the glory of God and the good of others ever before them. Never should one be exalted to a responsible position merely because he desires it. Those only should be chosen who are qualified for the position. Those who are to bear responsibilities should first be proved and given evidence that they are free from jealousy, that they will not take a dislike to this or that one, while they have a few favored friends and take no notice of others. God grant that all may move just right in that institution (*Counsels on Health*, p. 372).

Physicians should not allow their attention to be diverted from their work. Neither should they confine themselves so closely to professional work that health will be injured. In the fear of God they should be wise in the use of the strength that God has given them. Never should they disregard the means that God has provided for the preservation of health. It is their duty to bring under the control of reason every power that God has given them (*Medical Missionary*, p. 293).

The physician is never to lead his patients to fix their attention on him. He is to teach them to grasp with the trembling hand of faith the outstretched hand of the Saviour. Then the mind will be illuminated with the light radiating from the Light of the world (*Mind, Character and Personality*, Volume 2, p. 409).

The physician has precious opportunities for directing his patients to the promises of God's word. He is to bring from the treasure house things new and old, speaking here and there the words of comfort and instruction that are longed for. Let the physician make his mind a storehouse of fresh thoughts. Let him study the word of God diligently, that he may be familiar with its promises. Let him learn to repeat the comforting words that Christ spoke during His earthly ministry when giving His lessons and healing the sick. He should talk of the works of healing wrought by Christ, of His tenderness and love. Never should he neglect to direct the minds of his patients to Christ, the Chief Physician (*Ministry of Healing*, p. 121).

The physicians in our institutions must be imbued with the living principles of health reform. Men will never be truly temperate until the grace of Christ is an abiding principle in the heart (*Healthful Living*, p. 266).

Health reform will reach a class and has reached a class that otherwise would never have been reached by the truth. There is a great necessity for labor being put forth to help the people, believers and unbelievers, at the present time by health talks, and health publications. I cannot see why the health books should not have a permanent place as well as the other publications notwithstanding human prejudices to the contrary (*The Publishing Ministry*, p. 226).

Drugs never cure disease; they only change its form and location… When drugs are introduced into the system, for a time they seem to have a beneficial effect. A change may take place, but the disease is not cured. It will manifest itself in some other form … The disease which the drug was given to cure may disappear, but only to reappear in a new form, such as skin diseases, ulcers, painful, diseased joints, and sometimes in a more dangerous and deadly form … Nature keeps struggling, and the patient suffers with different ailments, until there is a sudden breaking down in her efforts, and death follows (*Healthful Living* 243).

Chapter 13

Dress

Correct taste is not to be despised or condemned. Our faith, if carried out, will lead us to be so plain in dress and zealous of good works that we shall be marked as peculiar. But when we lose taste for order and neatness in dress, we virtually leave the truth; for the truth never degrades but elevates (*Child Guidance*, p. 419).

Our dress is to be inexpensive,—not with "gold, or pearls, or costly array." Money is a trust from God. It is not ours to expend for the gratification of pride or ambition. In the hands of God's children it is food for the hungry and clothing for the naked. It is a defense to the oppressed, a means of health to the sick, or preaching the gospel to the poor. You could bring happiness to many hearts by using wisely the money that is now spent for show. Consider the life of Christ. Study His character, and be partakers with Him in His self-denial (*Messages to Young People*, p. 351).

Unto Adam also and to his wife did the LORD God make coats of skins, and clothed them (Genesis 3:21).

There is an ornament that will never perish, that will promote the happiness of all around us in this life, and will shine with undimmed luster in the immortal future. It is the adorning of a meek and lowly spirit. God has bidden us wear the richest dress upon the soul... Instead of seeking golden ornaments for the exterior, an earnest effort would be put forth to secure that wisdom which is of more value than fine gold (*Child Guidance*, p. 423).

Ye shall not make any cuttings in your flesh for the dead, nor print any marks upon you: I am the LORD (Leviticus 19:28).

In order to secure the most healthful clothing, the needs of every part of the body must be carefully studied. The character of the climate, the surroundings, the condition of the health, the age and occupation, must all be considered. Every article of dress should fit easily, obstructing neither the circulation of the blood nor a free, full, natural respiration. Everything worn should be so loose that when the arms are raised the clothing will be correspondingly lifted (*Counsels to Parents, Teachers and Students*, p. 306).

In dress and behavior we are to reveal propriety. Never are we to be slack or untidy in our appearance or our work (*Evangelism*, p. 672).

If they preserve to themselves sound constitutions and amiable tempers, they will possess true beauty that they can wear with a divine grace. And they will have no need to be adorned with artificials, for these are always expressive of an absence of the inward adorning of true moral worth. A beautiful character is of value in the sight of God. Such beauty will attract, but not mislead. Such charms are fast colors; they never fade (*Child Guidance*, p. 424).

We are living in an age represented as being like that before the Flood. All who now plead for souls should in their dress and deportment carry the modesty and marks of the Lord Jesus. They must wait, watch, and pray for the Holy Spirit to be abundantly bestowed. We must take in the idea of Christianity; in conversation and in dress we must represent the truth. A decided guard must be placed upon the human agents in regard to the impressions they are making upon others in deportment and in dress. The Bible is our guide; study its teachings with a purpose to obey, and you need make no mistakes (*Sons and Daughters of God*, p. 158).

The apostle presents the inward adorning, in contrast with the outward, and tells us what the great God values. The outward is corruptible. But the meek and quiet spirit, the development of a beautifully symmetrical character, will never decay. It is an adornment which is not perishable. In the sight of the Creator of everything that is valuable, lovely, and beautiful it is declared to be of great price (*My Life Today*, p. 123).

Special attention should be given to the extremities, that they may be as thoroughly clothed as the chest and the region over the heart, where is the greatest amount of heat. Parents who dress their children with the extremities naked, or nearly so, are sacrificing the health and lives of their children to fashion. If these parts are not so warm as the body, the circulation is not equalized. When the extremities, which are remote from the vital organs, are not properly clad, the blood is driven to the head, causing headache or nosebleed; or there is a sense of fullness about the chest, producing cough or palpitation of the heart, on account of too much blood in that locality; or the stomach has too much blood, causing indigestion (*Child Guidance*, p. 426).

There should be no carelessness in dress. For Christ's sake, whose witnesses we are, we should seek to make the best of our appearance. In the tabernacle service, God specified every detail concerning the garments of those who ministered before Him. Thus we are taught that He has a preference in regard to the dress of those who serve Him. Very specific were the directions given in regard to Aaron's robes, for his dress was symbolic. So the dress of Christ's followers should be symbolic. In all things we are to be representatives of Him. Our appearance in every respect should be characterized by neatness, modesty, and purity. But the word of God gives no sanction to the making of changes in apparel merely for the sake of fashion,--that we may appear like the world. Christians are not to decorate the person with costly array or expensive ornaments (*Messages to Young People*, p. 358).

For if there come unto your assembly a man with a gold ring, in goodly apparel, and there come in also a poor man in vile raiment; And ye have respect to him that weareth the gay clothing, and say unto him, Sit thou here in a good place; and say to the poor, Stand thou there, or sit here under my footstool: Are ye not then partial in yourselves, and are become judges of evil thoughts? (James 2:2–4).

The words of Scripture in regard to dress should be carefully considered. We need to understand that which the Lord of heaven appreciates in even the dressing of the body. All who are in earnest in seeking for the grace of Christ will heed the precious words of instruction inspired by God. Even the style of the apparel will express the truth of the gospel (*Messages to Young People*, p. 358).

Talk of the love and humility of Jesus, but do not encourage the brethren and sisters to engage in picking flaws in the dress or appearance of one another. Some take delight in this work; and when their minds are turned in this direction, they begin to feel that they must become church tinkers. They climb upon the judgment seat, and as soon as they see one of their brethren and sisters, they look to find something to criticize. This is one of the most effectual means of becoming narrow-minded and of dwarfing spiritual growth. God would have them step down from the judgment seat, for He has never placed them there (*Child Guidance*, p. 429).

But our clothing, while modest and simple, should be of good quality, of becoming colors, and suited for service. It should be chosen for durability rather than display. It should provide warmth and proper protection (*Messages to Young People*, p. 351).

There is danger of attaching too much importance to the matter of etiquette, and devoting much time to education upon the subject of manner and form, that can never be of any great use to many youth. Some are in danger of making the externals all-important, of overestimating the value of mere conventionalities. The results will not warrant the expenditure of time and thought given to these matters. Some who are trained to give much attention to these things, will manifest little true respect or sympathy for anything, however excellent, that in any way fails to meet their standard of conventionality. Anything that would encourage ungenerous criticism, a disposition to notice and expose every defect or error, is wrong. It fosters distrust and suspicion, which are contrary to the character of Christ, and detrimental to the mind thus exercised. Those who are engaged in this work, gradually depart from the true spirit of Christianity. While the gospel constantly sanctifies and ennobles the receiver, it will never lead us to cherish selfish and exalted ideas of our own ability or merit in contrast with that of others. It never nurtures pride and self-esteem. Every soul who sees Christ as he is, will abase self. He will exalt the Saviour as the "chiefest among ten thousand," the One "altogether lovely." (*Christian Education*, p. 201).

She is not afraid of the snow for her household: for all her household are clothed with scarlet (Proverbs 31:21).

In like manner also, that women adorn themselves in modest apparel, with shamefacedness and sobriety; not with broided hair, or gold, or pearls, or costly array; But (which becometh women professing godliness) with good works (1 Timothy 2:9–10).

Vainglory, the fashion of the world, the desire of the eye, and the lust of the flesh, are connected with the fall of the unfortunate. That which is pleasing to the natural heart and carnal mind is cherished. If the lust of the flesh had been rooted out of their hearts, they would not be so weak. If our sisters would feel the necessity of purifying their thoughts, and never suffer in themselves a carelessness of deportment which leads to improper acts, they need not in the least stain their purity. If they viewed the matter as God has presented it to me, they would have such an abhorrence of impure acts that they would not be found among those who fall through the temptations of Satan, no matter whom he might select as the medium (*Counsels on Health*, p. 570).

The idolatry of dress is a moral disease. It must not be taken over into the new life. In most cases, submission to the gospel requirements will demand a decided change in the dress (*Messages to Young People*, p. 358).

The woman shall not wear that which pertaineth unto a man, neither shall a man put on a woman's garment: for all that do so are abomination unto the LORD thy God (Deuteronomy 22:5).

I saw that the outside appearance is an index to the heart. When the exterior is hung with ribbons, collars, and needless things, it plainly shows that the love for all this is in the heart; unless such persons are cleansed from their corruption, they can never see God, for only the pure in heart will see Him (*Daughters of God*, p. 154).

There is an ornament that will never perish, that will promote the happiness of all around us in this life and will shine with undimmed luster in the immortal future. It is the adorning of a meek and lowly spirit. God has bidden us wear the richest dress upon the soul. By every look into the mirror the worshipers of fashion should be reminded of the neglected soul. Every hour squandered over the toilet should reprove them for leaving the intellect to lie waste. Then there might be a reformation that would elevate and ennoble all the aims and purposes of life. Instead of seeking golden ornaments for the exterior, an earnest effort would be put forth to secure that wisdom which is of more value than fine gold, yea, which is more precious than rubies (*Counsels on Health*, p. 601).

Our dress should be cleanly. Uncleanliness in dress is unhealthful, and thus defiling to the body and to the soul. "Ye are the temple of God... If any man defile the temple of God, him shall God destroy." 1 Cor. 3:16, 17 (*Messages to Young People*, p. 352).

There are many who try to correct the life of others by attacking what they consider are wrong habits. They go to those whom they think are in error, and point out their defects. They say, "You don't dress as you should." They try to pick off the ornaments, or whatever seems offensive, but they do not seek to fasten the mind to the truth. Those who seek to correct others should present the attractions of Jesus. They should talk of His love and compassion, present His example and sacrifice, reveal His Spirit, and they need not touch the subject of dress at all. There is no need to make the dress question the main point of your religion. There is something richer to speak of. Talk of Christ, and when the heart is converted, everything that is out of harmony with the Word of God will drop off. It is only labor in vain to pick leaves off a living tree. The leaves will reappear. The ax must be laid at the root of the tree, and then the leaves will fall off, never to return (*Evangelism*, p. 272).

Some receive the idea that in order to carry out that separation from the world that the Word of God requires, they must be neglectful of their apparel. There is a class of sisters who think they are carrying out the principle of nonconformity to the world by wearing an ordinary sun-bonnet, and the same dress worn by them through the week, upon the Sabbath when appearing in the assembly of the saints to engage in the worship of God. And some men who profess to be Christians view the matter of dress in the same light. These persons assemble with God's people upon the Sabbath, with their clothing dusty and soiled, and even with gaping rents in their garments, which are placed upon their persons in a slovenly manner (*Child Guidance*, p. 428).

Let the wearing of useless trimmings and adornments be discarded. Extravagance should never be indulged in to gratify pride. Our dress may be of good quality, made up with plainness and simplicity, for durability rather than for display (*Healthful Living*, p. 120).

There is an increasing tendency to have women in their dress and appearance as near like the other sex as possible and to fashion their dress very much like that of men, but God pronounces it abomination. "In like manner also, that women adorn themselves in modest apparel, with shamefacedness and sobriety" (1 Timothy 2:9) (*Child Guidance*, p. 427).

Many deceive themselves in thinking that good looks and a gay attire will gain for them consideration in the world. But the charms that consist only in the outward apparel are shallow and changeable; no dependence can be placed upon them. The adorning with Christ enjoins upon His followers will never fade. He says: "Whose adorning let it not be that outward adorning of plaiting the hair, and of wearing of gold, or of putting on of apparel; but let it be the hidden man of the heart, in that which is not corruptible, even the ornament of a meek and quiet spirit, which is in the sight of God of great price." (*Messages to Young People*, p. 345).

In like manner also, that women adorn themselves in modest apparel, with shamefacedness and sobriety; not with broided hair, or gold, or pearls, or costly array; But (which becometh women professing godliness) with good works (1 Timothy 2:9–10).

Why should not Christians living in these last days reveal the most attractive fruit in unselfish actions? Why should not the fruit of the commandment-keeping people of God appear in the very best representation of good works? Their words, their deportment, their dress, should bear fruit of the very best quality. "By their fruits," Christ said, "ye shall know them." (*The Upward Look*, p. 324).

We do not discourage neatness in dress. Correct taste is not to be despised nor condemned. Our faith, if carried out, will lead us to be so plain in dress, and zealous of good works, that we shall be marked as peculiar. But when we lose taste for order and neatness in dress, we virtually leave the truth; for the truth never degrades, but elevates. When believers are neglectful of their dress, and are coarse and rough in their manners, their influence hurts the truth. "We are," said the inspired apostle, "made a spectacle unto the world, and to angels, and to men." All heaven is marking the daily influence that the professed followers of Christ exert upon the world (*Messages to Young People*, p. 353).

We as a people do not believe it our duty to go out of the world to be out of the fashion. If we have a neat, plain, modest, and comfortable plan of dress, and worldlings choose to dress as we do, shall we change this mode of dress in order to be different from the world? No, we should not be odd or singular in our dress for the sake of differing from the world, lest they despise us for so doing. Christians are the light of the world, the salt of the earth. Their dress should be neat and modest, their conversation chaste and heavenly, and their deportment blameless (*Testimonies for the Church*, volume 1, p. 424).

Tight bands or waists hinder the action of the heart and lungs and should be avoided. No part of the body should at any time be made uncomfortable by clothing that compresses any organ or restricts its freedom of movement. The clothing of all children should be loose enough to admit of the freest and fullest respiration, and so arranged that the shoulders will support its weight (*Child Guidance*, p. 426).

Chapter 14

Romance & Marriage

Thou shalt not commit adultery (Exodus 20:14).

Young ladies connected with our institutions should keep a strict guard over themselves. In word and action, they should be reserved. Never when speaking to a married man should they show the slightest freedom. To my sisters who are connected with our sanitariums, I would say, gird on the armor. When talking to men, be kind and courteous, but never free. Observant eyes are upon you, watching your conduct, judging by it whether you are indeed children of God. Be modest. Abstain from every appearance of evil. Keep on the heavenly armor, or else for Christ's sake sever your connection with the sanitarium, the place where poor shipwrecked souls are to find a haven. Those connected with these institutions are to take heed to themselves. never, by word or action, are they to give the least occasion for wicked men to speak evil of the truth (*Counsels on Health*, p. 591).

Never should God's people venture upon forbidden ground. Marriage between believers and unbelievers is forbidden by God. But too often the unconverted heart follows its own desires, and marriages unsanctioned by God are formed. Because of this many men and women are without hope and without God in the world. Their noble aspirations are dead; by a chain of circumstances they are held in Satan's net. Those who are ruled by passion and impulse will have a bitter harvest to reap in this life, and their course may result in the loss of their souls (*Adventist Home*, p. 63).

Instituted by God, marriage is a sacred ordinance and should never be entered upon in a spirit of selfishness. Those who contemplate this step should solemnly and prayerfully consider its importance and seek divine counsel that they may know whether they are pursuing a course in harmony with the will of God. The instruction given in God's word on this point should be carefully considered. Heaven looks with pleasure upon a marriage formed with an earnest desire to conform to the directions given in the Scripture (*Adventist Home*, p. 70).

Wise parents will never select companions for their children without respect to their wishes (*Adventist Home*, p. 75).

Ye have heard that it was said by them of old time, Thou shalt not commit adultery: But I say unto you, That whosoever looketh on a woman to lust after her hath committed adultery with her already in his heart (Matthew 5:27, p. 28).

To gain a proper understanding of the marriage relation is the work of a lifetime. Those who marry enter a school from which they are never in this life to be graduated (*Adventist Home*, p. 105).

Neither husband nor wife is to make a plea for rulership. The Lord has laid down the principle that is to guide in this matter. The husband is to cherish his wife as Christ cherishes the church. And the wife is to respect and love her husband. Both are to cultivate the spirit of kindness, being determined never to grieve or injure the other (*Adventist Home*, p. 106).

Moreover thou shalt not lie carnally with thy neighbor's wife, to defile thyself with her (Leviticus 18:20).

The Lord Jesus has not been correctly represented in His relation to the church by many husbands in their relation to their wives, for they do not keep the way of the Lord. They declare that their wives must be subject to them in everything. But it was not the design of God that the husband should have control, as head of the house, when he himself does not submit to Christ. He must be under the rule of Christ that he may represent the relation of Christ to the church. If he is a coarse, rough, boisterous, egotistical, harsh, and overbearing man, let him never utter the word that the husband is the head of the wife, and that she must submit to him in everything; for he is not the Lord, he is not the husband in the true significance of the term (*Adventist Home*, p. 117).

We must have the Spirit of God, or we can never have harmony in the home. The wife, if she has the spirit of Christ, will be careful of her words; she will control her spirit, she will be submissive, and yet will not feel that she is a bondslave, but a companion to her husband. If the husband is a servant of God, he will not lord it over his wife; he will not be arbitrary and exacting. We cannot cherish home affection with too much care; for the home, if the Spirit of the Lord dwells there, is a type of heaven.... If one errs, the other will exercise Christlike forbearance and not draw coldly away (*Adventist Home*, p. 118).

I am pained when I see men praised, flattered, and petted. God has revealed to me the fact that some who receive these attentions are unworthy to take His name upon their lips; yet they are exalted to heaven in the estimation of finite beings, who read only from outward appearance. My sisters, never pet and flatter poor, fallible, erring men, either young or old, married or unmarried. You know not their weaknesses, and you know not but that these very attentions and this profuse praise may prove their ruin. I am alarmed at the shortsightedness, the want of wisdom, that many manifest in this respect (*Adventist Home*, p. 335).

Men who are doing God's work, and who have Christ abiding in their hearts, will not lower the standard of morality, but will ever seek to elevate it. They will not find pleasure in the flattery of women or in being petted by them. Let men, both single and married, say: "Hands off! I will never give the least occasion that my good should be evil spoken of. My good name is capital of far more value to me than gold or silver. Let me preserve it untarnished. If men assail that name, it shall not be because I have given them occasion to do so, but for the same reason that they spoke evil of Christ—because they hated the purity and holiness of His character, for it was a constant rebuke to them." (*Adventist Home*, p. 335).

And he saith unto them, Whosoever shall put away his wife, and marry another, committeth adultery against her (Mark 10:11).

Absolutely Positively

Never let a word of reproach or faultfinding fall upon the ears of your husband. You sometimes pass through strait places, but do not talk of these trials. Silence is eloquence. Hasty speech will only increase your unhappiness. Be cheerful and happy. Bring all the sunshine possible into your home, and shut out the shadows. Let the bright beams of the Sun of Righteousness shine into the chambers of your soul temple. Then the fragrance of the Christian life will be brought into your family. There will be no dwelling upon disagreeable things, which many times have no truth in them (*Adventist Home*, p. 349).

"And another said, I have married a wife, and therefore I cannot come." The sin of this man was not in marrying, but in marrying one who divorced his mind from the higher and more important interests of life (*Adventist Home*, p. 351).

Love "rejoiceth not in iniquity, but rejoiceth in the truth; beareth all things, believeth all things, hopeth all things, endureth all things." This love "never fails." It can never lose its value; it is a heavenly attribute. As a precious treasure, it will be carried by its possessor through the portals of the city of God (*Acts of the Apostles*, p. 319).

Flee fornication. Every sin that a man doeth is without the body; but he that committeth fornication sinneth against his own body (1 Corinthians 6:18).

The heart yearns for human love, but this love is not strong enough, or pure enough, or precious enough to supply the place of the love of Jesus. Only in her Saviour can the wife find wisdom, strength, and grace to meet the cares, responsibilities, and sorrows of life. She should make Him her strength and her guide. Let woman give herself to Christ before giving herself to any earthly friend, and enter into no relation which shall conflict with this. Those who would find true happiness must have the blessing of Heaven upon all that they possess and all that they do. It is disobedience to God that fills so many hearts and homes with misery. My sister, unless you would have a home where the shadows are never lifted, do not unite yourself with one who is an enemy of God (*Adventist Home*, p. 67).

The world is full of misery and sin today in consequence of ill-assorted marriages. In many cases it takes only a few months for husband and wife to realize that their dispositions can never blend; and the result is that discord prevails in the home, where only the love and harmony of heaven should exist (*Adventist Home*, p. 83).

The Scriptures state that both Jesus and His disciples were called to this marriage feast [at Cana]. Christ has given Christians no sanction to say when invited to a marriage, We ought not to be present on so joyous an occasion. By attending this feast Christ taught that He would have us rejoice with those who do rejoice in the observance of His statutes. He never discouraged the innocent festivities of mankind when carried on in accordance with the laws of Heaven. A gathering that Christ honored by His presence, it is right that His followers should attend. After attending this feast, Christ attended many others, sanctifying them by His presence and instruction (*Adventist Home*, p. 100).

If the sisters were elevated and possessed purity of heart, any corrupt advances, even from their minister, would be repulsed with such positiveness as would never need a repetition (*Adventist Home*, p. 336).

"Should parents," you ask, "select a companion without regard to the mind or feelings of son or daughter?" I put the question to you as it should be: Should a son or daughter select a companion without first consulting the parents, when such a step must materially affect the happiness of parents if they have any affection for their children? And should that child, notwithstanding the counsel and entreaties of his parents, persist in following his own course? I answer decidedly: No; not if he never marries. The fifth commandment forbids such a course. "Honor thy father and thy mother: that thy days may be long upon the land which the Lord thy God giveth thee." Here is a commandment with a promise which the Lord will surely fulfill to those who obey (*Adventist Home*, p. 75).

Nevertheless, to avoid fornication, let every man have his own wife, and let every woman have her own husband (1 Corinthians 7:2).

If a minister of the gospel does not control his baser passions, if he fails to follow the example of the apostle and so dishonors his profession and faith as to even name the indulgence of sin, our sisters who profess godliness should not for an instant flatter themselves that sin or crime loses its sinfulness in the least because their minister dares to engage in it. The fact that men who are in responsible places show themselves to be familiar with sin should not lessen the guilt and enormity of the sin in the minds of any. Sin should appear just as sinful, just as abhorrent, as it had been heretofore regarded; and the minds of the pure and elevated should abhor and shun the one who indulges in sin as they would flee from a serpent whose sting was deadly (*Adventist Home*, p. 336).

And unto the married I command, yet not I, but the Lord, Let not the wife depart from her husband (1 Corinthians 7:10).

Wives, submit yourselves unto your own husbands, as unto the Lord. For the husband is the head of the wife, even as Christ is the head of the church: and he is the savior of the body. Therefore as the church is subject unto Christ, so let the wives be to their own husbands in every thing. Husbands, love your wives, even as Christ also loved the church, and gave himself for it (Ephesians 5:22–25).

The slightest insinuations, from whatever source they may come, inviting you to indulge in sin or to allow the least unwarrantable liberty with your persons, should be resented as the worst of insults to your dignified womanhood. The kiss upon your cheek, at an improper time and place, should lead you to repel the emissary of Satan with disgust. If it is from one in high places, who is dealing in sacred things, the sin is of tenfold greater magnitude and should lead a God-fearing woman or youth to recoil with horror, not only from the sin he would have you commit, but from the hypocrisy and villainy of one whom the people respect and honor as God's servant. He is handling sacred things, yet hiding his baseness of heart under a ministerial cloak. Be afraid of anything like this familiarity. Be sure that the least approach to it is evidence of a lascivious mind and a lustful eye. If the least encouragement is given in this direction, if any of the liberties mentioned are tolerated, no better evidence can be given that your mind is not pure and chaste as it should be, and that sin and crime have charms for you. You lower the standard of your dignified, virtuous womanhood and give unmistakable evidence that a low, brutal, common passion and lust has been suffered to remain alive in your heart and has never been crucified (*Counsels on Health*, p. 612).

And Adam said, This is now bone of my bones, and flesh of my flesh: she shall be called Woman, because she was taken out of Man (Genesis 2:23).

Marriage is honorable in all, and the bed undefiled: but whoremongers and adulterers God will judge (Hebrews 13:4).

Marriage has received Christ's blessing, and it is to be regarded as a sacred institution. True religion is not to counterwork the Lord's plans. God ordained that man and woman should be united in holy wedlock, to raise up families that, crowned with honor, would be symbols of the family in heaven.And at the beginning of His public ministry Christ gave His decided sanction to the institution that had been sanctioned in Eden. Thus He declared to all that He will not refuse His presence on marriage occasions, and that marriage, when joined with purity and holiness, truth and righteousness, is one of the greatest blessings ever given to the human family (*Sons and Daughters of God*, p. 180).

I have often read these words: "Marriage is a lottery." Some act as if they believed the statement, and their married life testifies that it is such to them. But true marriage is not a lottery. Marriage was instituted in Eden. After the creation of Adam, the Lord said, "It is not good that the man should be alone; I will make him an help meet for him." When the Lord presented Eve to Adam, angels of God were witnesses to the ceremony. But there are few couples who are completely united when the marriage ceremony is performed. The form of words spoken over the two who take the marriage vow does not make them a unit. In their future life is to be the blending of the two in wedlock. It may be made a really happy union, if each will give to the other true heart affection (*In Heavenly Places*, p. 203).

A terrible picture of the condition of the world has been presented before me. Immorality abounds everywhere. Licentiousness is the special sin of this age. Never did vice lift its deformed head with such boldness as now. The people seem to be benumbed, and the lovers of virtue and true goodness are nearly discouraged by its boldness, strength, and prevalence. The iniquity which abounds is not merely confined to the unbeliever and the scoffer. Would that this were the case; but it is not. Many men and women who profess the religion of Christ are guilty. Even some who profess to be looking for His appearing are no more prepared for than event that Satan himself. They are not cleansing themselves from all pollution. They have so long served their lust that it is natural for their thoughts to be impure and their imaginations corrupt. It is as impossible to cause their minds to dwell upon pure and holy things as it would be to turn the course of Niagara and send its waters pouring up the falls (*Counsels on Health*, p. 615).

When a man hath taken a new wife, he shall not go out to war, neither shall he be charged with any business: but he shall be free at home one year, and shall cheer up his wife which he hath taken (Deuteronomy 24:5).

When the young adopt vile practices while the spirit is tender, they will never obtain force to fully and correctly develop physical, intellectual, and moral character. Here was a man debasing himself daily, and yet daring to venture into the presence of God and ask an increase of strength which he had vilely squandered and which, if granted, he would consume upon his lust. What forbearance has God! If He should deal with man according to his corrupt ways, who could live in His sight? What if we had been less cautious and carried the case of this man before God while he was practicing iniquity; would the Lord have heard? Would He have answered? "For Thou art not a God that hath pleasure in wickedness: neither shall evil dwell with Thee. The foolish shall not stand in Thy sight: Thou hatest all workers of iniquity." Psalm 5:4, 5. "If I regard iniquity in my heart, the Lord will not hear me." Psalm 66:18 (*Counsels on Health*, p. 620).

The man who stands in a position of responsibility in any of our schools cannot be too careful of his words and his acts. Never should he allow the least approach to familiarity in his relations to the students, such as placing his hand on the arm or shoulder of a girl student. He should in no case give the impression that commonness and familiarity are allowable. His lips and his hands are to express nothing that anyone could take advantage of (*Counsels to Parents, Teachers, and Students*, p. 256).

The wife is to respect her husband. The husband is to love and cherish his wife; and as their marriage vow unites them as one, so their belief in Christ should make them one in Him. What can be more pleasing to God than to see those who enter into the marriage relation seek together to learn of Jesus and to become more and more imbued with His Spirit? *(Sons and Daughters of God*, p. 181).

Marriage is honorable in all, and the bed undefiled: but whoremongers and adulterers God will judge (Hebrews 13:4).

Never should a man allow wife and home to draw his thoughts away from Christ or to lead him to refuse to accept the gracious invitations of the gospel (*Adventist Home*, p. 351).

Yours can yet be a happy family. Your wife needs your help. She is like a clinging vine; she wants to lean upon your strength. You can help her and lead her along. You should never censure her. Never reprove her if her efforts are not what you think they should be. Rather encourage her by words of tenderness and love. You can help your wife to preserve her dignity and self-respect. Never praise the work or acts of others before her to make her feel her deficiencies. You have been harsh and unfeeling in this respect. You have shown greater courtesy to your hired help than to her and have placed them Adventist Homestead of her in the house (*Sons and Daughters of God*, p. 181).

A woman that will submit to be ever dictated to in the smallest matters of domestic life, who will yield up her identity, will never be of much use or blessing in the world, and will not answer the purpose of God in her existence. She is a mere machine to be guided by another's will and another's mind. God has given each one, men and women, an identity, an individuality, that they must act in the fear of God for themselves (*Sons and Daughters of God*, p. 183).

Never earn the reputation of being a minister who is a particular favorite with the women. Shun the society of those who by their arts would weaken in the least your purpose to do right, or bring a stain upon the purity of your conscience. Do not give them your time or your confidence; for they will leave you feeling bereft of your spiritual strength. Do nothing among strangers, on the cars, in the home, in the street, that would have the least appearance of evil (*Evangelism*, p. 680).

When one who claims to be teaching the truth is inclined to be much in the company of young or even married women, when he familiarly lays his hand upon their person, or is often found conversing with them in a familiar manner, be afraid of him; the pure principles of truth are not wrought in his soul. Such are not workers with Jesus; they are not in Christ, and Christ is not abiding in them. They need a thorough conversion before God can accept their labors. The truth of heavenly origin never degrades the receiver, never leads him to the least approach to undue familiarity; on the contrary, it sanctifies the believer, refines his taste, elevates and ennobles him, and brings him into a close connection with Jesus. It leads him to regard the apostle Paul's injunction to abstain from even the appearance of evil, lest his good should be evil spoken of (*Evangelism*, p. 680).

Life is a precious gift of God and is not to be wasted in selfish regrets or more open indifference and dislike. Let the husband and wife talk things all over together. Renew the early attentions to each other, acknowledge your faults to each other, but in this work be very careful that the husband does not take it upon himself to confess his wife's faults or the wife her husband's. Be determined that you will be all that it is possible for you to be to each other, and the bonds of wedlock will be the most desirable of ties (*In Heavenly Places*, p. 203).

Even if an engagement has been entered into without a full understanding of the character of the one with whom you intend to unite, do not think that the engagement makes it a positive necessity for you to take upon yourself the marriage vow and link yourself for life to one whom you cannot love and respect. Be very careful how you enter into conditional engagements; but better, far better, break the engagement before marriage than separate afterward, as many do (*Adventist Home*, p. 48).

The young ladies connected with our institutions should keep a strict guard over themselves. In word and action they should be reserved. Never when speaking to a married man should they show the slightest freedom. To my sisters who are connected with our sanitariums I would say, Gird on the armor. When talking to men, be kind and courteous, but never free. Observant eyes are upon you, watching your conduct, judging by it whether you are indeed children of God. Be modest. Abstain from every appearance of evil. Keep on the heavenly armor, or else for Christ's sake sever your connection with the sanitarium, the place where poor, shipwrecked souls are to find a haven. Those connected with these institutions are to take heed to themselves. never, by word or action, are they to give the least occasion for wicked men to speak evil of the truth (*Medical Missionary*, p. 218).

The majority of the marriages of our time, and the way in which they are conducted, make them one of the signs of the last days. Men and women are so persistent, so headstrong, that God is left out of the question. Religion is laid aside, as if it had no part to act in this solemn and important matter. But unless those who profess to believe the truth are sanctified through it, and exalted in thought and character, they are not in as favorable a position before God as the sinner who has never been enlightened in regard to its claims (*Messages to Young People*, p. 460).

In the youthful mind marriage is clothed with romance, and it is difficult to divest it of this feature, with which imagination covers it, and to impress the mind with a sense of the weighty responsibilities involved in the marriage vow. This vow links the destinies of the two individuals with bonds which naught but the hand of death should sever (*Adventist Home*, p. 340).

Parents should never lose sight of their own responsibility for the future happiness of their children. Isaac's deference of his father's judgment was the result of the training that had taught him to love a life of obedience. While Abraham required his children to respect parental authority, his daily life testified that that authority was not a selfish or arbitrary control, but was founded in love, and had their welfare and happiness in view (*Messages to Young People*, p. 465).

Let a young woman accept as a life companion only one who possesses pure, manly traits of character, one who is diligent, aspiring, and honest, one who loves and fears God (*Adventist Home*, p. 47).

In regard to marriage, I would say, Read the Word of God. Even in this time, the last days of this world's history, marriages take place among Seventh-day Adventists….We have, as a people, never forbidden marriage, except in cases where there were obvious reasons that marriage would be misery to both parties. And even then, we have only advised and counseled (*Mind, Character and Personality*, Volume 1, p. 219).

Every marriage engagement should be carefully considered, for marriage is a step taken for life. Both the man and the woman should carefully consider whether they can cleave to each other through the vicissitudes of life as long as they both shall live (*Adventist Home*, p. 340).

God never designed that marriage should cover the multitude of sins that are practiced. Sensuality and base practices in a marriage relation are educating the mind and moral taste for demoralizing practices outside the marriage relation (*Mind, Character and Personality*, Volume 1, p. 223).

The animal passions, cherished and indulged, become very strong in this age, and untold evils in the marriage life are the sure results. In the place of the mind being developed and having the controlling power, the animal propensities rule over the higher and nobler powers until they are brought into subjection to the animal propensities. What is the result? Women's delicate organs are worn out and become diseased; childbearing is no more safe; sexual privileges are abused. Men are corrupting their own bodies; and the wife has become a bedservant to their inordinate, base lusts, until there is no fear of God before their eyes.... (*Testimonies on Sexual Behavior*, p. 115).

And said, For this cause shall a man leave father and mother, and shall cleave to his wife: and they twain shall be one flesh? Wherefore they are no more twain, but one flesh. What therefore God hath joined together, let not man put asunder (Matthew 19:5–6).

If men and women are in the habit of praying twice a day before they contemplate marriage, they should pray four times a day when such a step is anticipated. Marriage is something that will influence and affect your life, both in this world and in the world to come. A sincere Christian will not advance his plans in this direction without the knowledge that God approves his course. He will not want to choose for himself, but will feel that God must choose for him. We are not to please ourselves, for Christ pleased not Himself. I would not be understood to mean that anyone is to marry one whom he does not love. This would be sin. But fancy and the emotional nature must not be allowed to lead on to ruin. God requires the whole heart, the supreme affections (*Messages to Young People*, p. 460).

Let the husband and wife study each other's happiness, never failing in the small courtesies and little kindly acts that cheer and brighten the life. Perfect confidence should exist between husband and wife. Together they should consider their responsibilities. Together they should work for the highest good of their children. Never should they in the presence of the children criticize each other's plans or question each other's judgment. Let the wife be careful not to make the husband's work for the children more difficult. Let the husband hold up the hands of his wife, giving her wise counsel and loving encouragement (*Ministry of Healing*, p. 393).

Sexual excess will effectually destroy a love for devotional exercises, will take from the brain the substance needed to nourish the system, and will most effectively exhaust the vitality. No woman should aid her husband in this work of self-destruction. She will not do it if she is enlightened and has true love for him (*Adventist Home*, p. 124).

For this cause shall a man leave his father and mother, and cleave to his wife; And they twain shall be one flesh: so then they are no more twain, but one flesh (Mark 10:7–18).

The pure truth, which sanctifies the soul, will give you courage to cut yourself loose from the most pleasing acquaintance whom you know does not love and fear God, and knows nothing of the principles of true righteousness. We may always bear with a friend's infirmities and with his ignorance, but never with his vices. Never marry an unbeliever (*Our High Calling*, p. 257).

Before giving her hand in marriage, every woman should inquire whether he with whom she is about to unite her destiny is worthy. What has been his past record? Is his life pure? Is the love which he expresses of a noble, elevated character, or is it a mere emotional fondness? Has he the traits of character that will make her happy? Can she find true peace and joy in his affection? Will she be allowed to preserve her individuality, or must her judgment and conscience be surrendered to the control of her husband? …Can she honor the Saviour's claims as supreme? Will body and soul, thoughts and purposes, be preserved pure and holy? These questions have a vital bearing upon the well-being of every woman who enters the marriage relation (*Adventist Home*, p. 47).

Moral pollution has done more than every other evil to cause the race to degenerate. It is practiced to an alarming extent and brings on disease of almost every description. Even very small children, infants, being born with natural irritability of the sexual organs, find momentary relief in handling them, which only increases the irritation and leads to a repetition of the act, until a habit is established which increases with their growth (*Child Guidance*, p. 441).

Workers with marriage problems may present themselves as having been wronged, when it is their companions who have been most wronged.—I cannot appear to justify your course of action in your married life. Leaving your wife and family is an offense to God (*Pastoral Ministry* p. 87).

Chapter 15

Entertainment

There are men and women now in the decline of life who have never recovered from the effects of intemperance in reading. The habit formed in early years grew with their growth and strengthened with their strength. Their determined efforts to overcome the sin of abusing the intellect were partially successful, but they have never recovered the full vigor of mind that God bestowed upon them (*Counsels to Parents, Teachers, and Students*, p. 135).

There are modes of recreation which are highly beneficial to both mind and body. An enlightened, discriminating mind will find abundant means for entertainment and diversion, from sources not only innocent, but instructive. Recreation in the open air, the contemplation of the works of God in nature, will be of the highest benefit (*Adventist Home*, p. 496).

In referring to these races as a figure of the Christian warfare, Paul emphasized the preparation necessary to the success of the contestants in the race—the preliminary discipline, the abstemious diet, the necessity for temperance. "Every man that striveth for the mastery," he declared, "is temperate in all things." The runners put aside every indulgence that would tend to weaken the physical powers, and by severe and continuous discipline trained their muscles to strength and endurance, that when the day of the contest should arrive, they might put the heaviest tax upon their powers. How much more important that the Christian, whose eternal interests are at stake, bring appetite and passion under subjection to reason and the will of God! Never must he allow his attention to be diverted by amusements, luxuries, or ease. All his habits and passions must be brought under the strictest discipline. Reason, enlightened by the teachings of God's word and guided by His Spirit, must hold the reins of control (*Acts of the Apostles*, p. 311).

A little time spent in sowing your wild oats, dear young friends, will produce a crop that will embitter your whole life; an hour of thoughtlessness, once yielding to temptation, may turn the whole current of your life in the wrong direction. You can have but one youth; make that useful. When once you have passed over the ground, you can never return to rectify your mistakes. He who refuses to connect with God, and puts himself in the way of temptation will surely fall. God is testing every youth. Many have excused their carelessness and irreverence because of the wrong example given them by more experienced professors. But this should not deter any from right doing. In the day of final accounts you will plead no such excuses as you plead now (*Adventist Home*, p. 59).

Youthful minds fail to reach their noblest development when they neglect the highest source of wisdom—the word of God. That we are in God's world, in the presence of the Creator; that we are made in His likeness; that He watches over us and loves us and cares for us—these are wonderful themes for thought, and lead the mind into broad, exalted fields of meditation. He who opens mind and heart to the contemplation of such themes as these will never be satisfied with trivial, sensational subjects (*Counsels to Parents, Teachers, and Students*, p. 139).

The mind will never cease to be active. It is open to influences, good or bad. As the human countenance is stamped by the sunbeam on the polished plate of the artist, so are thoughts and impressions stamped on the mind of the child; and whether these impressions are of the earth earthy, or moral and religious, they are well-nigh ineffaceable. When reason is awakening, the mind is most susceptible; and so the very first lessons are of great importance. These lessons have a powerful influence in the formation of character. If they are of the right stamp, and if, as the child advances in years, they are followed up with patient perseverance, the earthly and the eternal destiny will be shaped for good. This is the word of the Lord: "Train up a child in the way he should go: and when he is old, he will not depart from it." Proverbs 22:6 (*Counsels to Parents, Teachers, and Students*, p. 143).

The world is deluged with books that might better be consumed than circulated. Books on sensational topics, published and circulated as a money-making scheme, might better never be read by the youth. There is a satanic fascination in such books (*Adventist Home*, p. 412).

By a life of easy indulgence a youth can never attain to real excellence as a man or as a Christian. God does not promise us ease, honor, or wealth in his service, but he assures us that all needed blessings will be ours, "with persecutions," and in the world to come "life everlasting." Nothing less than entire consecration to his service will Christ accept. This is the lesson which every one of us must learn (*Christian Education*, p. 240).

There are persons with a diseased imagination to whom religion is a tyrant, ruling them as with a rod of iron. Such are constantly mourning over their depravity and groaning over supposed evil. Love does not exist in their hearts; a frown is ever upon their countenances. They are chilled by the innocent laugh from the youth or from anyone. They consider all recreation or amusement a sin and think that the mind must be constantly wrought up to just such a stern, severe pitch. This is one extreme. Others think that the mind must be ever on the stretch to invent new amusements and diversions in order to gain health. They learn to depend on excitement and are uneasy without it. Such are not true Christians. They go to another extreme. The true principles of Christianity open before all a source of happiness, the height and depth, the length and breadth of which are immeasurable (*Adventist Home*, p. 493).

Never should books containing a perversion of truth be placed in the hands of children or youth. Let not our children, in the very process of obtaining an education, receive ideas that will prove to be seeds of sin. If those with mature minds had nothing to do with such books, they would themselves be far safer, and their example and influence on the right side would make it far less difficult to guard the youth from temptation (*Counsels to Parents, Teachers, and Students*, p. 385).

Never will these same opportunities offer themselves again. They had better been doing the hardest kind of labor on that holiday. They did not make the right use of their holiday, and it passed into eternity to confront them in the judgment as a day misspent (*Adventist Home*, p. 473).

The world is deluged with books that might better be consumed rather than circulated. Books upon Indian warfare and similar topics, published and circulated as a money-making scheme, might better Never be read. There is a satanic fascination in these books. The heart-sickening relation of crimes and atrocities has a bewitching power upon many youth, exciting in them the desire to bring themselves into notice, even by the most wicked deeds. There are many works more strictly historical whose influence is little better. The enormities, the cruelties, the licentious practices, portrayed in these writings, have acted as leaven in many minds, leading to the commission of similar acts. Books that delineate the satanic deeds of human beings are giving publicity to evil works. The horrible details of crime and misery need not be lived over, and none who believe the truth for this time should act a part in perpetuating their memory (*Colporteur Ministry*, p. 142).

After a day of pleasure seeking is ended, where is the satisfaction to the pleasure seeker? As Christian workers, whom have they helped to a better, higher, and purer life? What would they see if they should look over the record the angel wrote? A day lost! To their own souls a day lost, a day lost in the service of Christ, because no good was accomplished. They may have other days but never that day which was idled away in cheap, foolish talk, of girls with boys, and boys with girls (*Adventist Home*, p. 472).

There is no such thing as a truly converted person living a helpless, useless life. It is not possible for us to drift into heaven. No sluggard can enter there. If we do not strive to gain an entrance into the kingdom, if we do not seek earnestly to learn what constitutes its laws, we are not fitted for a part

Entertainment

in it. Those who refuse to co-operate with God on earth would not co-operate with Him in heaven. It would not be safe to take them to heaven (*Christ Object Lessons*, p. 280).

The value of time is beyond computation. Time squandered can never be recovered… The improvement of wasted moments is a treasure (*Child Guidance*, p. 123).

Children have active minds, and they need to be employed in lifting the burdens of practical life…. They should never be left to pick up their own employment. Parents should control this matter themselves (*Adventist Home*, p. 282).

Those who have indulged the habit of racing through exciting stories, are crippling, their mental strength, and disqualifying themselves for vigorous thought and research. There are men and women now in the decline of life who have never recovered from the effects of intemperate reading. The habit, formed in early years, has grown with their growth and strengthened with their strength; and their efforts to overcome it, though determined, have been only partially successful. Many have never recovered their original vigor of mind. All attempts to become practical Christians end with the desire. They cannot be truly Christlike, and continue to feed the mind upon this class of literature. Nor is the physical effect less disastrous. The nervous system is unnecessarily taxed by this passion for reading. In some cases, youth, and even those of mature age, have been afflicted with paralysis from no other cause than excess in reading. The mind was kept under constant excitement, until the delicate machinery of the brain became so weakened that it could not act, and paralysis was the result. *Christian Education*, p. 186).

Trust in the LORD with all thine heart; and lean not unto thine own understanding. In all thy ways acknowledge him, and he shall direct thy paths (Proverbs 3:5–6).

Those who have indulged the habit of racing through exciting stories, are crippling their mental strength, and disqualifying themselves for vigorous thought and research. There are men and women now in the decline of life who have never recovered from the effects of intemperate reading. The habit, formed in early years, has grown with their growth and strengthened with their strength; and their efforts to overcome it, though determined, have been only partially successful. Many have never recovered their original vigor of mind. All attempts to become practical Christians end with the desire. They cannot be truly Christ-like, and continue to feed the mind upon this class of literature. Nor is the physical effect less disastrous. The nervous system is unnecessarily taxed by this passion for reading. In some cases, youth, and even those of mature age, have been afflicted with paralysis from no other cause than excess in reading. The mind was kept under constant excitement, until the delicate machinery of the brain became so weakened that it could not act, and paralysis was the result (*Christian Temperance and Bible Hygiene*, p. 124).

On such occasions parents and children should feel free from care, labor, and perplexity. Parents should become children with their children, making everything as pleasant for them as possible. Let the whole day be given to recreation (*Messages to Young People*, p. 393).

Will you not arise, my Christian brethren and sisters, and gird yourselves for duty in the fear of God, so arranging this matter that it shall not be dry and uninteresting, but full of innocent enjoyment that shall bear the signet of Heaven? I know the poorer class will respond to these suggestions. The most wealthy should also show an interest and bestow their gifts and offerings proportionate to the means with which God has entrusted them. Let there be recorded in the heavenly books such a Christmas as has never yet been seen because of the donations which shall be given for the sustaining of the work of God and the upbuilding of His kingdom (*Adventist Home*, p. 483).

It is often asked, Are literary societies a benefit to our youth? To answer this question properly, we should consider not only the avowed purpose of such societies, but the influence which they have actually exerted, as proved by experience. The improvement of the mind is a duty which we owe to ourselves, to society, and to God. But we should never devise means for the cultivation of the intellect at the expense of the moral and the spiritual. And it is only by the harmonious development of both the mental and the moral faculties that the highest perfection of either can be attained. Are these results secured by literary societies as they are generally conducted? (*Counsels to Parents, Teachers, and Students*, p. 541).

These poor souls are engaged in a wild chase after worldly pleasure and earthly riches. They have no knowledge of anything more desirable. But games, theaters, horse races, will not satisfy the soul. Human beings were not created to be satisfied in this way, to spend their money for that which is not bread. Show them how infinitely superior to the fleeting joys and pleasures of the world is the imperishable glory of heaven. Seek to convince them of the freedom and hope and rest and peace there is in the gospel. "Whosoever drinketh of the water that I shall give him shall never thirst," Christ declared (*Evangelism*, p. 267).

Never let amusements, or the companionship of others, come between you and Jesus, your best Friend… When natural inclination draws you in the direction of fulfilling some selfish desire, set the Lord before you as your counselor, and ask, "Will this please Jesus? Will this increase my love for my best Friend? Will this course grieve my dear Saviour? Will it separate me from His company? Will Jesus accompany me to the pleasure party, where all will be lightness and gaiety, where there will be nothing of a religious nature, nothing serious, no thought of the things of God?" —*Faith I Live By*, p. 237).

By much slothfulness the building decayeth; and through idleness of the hands the house droppeth through (Ecclesiastes 10:18).

Books on sensational topics, published and circulated as a money-making scheme, might better never be read by the youth. There is a satanic fascination in such books. The heart-sickening recital of crimes and atrocities has a bewitching power upon many, exciting them to see what they can do to bring themselves into notice, even by the wickedest deeds. The enormities, the cruelties, the licentious practices, portrayed in some of the strictly historical writings have acted as leaven on many minds, leading to the commission of similar acts (*Messages to Young People*, p. 284).

I was shown that Sabbathkeepers as a people labor too hard without allowing themselves change or periods of rest. Recreation is needful to those who are engaged in physical labor and is still more essential for those whose labor is principally mental. It is not essential to our salvation, nor for the glory of God, to keep the mind laboring constantly and excessively, even upon religious themes. There are amusements, such as dancing, card playing, chess, checkers, etc., which we cannot approve, because Heaven condemns them. These amusements open the door for great evil. They are not beneficial in their tendency, but have an exciting influence, producing in some minds a passion for those plays which lead to gambling and dissipation. All such plays should be condemned by Christians, and something perfectly harmless should be substituted in their place (*Pastoral Ministry*, p. 247).

Those who are artificial in character and religious experience too readily gather for pleasure and amusement, and their influence attracts others. Sometimes young men and women who are trying to be Bible Christians are persuaded to join the party. Unwilling to be thought singular, and naturally inclined to follow the example of others, they place themselves under the influence of those who, perhaps, have never felt the divine touch on mind and heart. Had they prayerfully consulted the divine standard, to learn what Christ has said in regard to the fruit to be borne on the Christian tree, they would have discerned that these entertainments were really banquets prepared to keep souls from accepting the invitation to the marriage supper of the Lamb (*My Life Today*, p. 215).

Between the associations of the followers of Christ for Christian recreation and worldly gatherings for pleasure and amusement will exist a marked contrast. Instead of prayer and the mentioning of Christ and sacred things, will be heard from the lips of worldlings the silly laugh and the trifling conversation. The idea is to have a general high time. Their amusements commence in folly and end in vanity. Our gatherings should be so conducted, and we should so conduct ourselves, that when we return to our homes we can have a conscience void of offense toward God and man; a consciousness that we have not wounded or injured in any manner those with whom we have been associated, or had an injurious influence over them (*Messages to Young People*, p. 385).

Finally, brethren, whatsoever things are true, whatsoever things are honest, whatsoever things are just, whatsoever things are pure, whatsoever things are lovely, whatsoever things are of good report; if there be any virtue, and if there be any praise, think on these things… (Philippians 4:8).

Suffer not yourselves to open the lids of a book that is questionable. There is a hellish fascination in the literature of Satan. It is the powerful battery by which he tears down a simple religious faith. Never feel that you are strong enough to read infidel books; for they contain a poison like that of asps (*Faith I Live By*, p. 241).

Attention to recreation and physical culture will at times, no doubt, interrupt the regular routine of school-work; but the interruption will prove no real hindrance. In the invigoration of mind and body, the fostering of an unselfish spirit and the binding together of pupil and teacher by the ties of common interest and friendly association, the expenditure of time and effort will be repaid a hundredfold. A blessed outlet will be afforded for that restless energy which is so often a source of danger to the young. As a safeguard against evil, the preoccupation of the mind with good is worth more than unnumbered barriers of law and discipline (*Counsels on Health*, p. 192).

Happiness drawn from earthly sources is as changeable as varying circumstances can make it; but the peace of Christ is a constant and abiding peace. It does not depend upon any circumstances in life, on the amount of worldly goods or the number of earthly friends. Christ is the fountain of living water, and happiness drawn from Him can never fail (*Reflecting Christ*, p. 263).

There is a distinction between recreation and amusement. Recreation, when true to its name, re-creation, tends to strengthen and build up. Calling us aside from our ordinary cares and occupations, it affords refreshment for mind and body, and thus enables us to return with new vigor to the earnest work of life. Amusement, on the other hand, is sought for the sake of pleasure and is often carried to excess; it absorbs the energies that are required for useful work and thus proves a hindrance to life's true success (*Education* 207).

Chapter 16

The Church

Those who are placed in positions of trust must have the authority of action, but they are never to use this authority as a power to refuse and helpless. It is never to be exercised depress one struggling soul. Let those to given positions of influence ever remember them to carry out the mind of Christ, who, by creation and redemption, is the owner of all men (*Christian Leadership*, p. 27).

A minister's wife should ever have a leading influence on the minds of those with whom she associates, and she will be a help, or a great hindrance. She either gathers with Christ, or scatters abroad. A self-sacrificing missionary spirit is lacking among the companions of our ministers. It is self first, and then Christ secondly, and even thirdly. Never should a minister take his wife with him unless he knows that she can be a spiritual help; that she is one who can endure and suffer, to do good, and to benefit souls for Christ's sake. Those who accompany their husbands should go to labor unitedly with them. They must not expect to be free from trials and disappointments. They should not think too much of pleasant feelings. What have feelings to do with duty? (*Gospel Workers*, p. 213).

Could the instructors of children and youth have the result of their mistaken discipline mapped out before them, they would change their plan of education… God never designed that one human mind should be under the complete control of another. And those who make efforts to have the individuality of their pupils merged in themselves, to be mind, will, and conscience for them, assume fearful responsibilities. These scholars may, upon certain occasions, appear like well-drilled soldiers; but when the restraint is removed, there will be seen in them a want of independent action from firm principle (*Counsels to Parents, Teachers, and Students*, p. 76).

Never is such a man to manifest self-importance, or attempt to act as a dictator or a ruler. Let him watch and pray, and keep his eye single to the glory of God. As his imagination takes hold upon things unseen, and he contemplates the joy of the hope that is set before him,—even the precious boon of life eternal,—the commendation of man will not fill his mind with thoughts of pride. And at times when the enemy makes special efforts to spoil him by flattery and worldly honor, his brethren should faithfully warn him of his dangers; for, if left to himself, he will be prone to make mistakes, and reveal human frailties (*Counsels on Stewardship*, p. 147).

Absolutely Positively

Do not become discouraged or slacken your efforts when there are only a few to listen to a discourse. Even if there are but two or three, or no more than one, how do you know but that there may be one soul with whom the Spirit of God is striving? The Lord may give you a message for that soul, and he, if converted, may be the means of reaching many others. The results of your labor may, all unknown to you, be multiplied a thousand-fold. Do not look at the empty seats, and let your faith and courage sink, but think of what God is doing, in bringing his truth before the world. Remember that you are co-operating with divine agencies,—agencies that can never fail. Speak with as much earnestness, faith, and interest, as if there were thousands present to listen to your words (*Gospel Workers*, p. 268).

It is dangerous work to invest men with authority to judge and rule their fellow men. Not to you nor to any other man has been given power to control the actions of God's people, and the effort to do this must be no longer continued... God has been dishonored by the education that has been given to the churches in Southern California in looking to one man as conscience and judgment for them. God has never authorized any man to exercise a ruling power over his fellow-workers; and those who have allowed a dictatorial spirit to come into their official work need to experience the converting power of God upon their hearts. They have placed man where God should be (*Christian Leadership*, p. 33).

Then they that gladly received his word were baptized: and the same day there were added unto them about three thousand souls. And they continued stedfastly in the apostles' doctrine and fellowship, and in breaking of bread, and in prayers. And fear came upon every soul: and many wonders and signs were done by the apostles. And all that believed were together, and had all things common; And sold their possessions and goods, and parted them to all men, as every man had need. And they, continuing daily with one accord in the temple, and breaking bread from house to house, did eat their meat with gladness and singleness of heart, Praising God, and having favour with all the people. And the Lord added to the church daily such as should be saved (Acts 2:41–27)

Never should a young minister rest satisfied with a superficial knowledge of the truth, for he knows not where he may be required to bear witness for God. Many will have to stand before kings and before the learned of the earth, to answer for their faith. Those who have only a superficial understanding of the truth have failed to become workmen that need not be ashamed They will be confused, and will not be able clearly to expound the Scriptures (**Gospel Workers**, p. 93).

Never place as president of a conference a man who supposes that such a position gives him the power to dictate and control the consciences of others. It is natural for man to have a large estimate of self; old habits wrestle for the supremacy; but the man who occupies a position of trust should not glorify himself (*Christian Leadership*, p. 34).

The Church

The one who is in trust of sacred responsibilities should ever show forth the meekness and wisdom of Christ; for it is thus that he becomes a representative of Christ's character and methods. Never should he usurp authority, or command or threaten, saying, "Unless you do as I say, you will receive no pay from the conference." A man who would speak such words is out of his place as president of a conference. He would make men slaves to his judgment (*Christian Leadership*, p. 35).

Some of the servants of God have given up their lives to spend and be spent for the cause of God, until their constitutions are broken down, and they are almost worn out with mental labor, incessant care, toil, and privations. Others have not had, and would not take, the burden upon them. Yet just such ones think they have a hard time, because they have never experienced hardships. They never have been baptized into the suffering part, and never will be as long as they manifest so much weakness and so little fortitude, and love their ease so well (*Christian Experience and Teachings*, p. 160).

Those who have never experienced the tender, winning love of Christ cannot lead others to the fountain of life. His love in the heart is a constraining power, which leads men to reveal Him in the conversation, in the tender, pitiful spirit, in the uplifting of the lives of those with whom they associate. Christian workers who succeed in their efforts must know Christ; and in order to know Him, they must know His love. In heaven their fitness as workers is measured by their ability to love as Christ loved and to work as He worked (*Acts of the Apostles*, p. 550).

A pastor should mingle freely with the people for whom he labors, that by becoming acquainted with them he may know how to adapt his teaching to their needs. When a minister has preached a sermon, his work has but just begun. There is personal work for him to do. He should visit the people in their homes, talking and praying with them in earnestness and humility. There are families who will never be reached by the truths of God's word unless the stewards of His grace enter their homes and point them to the higher way. But the hearts of those who do this work must throb in unison with the heart of Christ (*Acts of the Apostles*, p. 363).

Those who bring in this unhappy chapter into the experiences of our work, and willingly accept the idea that the rulership of other men's conscience has been given to them, need to understand that they have made a grave mistake. Their office was never intended to give to them the responsibility which they have been led to think it bestowed. The danger signal is now lifted against this evil. Never, never let men consent to stand in a position which God alone should occupy (*Christian Leadership*, p. 28).

God never designed that one human mind should be under the complete control of another. And those who make efforts to have the individuality of their pupils merged in themselves, and to be mind, will, and conscience for them, assume fearful responsibilities. These scholars may, upon certain occasions, appear like well-drilled soldiers. But when the restraint is removed, there will be seen a want of independent action from firm principle existing in them (*Child Guidance*, p. 228).

I know thy works, that thou art neither cold nor hot: I would thou wert cold or hot. So then because thou art lukewarm, and neither cold nor hot, I will spue thee out of my mouth (Revelation 3:15–16).

Never should a laborer regard as a virtue the persistent maintenance of his position of independence, contrary to the decision of the general body… God has ordained that the representatives of His church from all parts of the earth, when assembled in a General Conference, shall have authority. The error that some are in danger of committing, is in giving to the mind and judgment of one man, or of a small group of men, the full measure of authority and influence that God has vested in His church, in the judgment and voice of the General Conference assembled to plan for the prosperity and advancement of His work (*Christian Leadership*, p. 1).

Those who have had no respect for order or discipline in this life would have no respect for the order which is observed in heaven. They can never be admitted into heaven, for all worthy of an entrance there will love order and respect discipline. The characters formed in this life will determine the future destiny. When Christ shall come, He will not change the character of any individual… Parents should neglect no duty on their part to benefit their children. They should so train them that they may be a blessing to society here and may reap the reward of eternal life hereafter (*Child Guidance*, p. 229).

God's chosen messengers, who are engaged in aggressive labor, should never be compelled to go a warfare at their own charges, unaided by the sympathetic and hearty support of their brethren. It is the part of church members to deal liberally with those who lay aside their secular employment that they may give themselves to the ministry. When God's ministers are encouraged, His cause is greatly advanced. But when, through the selfishness of men, their rightful support is withheld, their hands are weakened, and often their usefulness is seriously crippled (*Acts of the Apostles*, p. 340).

Our workers—ministers, teachers, physicians, directors—all need to remember that they are pledged to co-operate with Christ, to obey His directions, to follow His guidance. Every hour they are to ask and receive power from on high. They are to cherish a constant sense of the Saviour's love, of His efficiency, His watchfulness, His tenderness. They are to look to Him as the shepherd and bishop of their souls. Then they will have the sympathy and support of the heavenly angels. Christ will be their joy and crown of rejoicing. Their hearts will be controlled by the Holy Spirit, and they will have a knowledge of the truth which merely nominal believers can never gain (*Counsels to Parents, Teachers, and Students*, p. 284).

In the work of the gospel the Lord uses different instrumentalities, and nothing is to be allowed to separate these instrumentalities. Never should a sanitarium be established as an enterprise independent of the church. Our physicians are to unite with the work of the ministers of the gospel. Through their labors souls are to be saved, that the name of God may be magnified (*Counsels on Health*, p. 524).

The Lord's people are to be one. There is to be no separation in His work. Christ sent out the twelve apostles and afterward the seventy disciples to preach the gospel and to heal the sick. (Matthew 10:7, 8.) And as they went forth preaching the kingdom of God, power was given them to heal the sick and cast out evil spirits. In God's work teaching and healing are never to be separated (*A Call to Medical Evangelism and Health Education*, p. 42).

Levity is not appropriate in meetings where the solemn work and word of God are under consideration. The prayer has been offered that Christ shall preside in the assembly, and impart His wisdom, His grace and righteousness. Is it consistent to take a course that will be grievous to His Spirit and contrary to His work? (*Gospel Workers*, p. 447).

Upon Christian youth depend in a great measure the preservation and perpetuity of the institutions which God has devised as a means by which to advance His work. Never was there a period when results so important depended upon a generation of men. Then how important that the young should be qualified for this great work, that God may use them as His instruments! Their Maker has claims upon them which are paramount to all others. *Counsels to Parents, Teachers, and Students*, p. 99).

Never can the church reach the position that God desires it to reach until it is bound up in sympathy with its missionary workers. Never can the unity for which Christ prayed exist until spirituality is brought into missionary service, and until the church becomes an agency for the support of missions. The efforts of the missionaries will not accomplish what they should until the church members in the home field show, not only in word, but in deed, that they realize the obligation resting on them to give these missionaries their hearty support (*Counsels on Stewardship*, p. 47).

Our ideas of building and furnishing our institutions are to be molded and fashioned by a true, practical knowledge of what it means to walk humbly with God. Never should it be thought necessary to give an appearance of wealth. Never should appearance be depended on as a means of success. This is a delusion. The desire to make an appearance that is not in every way appropriate to the work that God has given us to do, an appearance that could be kept up only by expending a large sum of money, is a merciless tyrant. It is like a canker that is ever eating into the vitals (*Counsels on Health*, p. 277).

In the human brotherhood it takes all kinds of talents to make a perfect whole; and the church of Christ is composed of men and women of varied talents, and of all ranks and all classes. God never designed that the pride of men should dissolve that which His own wisdom had ordained,— the combination of all classes of minds, of all the varied talents that make a complete whole. There should be no depreciating of any part of God's great work, whether the agencies are high or lowly. All have their part to act in diffusing light in different degrees (*Gospel Workers*, p. 331).

Our institutions for any land are not to be crowded together in one locality. God never designed that the light of truth should be thus restricted. For a time the Jewish nation was required to worship at Jerusalem. But Jesus said to the Samaritan woman: "Believe Me, the hour cometh, when ye shall neither in this mountain, nor yet at Jerusalem, worship the Father." "The hour cometh, and now is, when the true worshipers shall worship the Father in spirit and in truth: for the Father seeketh such to worship Him. God is a Spirit: and they that worship Him must worship Him in spirit and in truth." John 4:21, 23, 24. Truth is to be planted in every place to which we can possibly gain access. It is to be carried to regions that are barren of the knowledge of God. Men will be blessed in receiving the One in whom their hopes of eternal life are centered. The acceptance of the truth as it is in Jesus will fill their hearts with melody to God (*Counsels on Health*, p. 216).

A responsibility rests upon the minister's wife which she should not and cannot lightly throw off. God will require the talent lent her, with usury. She should work earnestly, faithfully, and unitedly with her husband to save souls. She should never urge her wishes and desires, or express a lack of interest in her husband's labor, or dwell upon homesick, discontented feelings. All these natural feelings must be overcome. She should have a purpose in life which should be unfalteringly carried out. What if this conflicts with the feelings and pleasures and natural tastes! These should be cheerfully and readily sacrificed, in order to do good and save souls (*Gospel Workers*, p. 202).

The man who attempts to keep the commandments of God from a sense of obligation merely— because he is required to do so—will never enter into the joy of obedience. He does not obey. When the requirements of God are accounted a burden because they cut across human inclination, we may know that the life is not a Christian life. True obedience is the outworking of a principle within. It springs from the love of righteousness, the love of the law of God. The essence of all righteousness is loyalty to our Redeemer. This will lead us to do right because it is right—because right doing is pleasing to God (*Christ Object Lessons*, p. 97).

There is missionary labor to be done in the distribution of tracts and papers, and in canvassing for our different publications. Let none of you think that you cannot engage in this work because it is taxing, and requires time and thought. If it requires time, give it cheerfully; and the blessing of God will rest upon you. There never was a time when more workers were needed than at the present. There are brethren and sisters throughout all our ranks who should discipline themselves to engage in this work; in all our churches something should be done to spread the truth. It is the duty of all to study the various points of our faith, that they may be prepared to give a reason for the hope that is within them, with meekness and fear (*Colporteur Ministry*, p. 21).

Very much has been lost to the cause of God by a lack of attention to the young. Ministers should form an acquaintance with the youth in their congregations. Many are reluctant to do this, but their neglect is a sin in the sight of Heaven. There are among us many who are not ignorant of our faith, yet whose hearts have never been touched by the power of divine grace. Can we who claim to be servants of God pass on day after day, week after week, indifferent to these souls who are out of Christ? If they should die in their sins, unwarned, their blood would be required at the unfaithful watchman's hands (*Christian Education*, p. 222).

Never are we to rely upon worldly recognition and rank. Never are we, in the establishment of institutions, to try to compete with worldly institutions in size or splendor. We shall gain the victory, not by erecting massive buildings, in rivalry with our enemies, but by cherishing a Christlike spirit—a spirit of meekness and lowliness. Better far the cross and disappointed hopes, with eternal life at last, than to live with princes and forfeit heaven (*Counsels on Health*, p. 225).

A working church is a growing church. The members find a stimulus and a tonic in helping others. I have read of a man who, journeying on a winter's day through deep drifts of snow, became benumbed by the cold, which was almost imperceptibly freezing his vital powers. He was nearly chilled to death, and was about to give up the struggle for life, when he heard the moans of a fellow-traveler, who was also perishing with cold. His sympathy was aroused, and he determined to rescue him. He chafed the ice-cold limbs of the unfortunate man, and after considerable effort raised him to his feet. As the sufferer could not stand, he bore him in sympathizing arms through the very drifts he had thought he could never get through alone (*Gospel Workers*, p. 198).

Do not allow all your strength and energy to be given to worldly, temporal things during the week, and so have no energy and moral strength to give to the service of Christ on the Sabbath.

Absolutely Positively

There is earnest work to be done just now. We have not a moment's time to use selfishly. Let all we do be done with an eye single to the glory of God. Never rest till every child in your class is brought to the saving knowledge of Christ (*Counsels on Stewardship*, p. 125).

But never should it be forgotten that influence is no less a power for evil. To lose one's own soul is a terrible thing; but to cause the loss of other souls is still more terrible. That our influence should be a savor of death unto death is a fearful thought; yet this is possible. Many who profess to gather with Christ are scattering from Him. This is why the church is so weak. Many indulge freely in criticism and accusing. By giving expression to suspicion, jealousy, and discontent, they yield themselves as instruments to Satan. Before they realize what they are doing, the adversary has through them accomplished his purpose. The impression of evil has been made, the shadow has been cast, the arrows of Satan have found their mark. Distrust, unbelief, and downright infidelity have fastened upon those who otherwise might have accepted Christ. Meanwhile the workers for Satan look complacently upon those whom they have driven to skepticism, and who are now hardened against reproof and entreaty. They flatter themselves that in comparison with these souls they are virtuous and righteous. They do not realize that these sad wrecks of character are the work of their own unbridled tongues and rebellious hearts. It is through their influence that these tempted ones have fallen (*Christ Object Lessons*, p. 340).

Wickedness is reaching a height never before attained, and yet many ministers of the gospel are crying, "Peace and safety." But God's faithful messengers are to go steadily forward with their work. Clothed with the panoply of heaven, they are to advance fearlessly and victoriously, never ceasing their warfare until every soul within their reach shall have received the message of truth for this time (*Acts of the Apostles*, p. 220).

Never should we pass by one suffering soul without seeking to impart to him the comfort wherewith we are comforted of God (*Christ Object Lessons*, p. 387).

Let not the follower of Christ think, when he is no longer able to labor openly and actively for God and His truth, that he has no service to render, no reward to secure. Christ's true witnesses are never laid aside. In health and sickness, in life and death, God uses them still. When through Satan's malice the servants of Christ have been persecuted, their active labors hindered, when they have been cast into prison, or dragged to the scaffold or to the stake, it was that truth might gain a greater triumph. As these faithful ones sealed their testimony with their blood, souls hitherto in doubt and uncertainty were convinced of the faith of Christ and took their stand courageously for Him. From the ashes of the martyrs has sprung an abundant harvest for God (*Acts of the Apostles*, p. 465).

When a minister has presented the gospel message from the pulpit, his work is only begun. There is personal work for him to do. He should visit the people in their homes, talking and praying with them in earnestness and humility. There are families who will never be reached by the truths of God's word unless the stewards of His grace enter their homes and point them to the higher way. But the hearts of those who do this work must throb in unison with the heart of Christ (*Gospel Workers*, p. 187).

Let our periodicals be devoted to the publication of living, earnest matter. Let every article be full of practical, elevating, ennobling thoughts, thoughts that will give to the reader help and light and strength. Family religion, family holiness, is now to be honored as never before. If ever a people needed to walk before God as did Enoch, Seventh-day Adventists need to do so now, showing their sincerity by pure words, clean words, words full of sympathy, tenderness, and love (*Counsels to Writers and Editors*, p. 13).

It is the privilege of the watchmen on the walls of Zion to live so near to God, and to be susceptible to the impressions of His Spirit, that He can work through them to tell men and women of their peril and point them to the place of safety. Faithfully are they to warn them of the sure result of transgression, and faithfully are they to safeguard the interests of the church. At no time may they relax their vigilance. Theirs is a work requiring the exercise of every faculty of the being. In trumpet tones their voices are to be lifted, and never are they to sound one wavering, uncertain note. Not for wages are they to labor, but because they cannot do otherwise, because they realize that there is a woe upon them if they fail to preach the gospel. Chosen of God, sealed with the blood of consecration, they are to rescue men and women from impending destruction (*Acts of the Apostles*, p. 361).

I am warned that the less our ministers handle the subject of pantheism, the less they will help Satan to present his theories to the people. Let the truth for this time be kept before them. never, never repeat the spiritualistic sentiments, the strange, misleading theories, which have for years been coming in (*Counsels to Writers and Editors*, p. 93).

Many of those for whom our ministers labor are ignorant of the truths of the Bible and the requirements of God, and the simplest lessons on practical godliness come to them as a new revelation. These need to know what is truth, and in laboring for them the minister should not take up lines of thought that will simply please the fancy or gratify curiosity. Let him instead break the bread of life to these starving souls. Never should he preach a sermon that does not help his hearers to see more plainly what they must do to be saved (*Gospel Workers*, p. 153).

The workers must not spend their time in going over and over the ground among churches that are already confirmed in the truth, while on every hand are many who have never had the truth explained to them (*Evangelism*, p. 463).

My brethren, will you not give the flock of God bread, and not a stone? Never print in our papers a word that will lower the standard that God expects His people to meet. Call no man brilliant who has not the wisdom to choose the Lord Jesus Christ—the light and life of the world. The excellence of a man is determined by his possession of the virtues of Christ. Let us not look away from Christ to sinful human beings. The truth must be kept before the people. The standard of purity, temperance, and holiness must be uplifted (*Counsels to Writers and Editors*, p. 175).

The minister of Christ should be a man of prayer, a man of piety; cheerful, but never coarse and rough, jesting or frivolous. A spirit of frivolity may be in keeping with the profession of clowns and theatrical performers, but it is altogether beneath the dignity of a man who is chosen to stand between the living and the dead, and to be a mouthpiece for God (*Gospel Workers*, p. 132).

The reproach of indolence will never be wiped away from the church till every one who believes the truth shall be willing to labor as did our self-sacrificing Redeemer. Christ can not pronounce those good and faithful servants who have had the greatest advantages, the richest blessings, and yet have allowed a nation of helpless, dependent beings to remain degraded and unenlightened. Brethren, when you seek to help the ones who need education, that they may read the Word of God, when you say to every man, from the least to the greatest, Know the Lord, know Him for yourself, then your reproach will be wiped away. The Spirit of God will bless the means employed, even now (*Spaulding and Magan Collection*, p. 17).

Never should the laborer who raises up little companies here and there, give the impression to those newly come to the faith, that God does not require them to work systematically in helping to sustain the cause by their personal labors and by their means (*Evangelism*, p. 250).

Children and youth should never feel that it is something to be proud of to be indifferent and careless in meetings where God is worshiped. God sees every irreverent thought or action, and it is registered in the books of heaven. He says, "I know thy works." Nothing is hid from His all-searching eye. If you have formed in any degree the habit of inattention and indifference in the house of God, exercise the powers you have to correct it, and show that you have self-respect. Practice reverence until it becomes a part of yourself (*Child Guidance*, p. 546).

The Church

Christ has plainly taught that those who persist in open sin must be separated from the church, but He has not committed to us the work of judging character and motive. He knows our nature too well to entrust this work to us. Should we try to uproot from the church those whom we suppose to be spurious Christians, we should be sure to make mistakes. Often we regard as hopeless subjects the very ones whom Christ is drawing to Himself. Were we to deal with these souls according to our imperfect judgment, it would perhaps extinguish their last hope. Many who think themselves Christians will at last be found wanting. Many will be in heaven who their neighbors supposed would never enter there. Man judges from appearance, but God judges the heart. The tares and the wheat are to grow together until the harvest; and the harvest is the end of probationary time (*Christ Object Lessons*, p. 71).

The Lord requires that unity exist in every church, but the policy of consolidation must be guarded against. The workers in our institutions are to preserve their individuality; each is to sense the responsibility resting upon him, while he works under the divine leadership of the Lord Jesus. The workers are to counsel together, and to seek to bring in ideas that are in harmony with the teachings of truth, but never, as long as time shall last, is an arbitrary man-ruling power to come in to take the place and authority of God (*Spaulding and Magan Collection*, p. 377).

There are numbers that ought to become missionaries who never enter the field, because those who are united with them in church capacity or in our colleges, do not feel the burden of labor with them, to open before them the claims that God has upon all the powers, and do not pray with them and for them; and the eventful period which decides the plans and course of life passes, convictions, with them are stifled, other influences and inducements attract them, and temptations to seek worldly positions that will, they think, bring them money, take them into the worldly current. These young men might have been saved to the ministry through well-organized plans. If the churches in the different places do their duty, God will work with their efforts by his Spirit, and will supply faithful men to the ministry (*Christian Education*, p. 45).

Those who accept a position of responsibility in the cause of God should always remember that with the call to this work God has also called them to walk circumspectly before Him and before their fellow men. Instead of considering it their duty to order and dictate and command, they should realize that they are to be learners themselves. When a responsible worker fails to learn this lesson, the sooner he is released from his responsibilities the better it will be for him and for the work of God. Position never will give holiness and excellence of character. He who honors God and keeps His commandments is himself honored (*Christian Leadership*, p. 14).

The minister may think that with his fanciful eloquence he has done great things in feeding the flock of God; the hearers may suppose that they never before heard such beautiful themes, they have never seen the truth dressed up in such beautiful language, and as God was represented before them in His greatness, they felt a glow of emotion. But trace from cause to effect all this ecstasy of feeling caused by these fanciful representations. There may be truths, but too often they are not the food that will fortify them for the daily battles of life (*Evangelism*, p. 182).

I am instructed by the Lord to say that position never gives a man grace or makes him righteous. "The fear of the Lord is the beginning of wisdom." Some men entrusted with positions of responsibility entertain the idea that position is for the aggrandizement of self (*Medical Ministry*, p. 164, 165).

The church of Christ may be fitly compared to an army. The life of every soldier is one of toil, hardship, and danger. On every hand are vigilant foes, led on by the prince of the powers of darkness, who never slumbers and never deserts his post. Whenever a Christian is off his guard, this powerful adversary makes a sudden and violent attack. Unless the members of the church are active and vigilant, they will be overcome by his devices (*Christian Service*, p. 82).

The work of God in this earth can never be finished until the men and women comprising our church membership rally to the work, and unite their efforts with those of ministers and church officers (*Christian Service*, p. 68).

It is a solemn statement that I make to the church that not one in twenty whose names are registered upon the church books are prepared to close their earthly history, and would be as verily without God and without hope in the world as the common sinner. They are professionally serving God, but they are very earnestly serving mammon. This half and half work is a constant denying of Christ rather than a confessing of Christ. So many have brought their own unsubdued spirit, unrefined, their spiritual taste is perverted by their own immoral, debasing corruptions, symbolizing the world in spirit, in heart, in purpose, confirming themselves in lustful practices, and are full of deception through and through in their professed Christian life; living as sinners claiming to be Christians. Those who claim to be Christians and will confess Christ, should come out from among them and touch; not the unclean thing and to be separate (*GC Dailey Bulletin*, February 4, 1893).

Never weary the hearers by long discourses. This is not wise. For many years I have been laboring on this point, seeking to have our brethren sermonize less, and devote their time and strength to making important points of truth plain, for every point will be assailed by our opponents. Everyone connected with the work should keep fresh ideas; …and by tact and foresight bring all that is possible into your work to interest your hearers (*Evangelism*, p. 178).

Preaching is a small part of the work to be done for the salvation of souls. God's Spirit convicts sinners of the truth, and He places them in the arms of the church. The ministers may do their part, but they can never perform the work that the church should do (*Christian Service*, p. 68).

Decided proclamations are to be made. But in regard to this line of work, I am instructed to say to our people: Be guarded. In bearing the message, make no personal thrusts at other churches, not even the Roman Catholic Church. Angels of God see in the different denominations many who can be reached only by the greatest caution. Therefore let us be careful of our words. Let not our ministers follow their own impulses in denouncing and exposing the "mysteries of iniquity." Upon these themes silence is eloquence. Many are deceived. Speak the truth in tones and words of love. Let Christ Jesus be exalted. Keep to the affirmative of truth. Never leave the straight path God has marked out, for the purpose of giving someone a thrust. That thrust may do much harm and no good. It may quench conviction in many minds. Let the Word of God, which is the truth, tell the story of the inconsistency of those in error (*Evangelism*, p. 576).

The church of God below is one with the church of God above. Believers on the earth and the beings in heaven who have never fallen constitute one church. Every heavenly intelligence is interested in the assemblies of the saints who on earth meet to worship God. In the inner court of heaven they listen to the testimony of the witnesses for Christ in the outer court on earth, and the praise and thanksgiving from the worshipers below is taken up in the heavenly anthem, and praise and rejoicing sound through the heavenly courts because Christ has not died in vain for the fallen sons of Adam. While angels drink from the fountainhead, the saints on earth drink of the pure streams flowing from the throne, the streams that make glad the city of our God. Oh, that we could all realize the nearness of heaven to earth! …In every assembly of the saints below are angels of God, listening to the testimonies, songs, and prayers. Let us remember that our praises are supplemented by the choirs of the angelic host above (*God's Amazing Grace*, p. 75).

In the presentation of unpopular truth, which involves a heavy cross, preachers should be careful that every word is as God would have it. Their words should never cut. They should present the truth in humility, with the deepest love for souls, and an earnest desire for their salvation, and let the truth cut. They should not defy ministers of other denominations, and seek to provoke a debate. They should not stand in a position like that of Goliath when he defied the armies of Israel. Israel did not defy Goliath, but Goliath made his proud boasts against God and his people. The defying, the boasting, and the railing must come from the opposers of truth, who act the Goliath; but none of this spirit should be seen in those whom God has sent forth to proclaim the last message of warning to a doomed world (*Gospel Workers*, p. 187).

Absolutely Positively

The strength of an army is measured largely by the efficiency of the men in the ranks. A wise general instructs his officers to train every soldier for active service. He seeks to develop the highest efficiency on the part of all. If he were to depend on his officers alone, he could never expect to conduct a successful campaign. He counts on loyal and untiring service from every man in his army. The responsibility rests largely upon the men in the ranks (*Christian Service*, p. 74).

A minister should never think that he has learned enough, and may now relax his efforts. His education should continue throughout his lifetime; every day he should be learning, and putting to use the knowledge gained (*Gospel Workers*, p. 94).

The church of God upon the earth is one with the church of God above. Believers on the earth, and those who have never fallen in heaven, are one church. Every heavenly intelligence is interested in the assemblies of the saints, who on earth meet to worship God in spirit and truth, and in the beauty of holiness. In the inner court of heaven they listen to the testimonies of the witnesses for Christ in the outer court on earth, and the praise and thanksgiving that comes from the church below, is taken up in the heavenly anthem, and praise and rejoicing resounds through the heavenly court because Christ has not died in vain for the fallen sons of Adam. While angels drink from the fountainhead, the saints on earth drink of the pure streams flowing from the throne of God, making glad the city of God (*Our High Calling*, p. 167).

In the Scriptures thousands of gems of truth lie hidden from the surface seeker. The mine of truth is never exhausted. The more you search the Scriptures with humble hearts, the greater will be your interest, and the more you will feel like exclaiming with Paul: "O the depth of the riches both of the wisdom and knowledge of God!" (*My Life Today*, p. 22).

The true minister of God will not shun hardship or responsibility. From the Source that never fails those who sincerely seek for divine power, he draws strength that enables him to meet and overcome temptation, and to perform the duties that God places upon him. The nature of the grace that he receives, enlarges his capacity to know God and His Son. His soul goes out in longing desire to do acceptable service for the Master. And as he advances in the Christian pathway, he becomes "strong in the grace that is in Christ Jesus." This grace enables him to be a faithful witness of the things that he has heard. He does not despise or neglect the knowledge that he has received from God, but commits this knowledge to faithful men, who in their turn teach others (*Gospel Workers*, p. 108).

Give the Word its honored position as a guide in the home. Let it be regarded as the Counselor in every difficulty, the standard of every practice.... There can never be true prosperity to any soul in the family circle unless the truth of God, the wisdom of righteousness, presides (*My Life Today*, p. 25).

In ancient times God spoke to men by the mouth of prophets and apostles. In these days He speaks to them by the Testimonies of His Spirit. There was never a time when God instructed His people more earnestly than He instructs them now concerning His will and the course that He would have them pursue (*My Life Today*, p. 40).

If the church will put on the robe of Christ's righteousness, withdrawing from all allegiance with the world, there is before her the dawn of a bright and glorious day. God's promise to her will stand fast forever. He will make her an eternal excellency, a joy of many generations. Truth, passing by those who despise and reject it, will triumph. Although at times apparently retarded, its progress has never been checked. When the message of God meets with opposition, He gives it additional force, that it may exert greater influence. Endowed with divine energy, it will cut its way through the strongest barriers, and triumph over every obstacle (*My Life Today*, p. 266).

Those who are of the household of faith should never neglect the assembling of themselves together; for this is God's appointed means of leading His children into unity, in order that in Christian love and fellowship they may help, strengthen, and encourage one another (*Our High Calling*, p. 166).

The use of musical instruments to create a bedlam of noise, shocks the senses and perverts the worship. The Holy Spirit never reveals itself in such methods, in such a bedlam of noise. This is an invention of Satan to cover up his ingenious methods for making of none effect the pure, sincere, elevating, ennobling, sanctifying truth for this time. Better never have the worship of God blended with music than to use musical instruments to do the work which last January was represented to me would be brought into our camp meetings. The truth for this time needs nothing of this kind in its work of converting souls. A bedlam of noise shocks the senses and perverts that which if conducted aright might be a blessing. The powers of satanic agencies blend with the din and noise, to have a carnival, and this is termed the Holy Spirit's working (*Pastoral Ministry*, p.178).

Not forsaking the assembling of ourselves together, as the manner of some is; but exhorting one another: and so much the more, as ye see the day approaching (Hebrews 10:25)

Chapter 17

Evangelism

Then saith he unto his disciples, The harvest truly is plenteous, but the labourers are few; Pray ye therefore the Lord of the harvest, that he will send forth labourers into his harvest (Matthew 9:37–38).

How many who know the truth for this time are working in harmony with its principles? It is true that something is being done; but more, far more, should have been done. The work is accumulating, and the time for doing it is diminishing. All should now be burning and shining lights, and yet many are failing to keep their lamps supplied with the oil of grace, trimmed and burning, so that light may gleam out today. Too many are counting on a long stretch of tomorrow, but this is a mistake. Let everyone be educated in such a way as to show the importance of the special work for today. Let everyone labor for God and for souls; let each show wisdom and never be found in idleness, waiting for someone to set him to work. The "someone" who could set you to work is overcrowded with responsibilities, and time is lost in waiting for his directions (*Counsels to Parents, Teachers, and Students*, p. 418).

We should all become witnesses for Jesus. Social power, sanctified by the grace of Christ, must be improved in winning souls to the Saviour. Let the world see that we are not selfishly absorbed in our own interests, but that we desire others to share our blessings and privileges. Let them see that our religion does not make us unsympathetic or exacting. Let all who profess to have found Christ minister as He did for the benefit of men. We should never give to the world the false impression that Christians are a gloomy, unhappy people (*Adventist Home*, p. 428).

And into whatsoever city or town ye shall enter, enquire who in it is worthy; and there abide till ye go thence. And when ye come into an house, salute it. And if the house be worthy, let your peace come upon it: but if it be not worthy, let your peace return to you. And whosoever shall not receive you, nor hear your words, when ye depart out of that house or city, shake off the dust of your feet (Matthew 10:11–14).

The talent of knowledge, sanctified and put to use in the Master's service, is never lost. A self-sacrificing effort to do good will be crowned with success. "We are laborers together with God."

I Corinthians 3:9. The Lord will co-operate with the human worker. To Him is to be given the praise and the glory for what we are able to accomplish (*Counsels to Parents, Teachers, and Students*, p. 451).

You have neighbors. Will you give them the message? You may never have had the hands of ordination laid upon you, but you can humbly carry the message. You can testify that God has ordained that all for whom Christ died shall have everlasting life, if they believe on Him (*Spaulding and Magan Collection*, p. 372).

Then said Jesus to them again, Peace be unto you: as my Father hath sent me, even so send I you (John 20:21).

There is to be a time of trouble such as never was since there was a nation. Our work is to study to weed out of all our discourses everything that savors of retaliation and defiance and making a drive against churches and individuals, because this is not Christ's way and method (*Counsels to Writers and Editors, p. 64*).

Christ did not tell His disciples that their work would be easy. He showed them the vast confederacy of evil arrayed against them. They would have to fight "against principalities, against powers, against the rulers of the darkness of this world, against spiritual wickedness in high places." Ephesians 6:12. But they would not be left to fight alone. He assured them that He would be with them; and that if they would go forth in faith, they should move under the shield of Omnipotence. He bade them be brave and strong; for One mightier than angels would be in their ranks—the General of the armies of heaven. He made full provision for the prosecution of their work and took upon Himself the responsibility of its success. So long as they obeyed His word, and worked in connection with Him, they could not fail. Go to all nations, He bade them. Go to the farthest part of the habitable globe and be assured that My presence will be with you even there. Labor in faith and confidence; for the time will never come when I will forsake you. I will be with you always, helping you to perform your duty, guiding, comforting, sanctifying, sustaining you, giving you success in speaking words that shall draw the attention of others to heaven (*Acts of the Apostles*, p. 29).

And he said unto them, Go ye into all the world, and preach the gospel to every creature (Mark 16:15).

Let it never be forgotten that these institutions are to cooperate with the ministry of the delegates of heaven. They are among the agencies represented by the angel flying "in the midst of heaven, having the everlasting gospel to preach unto them that dwell on the earth, and to every nation, and kindred, and tongue, and people, saying with a loud voice, Fear God, and give glory to Him; for the hour of His judgment is come." Revelation 14:6, 7 (*Counsels to Writers and Editors*, p. 179).

In his ministry, Paul was often compelled to stand alone. He was specially taught of God and dared make no concessions that would involve principle. At times the burden was heavy, but Paul stood firm for the right. He realized that the church must never be brought under the control of human power. The traditions and maxims of men must not take the place of revealed truth. The advance of the gospel message must not be hindered by the prejudices and preferences of men, whatever might be their position in the church (*Acts of the Apostles*, p. 199).

I must tell you from the light given me by God, I know that much time and money are spent by students in acquiring a knowledge that is as chaff to them; for it does not enable them to help their fellow-men to form characters that will fit them to unite with saints and angels in the higher school. In the place of crowding youthful minds with a mass of things that are distasteful, and that in many cases will never be of any use to them, a practical education should be given. Time and money is spent in gaining useless knowledge. The mind should be carefully and wisely taught to dwell upon Bible truth. The main object of education should be to gain a knowledge of how we can glorify God, whose we are by creation and by redemption (*Spaulding and Magan Collection*, p. 56).

Pray ye therefore the Lord of the harvest, that he will send forth labourers into his harvest (Matthew 9:38).

He who has appointed "to every man his work" (Mark 13:34) according to his ability, will never let the faithful performance of duty go unrewarded. Every act of loyalty and faith will be crowned with special tokens of God's favor and approbation. To every worker is given the promise, "He that goeth forth and weepeth, bearing precious seed, shall doubtless come again with rejoicing, bringing his sheaves with him." Psalm 126:6 (*Counsels to Parents, Teachers, and Students*, p. 518).

We are not to wait for souls to come to us; we must seek them out where they are. When the word has been preached in the pulpit, the work has but just begun. There are multitudes who will never be reached by the gospel unless it is carried to them (*Christ Object Lessons*, p. 229).

From Paul's day to the present time, God by His Holy Spirit has been calling after the Jew as well as the Gentile. "There is no respect of persons with God," declared Paul. The apostle regarded himself as "debtor both to the Greeks, and to the barbarians," as well as to the Jews; but he never lost sight of the decided advantages possessed by the Jews over others, "chiefly, because that unto them were committed the oracles of God." "The gospel," he declared, "is the power of God unto salvation to everyone that believeth; to the Jew first, and also to the Greek. For therein is the righteousness of God revealed from faith to faith: as it is written, The just shall live by faith." It is of this gospel of Christ, equally efficacious for Jew and Gentile, that Paul in his epistle to the Romans declared he was not ashamed (*Acts of the Apostles*, p. 380).

For the Son of man is come to seek and to save that which was lost (Luke 19:10).

In their efforts to reach the people, the Lord's messengers are not to follow the ways of the world. In the meetings that are held, they are not to depend on worldly singers and theatrical display to awaken an interest. How can those who have no interest in the Word of God, who have never read His Word with a sincere desire to understand its truths, be expected to sing with the spirit and the understanding? How can their hearts be in harmony with the words of sacred song? How can the heavenly choir join in music that is only a form? (*Evangelism*, p. 508).

Go ye therefore, and teach all nations, baptizing them in the name of the Father, and of the Son, and of the Holy Ghost: Teaching them to observe all things whatsoever I have commanded you: and, lo, I am with you always, even unto the end of the world. Amen (Matthew 28:19–20).

The command given in the parable, to "compel them to come in," has often been misinterpreted. It has been regarded as teaching that we should force men to receive the gospel. But it denotes rather the urgency of the invitation, and the effectiveness of the inducements presented. The gospel never employs force in bringing men to Christ. Its message is "Ho, every one that thirsteth, come ye to the waters." Isaiah 55:1. "The Spirit and the bride say, Come... And whosoever will, let him take the water of life freely." Revelation 22:17. The power of God's love and grace constrains us to come (*Christ Object Lessons*, p. 235).

Therefore they that were scattered abroad went every where preaching the word (Acts 8:4).

Wake up, wake up, my brethren and sisters, and enter the fields in America that have never been worked. After you have given something for foreign fields, do not think your duty done. There is a work to be done in foreign fields, but there is a work to be done in America that is just as important. In the cities of America there are people of almost every language. These need the light that God has given to His church (*Christian Service*, p. 199).

It is important that in defending the doctrines which we consider fundamental articles of faith, we should never allow ourselves to employ arguments that are not wholly sound. These may avail to silence an opposer, but they do not honor the truth. We should present sound arguments, that will not only silence our opponents, but will bear the closest and most searching scrutiny (*Evangelism*, p. 166).

And said unto them, Thus it is written, and thus it behooved Christ to suffer, and to rise from the dead the third day: And that repentance and remission of sins should be preached in his name among all nations, beginning at Jerusalem. And ye are witnesses of these things (Luke 24:46–48).

Let every one labor for God and for souls; let each show wisdom, and never be found in idleness, waiting for some one to set him to work. The "some one" who could set you to work is overcrowded with responsibilities, and time is lost in waiting for his directions. God will give you wisdom in reforming at once; for the call is still made, "Son, go work today in My vineyard." "Today if ye will hear His voice, harden not your hearts." (Hebews 3:7, 8). The Lord prefaces the requirement with the endearing word "son." How tender, how compassionate, yet withal, how urgent! His invitation is also a command (*Christian Service*, p. 100).

Workers for Christ are never to think, much less to speak, of failure in their work. The Lord Jesus is our efficiency in all things; His Spirit is to be our inspiration; and as we place ourselves in His hands, to be channels of light, our means of doing good will never be exhausted. We may draw upon His fullness, and receive of that grace which has no limit (*Christian Service*, p. 261).

The places in which the truth has never been proclaimed are the best places in which to work. The truth is to take possession of the will of those who have never before heard it. They will see the sinfulness of sin, and their repentance will be thorough and sincere. The Lord will work upon hearts that in the past have not often been appealed to, hearts that heretofore have not seen the enormity of sin (*Evangelism*, p. 21).

But watch thou in all things, endure afflictions, do the work of an evangelist, make full proof of thy ministry (2 Timothy 4:5).

The world must be warned of the soon coming of the Lord. We have but a little time in which to work. Years have passed into eternity that might have been improved in seeking first the kingdom of God and His righteousness, and in diffusing the light to others. God now calls upon His people who have great light and are established in the truth, having had much labor bestowed upon them, to work for themselves and for others as they have never done before. Make use of every ability; bring into exercise every power, every entrusted talent; use all the light that God has given you to do others good. Do not try to become preachers, but become ministers for God (*Christian Service*, p. 92).

We must never forget how hard it is to remove long-cherished errors from the minds of men, which have been taught from childhood. We must bear in mind that earth is not heaven, and that there will be discouragements to meet and to overcome, but forbearance and tenderness and pity should be exercised toward all who are in darkness. If we bring them to see the light, it will not be solely by arguments, it must be by the work of the grace of Christ on your own hearts, revealed in your own characters with firmness, yet with the meekness and simplicity of Christ. Through much prayer you must labor for souls, for this is the only method by which you can reach hearts. It is not your work, but the work of Christ who is by your side, that impresses hearts (*Evangelism*, p. 341).

But ye shall receive power, after that the Holy Ghost is come upon you: and ye shall be witnesses unto me both in Jerusalem, and in all Judaea, and in Samaria, and unto the uttermost part of the earth (Acts 1:8).

Let us take heed to our words. Let us talk faith, and we shall have faith. Never give place to a thought of discouragement in the work of God. Never utter a word of doubt. It is as seed sown in the heart of both speaker and hearers, to produce a harvest of discouragement and unbelief (*Evangelism*, p. 633).

We become too easily discouraged over the souls who do not at once respond to our efforts. Never should we cease to labor for a soul while there is one gleam of hope. Precious souls cost our self-sacrificing Redeemer too dear a price to be lightly given up to the tempter's power ... Without a helping hand many would never recover themselves, but by patient, persistent effort they may be uplifted. Such need tender words, kind consideration, tangible help... Christ is able to uplift the most sinful and place them where they will be acknowledged as children of God, joint heirs with Christ to the immortal inheritance. By the miracle of divine grace many may be fitted for lives of usefulness (*God's Amazing Grace*, p. 127).

And this gospel of the kingdom shall be preached in all the world for a witness unto all nations; and then shall the end come (Matthew 24:14).

My brethren, enter the cities while you can. In the cities that have been already entered there are many who have never heard the message of truth. Some who have heard have been converted, and some have died in the faith. There are many others who, if they were given an opportunity, might hear and accept the message of salvation ... These, our last efforts for the work of God in the earth, must bear decidedly the impress of the divine (*Evangelism*, p. 33).

Absolutely Positively

There is nothing in us of ourselves by which we can influence others for good. If we realize our helplessness and our need of divine power, we shall not trust to ourselves. We know not what results a day, an hour, or a moment may determine, and never should we begin the day without committing our ways to our heavenly Father. His angels are appointed to watch over us, and if we put ourselves under their guardianship, then in every time of danger they will be at our right hand. When unconsciously we are in danger of exerting a wrong influence, the angels will be by our side, prompting us to a better course, choosing our words for us, and influencing our actions. Thus our influence may be a silent, unconscious, but mighty power in drawing others to Christ and the heavenly world (*God's Amazing Grace*, p. 272).

Christ drew the hearts of his hearers to him by the manifestation of his love, and then, little by little, as they were able to bear it, he unfolded to them the great truths of the kingdom. We also must learn to adapt our labors to the condition of the people,—to meet men where they are. While the claims of the law of God are to be presented to the world, we should never forget that love—the love of Christ—is the only power that can soften the heart, and lead to obedience. All the great truths of the Scriptures center in Christ; rightly understood, all lead to him. Let Christ be presented as the Alpha and Omega, the beginning and the end, of the great plan of redemption. Present to the people such subjects as will strengthen their confidence in God and in his word, and lead them to investigate its teachings for themselves. And as they go forward, step by step, in the study of the Bible, they will be better prepared to appreciate the beauty and harmony of its precious truths (*Gospel Workers*, p. 301).

Dear young friends, remember that it is not necessary to be an ordained minister in order to serve the Lord. There are many ways of working for Christ. Human hands may never have been laid on you in ordination, but God can give you fitness for His service. He can work through you to the saving of souls. If, having learned in the school of Christ, you are meek and lowly in heart, He will give you words to speak for Him (*Messages to Young People*, p. 226).

The evangelization of the world is the work that God has given to those who go forth in His name. They are to be co-laborers with Christ, revealing to those ready to perish His tender, pitying love. God calls for thousands to work for Him, not by preaching to those who know the truth, going over and over the same ground, but by warning those who have never heard the last message of mercy. Work, with a heart filled with an earnest longing for souls. Do medical missionary work. Thus you will gain access to the hearts of the people. The way will be prepared for more decided proclamation of the truth. You will find that relieving their physical suffering gives you opportunity to minister to their spiritual needs (*My Life Today*, p. 224).

Those who have been most successful in winning souls, were men and women who did not pride themselves in their ability, but who went in humility and faith, and the power of God worked with their efforts in convicting and converting the hearts of those to whom they appealed. Jesus did this very work. He came close to those whom he desired to benefit. How often, with a few gathered about him, he began the precious lessons, and one by one the passers-by paused to listen, until a great multitude heard with wonder and awe the words of God through the heaven-sent Teacher. He did not wait for congregations to assemble. The grandest truths were spoken to single individuals. The woman at the well in Samaria heard the wonderful words, "Whosoever drinketh of the water that I shall give him shall never thirst; but the water that I shall give him shall be in him a well of water springing up into everlasting life" (John 4:14) (*Gospel Workers*, p. 337).

Millions upon millions of human souls ready to perish, bound in chains of ignorance and sin, have never so much as heard of Christ's love for them. Were our condition and theirs to be reversed, what would we desire them to do for us? All this, so far as lies in our power, we are under the most solemn obligation to do for them." Christ's rule of life, by which every one of us must stand or fall in the judgment, is, "Whatsoever ye would that men should do to you, do ye even so to them" (*My Life Today*, p. 225).

Chapter 18

Heaven

For the Lord himself shall descend from heaven with a shout, with the voice of the archangel, and with the trump of God: and the dead in Christ shall rise first: Then we which are alive and remain shall be caught up together with them in the clouds, to meet the Lord in the air: and so shall we ever be with the Lord. Wherefore comfort one another with these words. (1 Thessalonians 4:16-20)

In heaven there is perfect order, perfect obedience, perfect peace and harmony. Those who have had no respect for order or discipline in this life, would have no respect for the order which is observed in heaven. They can never be admitted into heaven, for all worthy of an entrance there will love order and respect discipline. The characters formed in this, will determine the future life. When Christ shall come, he will not change the character of any individual. Precious, probationary time is given to be improved in washing our robes of character, and making them white in the blood of the Lamb. *Christian Education*, p. 237).

All heaven appreciates the struggles of those who are fighting for the crown of everlasting life, that they may be partakers with Christ in the city of God.... God wants you there, Christ wants you there, the heavenly host wants you there. The angels are willing to stand in the outer circle, and let those who have been redeemed by the blood of Jesus stand in the inner circle... A crown of glory waits for all who fight the good fight of faith (*Our High Calling*, p. 368).

The inhabitants of Heaven are perfect, because the will of God is their joy, and supreme delight. Many here destroy their own comfort injure their health, and violate a good conscience, because they will not cease to do wrong. The injunctions to mortify the deeds of the body, with its affections and lusts, has no effect upon them. They profess Christ, but are not his followers, and never can be, until they cease their wrong-doing, and work the work of righteousness (*An Appeal to Mothers*, p. 26).

Thus saith the LORD, The heaven is my throne, and the earth is my footstool: where is the house that ye build unto me? and where is the place of my rest? (Isaiah 66:1).

Angels work harmoniously. Perfect order characterizes all their movements. The more closely we imitate the harmony and order of the angelic host, the more successful will be the efforts of these heavenly agents in our behalf. If we see no necessity for harmonious action, and are disorderly, undisciplined, and disorganized in our course of action, angels, who are thoroughly organized and move in perfect order, cannot work for us successfully. They turn away in grief, for they are not authorized to bless confusion, distraction, and disorganization. All who desire the co-operation of the heavenly messengers, must work in unison with them. Those who have the unction from on high, will in all their efforts encourage order, discipline, and union of action, and then the angels of God can co-operate with them. But never, never will these heavenly messengers place their endorsement upon irregularity, disorganization, and disorder. All these evils are the result of Satan's efforts to weaken our forces, to destroy our courage, and prevent successful action (*Christian Experience and Teachings*, p. 199).

Jesus is today in heaven preparing mansions for those who love Him; yes, more than mansions, a kingdom which is to be ours. But all who shall inherit these blessings must be partakers of the self-denial and self-sacrifice of Christ for the good of others (*God's Amazing Grace*, p. 62).

I saw Jesus lead the redeemed company to the gate of the city. He laid hold of the gate and swung it back on its glittering hinges, and bade the nations that had kept the truth enter in. Within the city there was everything to feast the eye. Rich glory they beheld everywhere. Then Jesus looked upon His redeemed saints; their countenances were radiant with glory; and as He fixed His loving eyes upon them, He said, with His rich, musical voice, "I behold the travail of My soul, and am satisfied. This rich glory is yours to enjoy eternally. Your sorrows are ended. There shall be no more death, neither sorrow nor crying, neither shall there be any more pain" (*God's Amazing Grace*, p. 359).

And I John saw the holy city, new Jerusalem, coming down from God out of heaven, prepared as a bride adorned for her husband. And I heard a great voice out of heaven saying, Behold, the tabernacle of God is with men, and he will dwell with them, and they shall be his people, and God himself shall be with them, and be their God. And God shall wipe away all tears from their eyes; and there shall be no more death, neither sorrow, nor crying, neither shall there be any more pain: for the former things are passed away. And he that sat upon the throne said, Behold, I make all things new. And he said unto me, Write: for these words are true and faithful. And he said unto me, It is done. I am Alpha and Omega, the beginning and the end. I will give unto him that is athirst of the fountain of the water of life freely. He that overcometh shall inherit all things; and I will be his God, and he shall be my son. But the fearful, and unbelieving, and the abominable, and murderers, and whoremongers, and sorcerers, and idolaters, and all liars, shall have their part in the lake which burneth with fire and brimstone: which is the second death. And there came unto me one of the seven angels which had the seven vials full of the seven last plagues, and talked with me, saying, Come hither, I will shew thee the bride, the Lamb's wife. And he carried me away in the spirit to a great and high mountain, and shewed me that great city, the holy Jerusalem, descending out of heaven from God, Having the glory of God: and her light was like unto a stone most precious, even like a jasper stone, clear as crystal; And had a wall great and high, and had twelve gates, and at the gates twelve angels, and names written thereon, which are the names of the twelve tribes of the children of Israel: On the east three gates; on the north three gates; on the south three gates; and on the west three gates. And the wall of the city had twelve foundations, and in them the names of the twelve apostles of the Lamb. And he that talked with me had a golden reed to measure the city, and the gates thereof, and the wall thereof. And the city lieth foursquare, and the length is as large as the breadth: and he measured the city with the reed, twelve thousand furlongs. The length and the breadth and the height of it are equal. And he measured the wall thereof, an hundred and forty and four cubits, according to the measure of a man, that is, of the angel. And the building of the wall of it was of jasper: and the city was pure gold, like unto clear glass. And the foundations of the wall of the city were garnished with all manner of precious stones. The first foundation was jasper; the second, sapphire; the third, a chalcedony; the fourth, an emerald; The fifth, sardonyx; the sixth, sardius; the seventh, chrysolyte; the eighth, beryl; the ninth, a topaz; the tenth, a chrysoprasus; the eleventh, a jacinth; the twelfth, an amethyst. And the twelve gates were twelve pearls: every several gate was of one pearl: and the street of the city was pure gold, as it were transparent glass. And I saw no temple therein: for the Lord God Almighty and the Lamb are the temple of it. And the city had no need of the sun, neither of the moon, to shine in it: for the glory of God did lighten it, and the Lamb is the light thereof. And the nations of them which are saved shall walk in the light of it: and the kings of the earth do bring their glory and honour into it. And the gates of it shall not be shut at all by day: for there shall be no night there. And they shall bring the glory and honour of the nations into it. And there shall in no wise enter into it any thing that defileth, neither whatsoever worketh abomination, or maketh a lie: but they which are written in the Lamb's book of life (Revelation 21:2–27).

Those who take no pleasure in thinking and talking of God in this life, will not enjoy the life that is to come, where God is ever present, dwelling among his people. But those who love to think of God will be in their element, breathing in the atmosphere of heaven. Those who on earth love the thought of heaven, will be happy in its holy associations and pleasures. The prophet says, "And God shall wipe away all tears from their eyes; and there shall be no more death, neither sorrow, nor crying, neither shall there be any more pain; for the former things are passed away." "And there shall be no more curse; but the throne of God and of the Lamb shall be in it; and his servants shall serve him; and they shall see his face; and his name shall be in their foreheads." (*Review and Herald*, May 13, 1890).

After this I beheld, and, lo, a great multitude, which no man could number, of all nations, and kindreds, and people, and tongues, stood before the throne, and before the Lamb, clothed with white robes, and palms in their hands; And cried with a loud voice, saying, Salvation to our God which sitteth upon the throne, and unto the Lamb (Revelation 7:9–10).

Could those whose lives have been spent in rebellion against God be suddenly transported to heaven and witness the high, the holy state of perfection that ever exists there,—every soul filled with love, every countenance beaming with joy, enrapturing music in melodious strains rising in honor of God and the Lamb, and ceaseless streams of light flowing upon the redeemed from the face of Him who sitteth upon the throne,—could those whose hearts are filled with hatred of God, of truth and holiness, mingle with the heavenly throng and join their songs of praise? Could they endure the glory of God and the Lamb? No, no; years of probation were granted them, that they might form characters for heaven; but they have never trained the mind to love purity; they have never learned the language of heaven, and now it is too late. A life of rebellion against God has unfitted them for heaven. Its purity, holiness, and peace would be torture to them; the glory of God would be a consuming fire. They would long to flee from that holy place. They would welcome destruction, that they might be hidden from the face of Him who died to redeem them. The destiny of the wicked is fixed by their own choice. Their exclusion from heaven is voluntary with themselves, and just and merciful on the part of God (*The Great Controversy*, p. 542).

In my Father's house are many mansions: if it were not so, I would have told you. I go to prepare a place for you (John 14:2).

We shall never know what dangers, seen and unseen, we have been delivered from through the interposition of the angels until we shall see in the light of eternity the providences of God. Then we shall better understand what God has done for us all the days of our life. We shall know then that the whole heavenly family watched to see our course of action from day to day (*In Heavenly Places*, p. 101).

As your senses delight in the attractive loveliness of the earth, think of the world that is to come, that shall never know the blight of sin and death; where the face of nature will no more wear the shadow of the curse. Let your imagination picture the home of the saved, and remember that it will be more glorious than your brightest imagination can portray. In the varied gifts of God in nature we see but the faintest gleaming of His glory (*God's Amazing Grace*, p. 359).

As your senses delight in the attractive loveliness of the earth, think of the world that is to come, that shall never know the blight of sin and death; where the face of nature will no more wear the shadow of the curse. Let your imagination picture the home of the saved, and remember that it will be more glorious than your brightest imagination can portray. In the varied gifts of God in nature we see but the faintest gleaming of His glory. It is written, "Eye hath not seen, nor ear heard, neither have entered into the heart of man, the things which God hath prepared for them that love him" 1 Corinthians 2:9 (*Maranatha* 319).

Chapter 19

Encouragement

As His representatives among men, Christ does not choose angels who have never fallen, but human beings, men of like passions with those they seek to save (*Conflict and Courage*, p. 289).

The cost of the redemption of the race can never be fully realized until the redeemed shall stand with the Redeemer, by the throne of God. And as they have capacity to appreciate the value of immortal life, and the eternal reward, they will swell the song of victory and immortal triumph, "Saying with a loud voice, Worthy is the Lamb that was slain to receive power, and riches, and wisdom, and strength, and honour, and glory, and blessing. And every creature," says John, "which is in heaven, and on the earth, and under the earth, and such as are in the sea, and all that are in them, heard I saying, Blessing, and honour, and glory, and power, be unto him that sitteth upon the throne, and unto the Lamb for ever and ever" (*Confrontation, p.* 55).

There hath no temptation taken you but such as is common to man: but God is faithful, who will not suffer you to be tempted above that ye are able; but will with the temptation also make a way to escape, that ye may be able to bear it (1 Corinthians 10:13).

Those who really enjoy the love of God will have joy and peace. Religion was never designed to make one pleasureless. What can be productive of greater happiness than to enjoy the peace of Christ, the bright sunshine of His presence? (*Faith I Live By*, p. 237).

What was the strength of those who in the past have suffered persecution for Christ's sake? It was union with God, union with the Holy Spirit, union with Christ. Reproach and persecution have separated many from earthly friends, but never from the love of Christ. Never is the tempest-tried soul more dearly loved by His Saviour than when he is suffering reproach for the truth's sake. "I will love him," Christ said, "and will manifest Myself to him." John 14:21. When for the truth's sake the believer stands at the bar of earthly tribunals, Christ stands by his side. When he is confined within prison walls, Christ manifests Himself to him and cheers his heart with His love. When he suffers death for Christ's sake, the Saviour says to him, They may kill the body, but they cannot hurt the soul. "Be of good cheer; I have overcome the world." "Fear thou not; for I am with thee: be not dismayed; for I am thy God: I will strengthen thee; yea, I will help thee; yea,

Absolutely Positively

I will uphold thee with the right hand of My righteousness" John 16:33; Isaiah 41:10 (*Acts of the Apostles*, p. 85).

Be strong and of a good courage, fear not, nor be afraid of them: for the LORD thy God, he it is that doth go with thee; he will not fail thee, nor forsake thee (Deuteronomy 31:6).

You can fight against the enemy, not in your own strength, but in the strength God is ever ready to give you. Trusting in His word, you will never say, "I can't" (*Adventist Home*, p. 357).

A person whose mind is quiet and satisfied in God is in the pathway to health. To have a consciousness that the eyes of the Lord are upon us, and His ears open to hear our prayers, is a satisfaction indeed. To know that we have a never-failing Friend in whom we can confide all the secrets of the soul, is a privilege which words can never express (*Faith I Live By*, p. 229).

God designs that the sick, the unfortunate, those possessed with evil spirits, shall hear his voice through us. Through his human agents he desires to be a comforter such as the world has never before seen. His words are to be voiced by his followers: "Let not your heart be troubled, neither let it be afraid. Ye believe in God, believe also in me" (*Spaulding and Magan Collection*, p. 89).

If we surrender our lives to His service, we can never be placed in a position for which God has not made provision. Whatever may be our situation, we have a Guide to direct our way; whatever our perplexities, we have a sure Counselor; whatever our sorrow, bereavement, or loneliness, we have a sympathizing Friend. If in our ignorance we make missteps, Christ does not leave us. His voice, clear and distinct, is heard saying,"I am the Way, the Truth, and the Life." John 14:6. "He shall deliver the needy when he crieth; the poor also, and him that hath no helper." Psalms 72:12 (*Christ Object Lessons*, p. 173).

Pentecost brought them the heavenly illumination. The truths they could not understand while Christ was with them were now unfolded. With a faith and assurance that they had never before known, they accepted the teachings of the Sacred Word. No longer was it a matter of faith with them that Christ was the Son of God. They knew that, although clothed with humanity, He was indeed the Messiah, and they told their experience to the world with a confidence which carried with it the conviction that God was with them (*Acts of the Apostles*, p. 45).

Why art thou cast down, O my soul? and why art thou disquieted in me? hope thou in God: for I shall yet praise him for the help of his countenance (Psalms 42:5).

God's promises to us are so rich, so full, that we need never hesitate or doubt; we need never waver or backslide. In view of the encouragements that are found all through the Word of God, we have no right to be gloomy or despondent (*The Later Elmshaven Years, Volume 6*, by Arthur L. White, p. 376).

"There has never been a time since we first embraced the Advent faith, that our position looked so clear and satisfactory as at the present. Our pathway, like 'the shining light that shineth more and more unto the perfect day,' is brightening at every step we take. This was to be the portion of the 'just,' who in the waiting, watching time, should 'live by faith.' — *The Later Elmshaven Years, Volume 6*, by Arthur L. White, p. 255).

God invites us to prove for ourselves the reality of His Word, the truth of His promises. He bids us "taste and see that the Lord is good." Psalms 34:8 He declares, "Ask, and ye shall receive." John 16:24. His promises will be fulfilled. They have never failed; they never can fail (*Faith I Live By*, p. 123).

For the disheartened there is a sure remedy,—faith, prayer, work. Faith and activity will impart assurance and satisfaction that will increase day by day. Are you tempted to give way to feelings of anxious foreboding or utter despondency? In the darkest days, when appearances seem most forbidding, fear not. Have faith in God. He knows your need. He has all power. His infinite love and compassion never weary. Fear not that He will fail of fulfilling His promise. He is eternal truth. Never will He change the covenant He has made with those who love Him. And He will bestow upon His faithful servants the measure of efficiency that their need demands (*Christian Service*, p. 107).

Therefore I take pleasure in infirmities, in reproaches, in necessities, in persecutions, in distresses for Christ's sake: for when I am weak, then am I strong (2 Corinthians 2:10).

All Heaven is interested in the happiness of man. Our heavenly Father does not close the avenues of joy to any of His creatures. The divine requirements call upon us to shun those indulgences that would bring suffering and disappointment, that would close to us the door of happiness and heaven... He [the world's Redeemer] requires us to perform only those duties that will lead our steps to heights of bliss to which the disobedient can never attain. The true, joyous life of the soul is to have Christ formed within, the hope of glory (*Faith I Live By*, p. 226).

But though the conflict is a ceaseless one, none are left to struggle alone. Angels help and protect those who walk humbly before God. Never will our Lord betray one who trusts in Him. As His children draw near to Him for protection from evil, in pity and love He lifts up for them a standard against the enemy. Touch them not, He says; for they are Mine. I have graven them upon the palms of My hands (*Christian Service*, p. 166).

Heaven's forgiveness and peace and love in the soul. Money cannot buy it, intellect cannot procure it, wisdom cannot attain to it; you can never hope, by your own efforts, to secure it. But God offers it to you as a gift, "without money and without price." Isaiah 55:1 (*Faith I Live By*, p. 103).

Blessed is the man that endureth temptation: for when he is tried, he shall receive the crown of life, which the Lord hath promised to them that love him (James 1:12).

The Lord sets men in responsible places, not to act out their own wills, but His will. So long as they cherish His pure principles of government, He will bless and strengthen them, recognizing them as His instrumentalities. God never forsakes the one who is true to principle (*Conflict and Courage*, p. 188).

We should never give to the world the false impression that Christians are a gloomy, unhappy people. If our eyes are fixed on Jesus, we shall see a compassionate Redeemer, and shall catch light from His countenance. Wherever His Spirit reigns, there peace abides. And there will be joy also, for there is a calm, holy trust in God (*Desire of Ages*, p. 152).

Christians who are constantly growing in earnestness, in zeal, in fervor, in love,—such Christians never backslide (*Christian Service*, p. 107).

To the believer, death is but a small matter. Christ speaks of it as if it were of little moment. "If a man keep my saying, he shall never see death," "he shall never taste of death" (John 8:51, 52). To the Christian, death is but a sleep, a moment of silence and darkness. The life is hid with Christ in God, and "when Christ, who is our life, shall appear, then shall ye also appear with him in glory" (Colossians. 3:4) (*Faith I Live By*, p. 187).

Come to Jesus, and receive rest and peace. You may have the blessing even now. Satan suggests that you are helpless and cannot bless yourself. It is true; you are helpless. But lift up Jesus before him: "I have a risen Saviour. In Him I trust, and He will never suffer me to be confounded. In His name I triumph. He is my righteousness and my crown of rejoicing." Let no one here feel that his case is hopeless, for it is not. You may see that you are sinful and undone, but it is just on this account that you need a Saviour. If you have sins to confess, lose no time. These moments are golden. "If we confess our sins, He is faithful and just to forgive us our sins, and to cleanse us from all unrighteousness" (1 John 1:9). Those who hunger and thirst after righteousness will be filled, for Jesus has promised it. Precious Saviour! His arms are open to receive us, and His great heart of love is waiting to bless us (*Faith and Works*, p. 37).

Blessed are they that mourn: for they shall be comforted. Blessed are the meek: for they shall inherit the earth. Blessed are they which do hunger and thirst after righteousness: for they shall be filled. Blessed are the merciful: for they shall obtain mercy. Blessed are the pure in heart: for they shall see God. Blessed are the peacemakers: for they shall be called the children of God. Blessed are they which are persecuted for righteousness' sake: for theirs is the kingdom of heaven. Blessed are ye, when men shall revile you, and persecute you, and shall say all manner of evil against you falsely, for my sake. Rejoice, and be exceeding glad: for great is your reward in heaven: for so persecuted they the prophets which were before you (Matthew 5:4–12).

The Lord seeks to save, not to destroy. He delights in the rescue of sinners. "As I live, saith the Lord God, I have no pleasure in the death of the wicked" (Ezekiel 33:11). By warnings and entreaties He calls the wayward to cease from their evil-doing and to turn to Him and live. He gives His chosen messengers a holy boldness, that those who hear may fear and be brought to repentance. How firmly the man of God rebuked the king! And this firmness was essential; in no other way could the existing evils have been rebuked. The Lord gave His servant boldness, that an abiding impression might be made on those who heard. The messengers of the Lord are never to fear the face of man, but are to stand unflinchingly for the right. So long as they put their trust in God, they need not fear; for He who gives them their commission gives them also the assurance of His protecting care (*Conflict and Courage*, p. 202).

When the soul surrenders itself to Christ, a new power takes possession of the new heart. A change is wrought which man can never accomplish for himself. It is a supernatural work, bringing a supernatural element into human nature. The soul that is yielded to Christ becomes His own fortress, which He holds in a revolted world, and He intends that no authority shall be known in it but His own (*Desire of Ages*, p. 324).

God never leads His children otherwise than they would choose to be led, if they could see the end from the beginning and discern the glory of the purpose which they are fulfilling as co-workers with Him (*Faith I Live By*, p. 64).

This promise will never fail. We cannot enjoy the favor of God unless we comply with the conditions upon which His favor is bestowed. By so doing there will come to us that peace, contentment, and wisdom that the world can neither give nor take away… A humble mind and a grateful heart will elevate us above petty trials and real difficulties. The less earnest, energetic, and vigilant we are in the service of the Master, the more will the mind dwell upon self, magnifying molehills into mountains of difficulty (*Conflict and Courage*, p. 370).

Victories are not gained by ceremonies or display, but by simple obedience to the highest General, the Lord God of heaven. He who trusts in this Leader will never know defeat (*God's Amazing Grace*, p. 39).

If you take even one step toward Him in repentance, He will hasten to enfold you in His arms of infinite love. His ear is open to the cry of the contrite soul. The very first reaching out of the heart after God is known to Him. Never a prayer is offered, however faltering, never a tear is shed, however secret, never a sincere desire after God is cherished, however feeble, but the Spirit of God goes forth to meet it. Even before the prayer is uttered or the yearning of the heart made known, grace from Christ goes forth to meet the grace that is working upon the human soul (*Faith I Live By*, p. 129).

Summon all your powers to look up, not down at your difficulties; then you will never faint by the way. You will soon see Jesus behind the cloud, reaching out His hand to help you; and all you have to do is to give Him your hand in simple faith and let Him lead you... A great name among men is as letters traced in sand, but a spotless character will endure to all eternity. God gives you intelligence and a reasoning mind, whereby you may grasp His promises; and Jesus is ready to help you in forming a strong, symmetrical character (*God's Amazing Grace*, p. 81).

The humblest and poorest of the disciples of Jesus can be a blessing to others. They may not realize that they are doing any special good, but by their unconscious influence they may start waves of blessing which will widen and deepen, and the happy result of their words and consistent deportment they may never know until the final distribution of rewards. They do not feel or know that they are doing anything great. They are not required to weary themselves with anxieties about success. They have only to go forward, not with many words, and vain-glorying, and boasting, but quietly, faithfully doing the work which God's providence has assigned them, and they will not lose their reward (*Gospel Workers*, p. 379).

Those who surrender their lives to His guidance and to His service will never be placed in a position for which He has not made provision. Whatever our situation, if we are doers of His word, we have a Guide to direct our way; whatever our perplexity, we have a sure Counselor; whatever our sorrow, bereavement, or loneliness, we have a sympathizing Friend (*God's Amazing Grace*, p. 114).

If you would find happiness and peace in all you do, you must do everything in reference to the glory of God. If you would have peace in your hearts, you must seek earnestly to imitate the life of Christ. Then there will be no need of affecting cheerfulness, or of your seeking for pleasure in the indulgence of pride and the frivolities of the world. You will have a serenity and happiness in right doing that you can never realize in a course of wrong (*Lift Him Up*, p. 91).

For every class of temptations there is a remedy. We are not left to ourselves to fight the battle against self and our sinful natures in our own finite strength. Jesus is a mighty helper, a never-failing support.... None need fail or become discouraged, when such ample provision has been made for us (*Our High Calling*, p. 88).

Come to Jesus, and receive rest and peace. You may have the blessing even now. Satan suggests that you are helpless, and cannot bless yourself. It is true; you are helpless. But lift up Jesus before him: "I have a risen Saviour. In him I trust, and he will never suffer me to be confounded. In his name I triumph. He is my righteousness, and my crown of rejoicing." Let no one here feel that his case is hopeless; for it is not. You may see that you are sinful and undone; but it is just on this account that you need a Saviour. If you have sins to confess, lose no time. These moments are golden. "If we confess our sins, he is faithful and just to forgive us our sins, and to cleanse us from all unrighteousness." (1 John 1:9.) Those who hunger and thirst after righteousness will be filled; for Jesus has promised it. Precious Saviour! his arms are open to receive us, and his great heart of love is waiting to bless us (*Gospel Workers*, p. 413).

While God has given ample evidence for faith, he will never remove all excuse for unbelief. All who look for hooks to hang their doubts upon, will find them. And those who refuse to accept and obey God's Word until every objection has been removed, and there is no longer an opportunity for doubt, will never come to the light (*Great Controversy*, p. 527).

God loves His creatures with a love that is both tender and strong. He has established the laws of nature, but His laws are not arbitrary exactions. Every "thou shalt not," whether in physical or moral law, contains or implies a promise. If it is obeyed, blessings will attend our steps; if it is disobeyed, the result is danger and unhappiness. The laws of God are designed to bring His people closer to Himself. He will save them from the evil and lead them to the good if they will be led, but force them He never will (*God's Amazing Grace*, p. 266).

The Scriptures plainly show that the work of sanctification is progressive. When in conversion the sinner finds peace with God through the blood of the atonement, the Christian life has but just begun. Now he is to "go on unto perfection;" to grow up "unto the measure of the stature of the fullness of Christ." Says the apostle Paul: "This one thing I do, forgetting those things which are behind, and reaching forth unto those things which are before, I press toward the mark for the prize of the high calling of God in Christ Jesus" (Philippians 3:13, 14). And Peter sets before us the steps by which Bible sanctification is to be attained: "Giving all diligence, add to your faith virtue; and to virtue knowledge; and to knowledge temperance; and to temperance patience; and to patience godliness; and to godliness brotherly kindness; and to brotherly kindness charity... If ye do these things, ye shall never fall." 2 Peter 1:5–10 (*Great Controversy*, p. 470).

For every class of temptations there is a remedy. We are not left to ourselves to fight the battle against self and our sinful natures in our own finite strength. Jesus is a mighty helper, a never-failing support. His followers should develop symmetrical characters by strengthening weak traits. They must become Christ-like in disposition and pure and holy in life. None can do this in their own strength, but Jesus can give the daily grace needed to do this work. None need fail or become discouraged, when such ample provision has been made for us (*Gospel Workers*, p. 418).

Not without a purpose does God send trial to His children. He never leads them otherwise than they would choose to be led if they could see the end from the beginning, and discern the glory of the purpose which they are fulfilling as workers together with Him. He subjects them to discipline to humble them, to lead them, through trial and affliction, to see their weakness and draw near to Him (*In Heavenly Places*, p. 267).

The whole universe will have become witnesses to the nature and results of sin. And its utter extermination, which in the beginning would have brought fear to angels and dishonor to God, will now vindicate His love and establish His honor before the universe of beings who delight to do His will, and in whose heart is His law. Never will evil again be manifest. Says the word of God: "Affliction shall not rise up the second time" (Nahum 1:9). The law of God, which Satan has reproached as the yoke of bondage, will be honored as the law of liberty. A tested and proved creation will never again be turned from allegiance to Him whose character has been fully manifested before them as fathomless love and infinite wisdom (*Great Controversy*, p. 504).

The Lord looks with deepest interest upon each striving soul. He loves each one. Did He not, He never would have given His only-begotten Son to die for us (*In Heavenly Places*, p. 278).

God never leaves the world without men who can discern between good and evil, righteousness and unrighteousness. He has men whom He has appointed to stand in the forefront of the battle in times of emergency (*Gospel Workers*, p. 263).

Man will be left without excuse. God has given sufficient evidence upon which to base faith if he wish to believe. In the last days the earth will be almost destitute of true faith. Upon the merest pretense, the Word of God will be considered unreliable, while human reasoning will be received, though it be in opposition to plain Scripture facts. Men will endeavor to explain from natural causes the work of creation, which God has never revealed. But human science cannot search out the secrets of the God of heaven, and explain the stupendous works of creation, which were a miracle of Almighty power, any sooner than it can show how God came into existence (*Lift Him Up*, p. 59).

The Lord desires us to act sensibly. We shall have trials; we need never expect anything else; for the time has not yet come when Satan is to be bound. Wherever we may be, we shall continue to have trials. But if we give up to the suggestions of the enemy, we lose the battle. Can we afford to yield to the arch-deceiver? Oh, no! We are to turn for help and deliverance to Him who "according to His abundant mercy hath begotten us again unto a lively hope by the resurrection of Jesus Christ," even the hope of an eternal inheritance reserved for those "who are kept by the power of God through faith unto salvation" (*Loma Linda Messages*, p. 613).

In the plan of God, all the riches of heaven are to be drawn upon by men. Nothing in the treasury of divine resources is deemed too costly to accompany the great gift of the only begotten Son of God... Christ was empowered to breathe into fallen humanity the breath of life. Those who receive Him will never hunger, never thirst; for greater joy than that found in Christ there cannot be. Study the words spoken by the Saviour from the Mount of Blessing. How the divine nature shone through His humanity as His lips uttered the benedictions upon those who were the objects of His mercy and love. He blessed them with a fullness that showed that He was drawing from the inexhaustible store of the richest treasures. The treasures of eternity were at His command. The Father committed the riches of heaven to Him, and in the disposal of them He knew no bound. Those who accept Him as their Saviour, their Redeemer, the Prince of life, he acknowledges before the heavenly host, before the worlds unfallen, and before the fallen world, as His peculiar treasure (*Lift Him Up*, p. 230).

The thought that we are in God's world and in the presence of the great Creator of the universe, who made man in His own image, after His own likeness, will lift the mind into broader, higher fields for meditation than any fictitious story. The thought that God's eye is watching us, that He loves us and cared so much for fallen man as to give His dearly beloved Son to redeem us that we might not miserably perish, is a great one, and whoever opens his heart to the acceptance and contemplation of these great themes will never be satisfied with trivial, sensational subjects (*Review and Herald*, Nov 9, 1886).

Let us never forget, even when we walk in the valley, that Christ is as much with us when we walk trustingly there as when we are on the mountaintop (*Mind, Character and Personality*, Volume 2, p. 811).

Absolutely Positively

Faith in God's love and overruling providence lightens the burdens of anxiety and care. It fills the heart with joy and contentment in the highest or the lowliest lot. Religion tends directly to promote health, to lengthen life, and to heighten our enjoyment of all its blessings. It opens to the soul a never-failing fountain of happiness (*My Life Today*, p. 158).

Temptation and trial will come to us all, but we need never be worsted by the enemy. Our Saviour has conquered in our behalf. Satan is not invincible... Christ was tempted that He might know how to help every soul that should afterward be tempted. Temptation is not sin; the sin lies in yielding. To the soul who trusts in Jesus, temptation means victory and greater strength (*Our High Calling*, p. 87).

Let us never lose sight of the fact that Jesus is a wellspring of joy. He does not delight in the misery of human beings, but loves to see them happy (*Adventist Home*, p. 513).

Take the word of Christ as your assurance. Has He not invited you to come unto Him? Never allow yourself to talk in a hopeless, discouraged way. If you do you will lose much. By looking at appearances and complaining when difficulties and pressure come, you give evidence of a sickly, enfeebled faith. Talk and act as if your faith was invincible. The Lord is rich in resources; He owns the world. Look heavenward in faith. Look to Him who has light and power and efficiency (*Christ Object Lessons*, p. 146).

Had the Christian never experienced the storms of affliction in this world, had his heart never been chilled by disappointment or oppressed by fear, he would scarcely know how to appreciate heaven. We will not be despondent, though often weary, sad, and heartsick; the winter will not always last. The summer of peace, joy, and eternal gladness soon will come. Then Christ will dwell with us and will lead us to fountains of living waters, and will wipe all tears from our eyes (*Our High Calling*, p. 158).

Do not listen to the enemy's suggestion to stay away from Christ until you have made yourself better; until you are good enough to come to God. If you wait until then, you will never come. When Satan points to your filthy garments, repeat the promise of Jesus, "Him that cometh to Me I will in no wise cast out." John 6:37. Tell the enemy that the blood of Jesus Christ cleanses from all sin. Make the prayer of David your own, "Purge me with hyssop, and I shall be clean; wash me, and I shall be whiter than snow." Psalms 51:7 (*Christ Object Lessons*, p. 205).

If you take hold of the strength of the mighty Helper, and not reason with your adversary and never complain of God, His promises will be verified. The experience that you gain today in trusting

Him will help you in meeting the difficulties of tomorrow. Each day you are to come, trusting as a little child drawing nearer to Jesus and heaven. In meeting with unwavering trust in God the daily trials and difficulties, you will again and again test the promises of Heaven, and each time you will learn a lesson of faith. Thus you will gain strength to resist temptation, and when the harder trials come, you will be able to endure (*Our High Calling*, p. 326).

We invite you to view the complete
selection of titles we publish at:

www.TEACHServices.com

Scan with your mobile
device to go directly
to our website.

Please write or email us your praises, reactions, or
thoughts about this or any other book we publish at:

P.O. Box 954
Ringgold, GA 30736

info@TEACHServices.com

TEACH Services, Inc., titles may be purchased in bulk for
educational, business, fund-raising, or sales promotional use.
For information, please e-mail:

BulkSales@TEACHServices.com

Finally, if you are interested in seeing
your own book in print, please contact us at

publishing@TEACHServices.com

We would be happy to review your manuscript for free.

www.ingramcontent.com/pod-product-compliance
Lightning Source LLC
Chambersburg PA
CBHW081837170426
43199CB00017B/2764